Venerable Master Hsing Yun

A historical meeting between two religions - the master greeted by His Holiness, Pope John Paul II at Vatican City

Extending a warm welcome to the Dalai Lama

Escorted by the abbot of the Dhammakaya Foundation, Thailand for a tour of the grounds

Ordaining the first-ever Buddhist monastics in Africa

A Ch'an, Pureland, Tantric rally in Taiwan

Giving a Dharma speech

A group photo with delegates at the World Fellowship of Buddhists Conference at Nan Tien Temple, Australia

Leading the opening ceremony of the International Outstanding Buddhist Women Conference at Fo Guang Shan, Taiwan

A family portrait with his mother and family members

Enjoying the serenity of Hsi Lai Temple

A noted calligraphist
(Courtesy of Chen Chih-min)

With the President of the Republic of China, Li Teng-hui

The master leading a sea of BLIA members in the campaign for universal compassion and loving kindness toward all, in Taipei.

The master leading the Welcoming Ceremony to receive the Buddha's Tooth Relic, originating from Tibet, in a joint Sutric and Tantric Dharma Service held in Taiwan

A portrait in oils by Li Zijian

Fo Guang Shan by day
...and by night

The master played a major role in the re-establishment of the Bhiksuni Order in both the Tibetan and Theravadan Traditions in Bodhgaya, India

Youth members from around the world gathered for the BLIA Youth Conference in 1999

THE BIOGRAPHY OF
VENERABLE MASTER HSING YUN

HANDING DOWN THE LIGHT

Original Chinese Text by Fu Chi-ying
Translated by Amy Lui-Ma

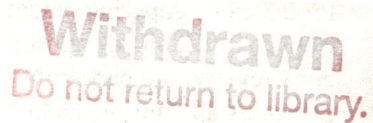

HSI LAI UNIVERSITY PRESS
LOS ANGELES, U.S.A.

© 2000 Hsi Lai University Press, in arrangement with
Commonwealth Publishing Co., Ltd.

Chinese language © 1995 Fu Chi-ying and
Venerable Master Hsing Yun

Published by Hsi Lai University Press
3456 S. Glenmark Drive
Hacienda Heights, CA 91745.
Telephone: 626-961-9697

Protected by copyright under the terms of the International Copyright Union; all rights reserved. Except for fair use in book reviews, no part of this book may be reproduced for any reason by any means, including any method of photographic reproduction, without permission of the publisher.

ISBN: 0-964261-29-4
Library of Congress Catalog Card Number: 00-101401

Cover design by Shih Mei-chi
Cover calligraphy: The characters *ch'uan* (top) by Su Teng-po (1037-1101) and *teng* (bottom) by Wang Hsi-chih (303-361), both in running script.

Printed in Los Angeles, U.S.A.

CONTENTS

Master's note	*i*
Author's note	*iii*
Translator's note	*vii*
A note on the revised edition	*viii*
Preface	*ix*

Part One
Many, many returns in Buddha karma

1.	To the delight of all Buddhas	*5*
2.	Promise on Cloud Dwelling Mountains	*19*
3.	Facing the turbulent times	*35*

Part Two
Crossing the nighted sea, light in hand

4.	The T'ang monk sets sail	*51*
5.	Ilan, the cradle	*61*
6.	Master of innovation	*73*

Part Three
'Tis with him perpetual Buddha truth

7.	Heading south	*95*
8.	Epoch of Buddha's light	*107*
9.	An outstanding disciple of Buddhism	*119*
10.	Traditional monastery, modern visions	*137*
11.	Dharma should not be separated from worldly awakening	*153*
12.	Good affinities around the world	*169*

Part Four
Spreading the Dharma to deliver all beings

13. The baton, its passing and receiving	191
14. Like clouds and water	203
15. Heart for the isle, soul for the mainland	217

Part Five
Buddha's light held high

16. The Dharma coming west	239
17. Buddha's Light International Association	255
18. Holding space in an embrace	269

Part Six
Returning on wings of his vows

19. Heart of a child	289
20. Devoted to the Buddhist path	311
21. No regrets whatsoever	321

Appendix 1 The chronology of Venerable Master Hsing Yun	333
Appendix 2 Fo Guang Shan: Global distribution of branch temples, 1999	342
Appendix 3 Buddha's Light Int'l Association: Global distribution of chapters, 1999	344
Appendix 4 Fo Guang Shan: Distribution of branch temples in Taiwan, 1999	346

Master's note

Having marched through life for close to seventy years, I am but an ordinary monk who deems "preaching the Dharma a daily duty and benefiting all living beings a lifetime career." Whatever transpires in the outer conditions, I have always felt profoundly blessed to be in the favor of the Buddhas from the ten directions and with the affinity of all living beings. With them watching over and caring for me, little by little I have been able to carry out the sacred mission that pertains to a monastic. These past few years, friends have taken such an interest in my life that they have been quite vehement in writing about it. Some of the results are exalting, others critical; some well-intentioned, others without much intention. All of them I invariably choose to regard as references for my practice and mirrors for my doings.

For some time now I have enjoyed the congeniality of those at Commonwealth Publishing Company, a refreshing bunch of idealists, enthusiasts, and professionals under publisher Kao Hsi-chun. When the group came up with the notion of doing my biography, I was only too glad to comply.

Commonwealth's chief editor Fu Chi-ying was the one to author the text. After working closely with her the next two years, I was left with no doubt that the task had fallen on the right shoulders. A receptive yet independent thinker, the skilled journalist persisted in taking her subject back in time without appearing to cross-examine me. I have only good things to say about the thoroughness of her research and investigation. The first draft alone struck me as being incredibly complete in its portrayal of my disposition, thinking, and spirituality. The essentials were all there in one articulate flow. I was won over instantly, which was not much of a surprise; so were the senior disciples of Fo Guang Shan, which, in a way, was a surprise.

Too insignificant are personal footprints along the river of no return that is history. That I am prepared to disclose my life, work, faith, experience, thoughts, and feelings is because, in so doing, Buddhists may be able to draw cross-references for their own cultivation. But most of all, I hope this offering of the records of my inner growth and outer journey should prompt everyone to rise in unison to extinguish the flare of worldly strife, to light in its place the light within each of us, and to create the joyful, harmonious Pureland on earth.

Once again, my thanks to friends at Commonwealth and to Chi-ying for this book. Let me pray that the compassionate light of the Triple Gems be around you, dear readers, and that health in body and mind, and propitiousness be yours!

Hsing Yun
Taipei Temple
December 1994.

Author's Note

From reporter, copy-editor, producer, to chief editor, I have a career that is composed of my favorite thing – words. Since leaving school over ten years ago, I have been counting my blessings daily. But never have I thought of penning a book.

How strange are the causes and conditions taught in Buddhism! How wondrous they are!

I first had a personal interview with Venerable Master Hsing Yun six years ago for *Global View Monthly*. Two years later, a proposed biographical series by the Commonwealth Publishing Company featuring contemporary figures triggered off unanimous efforts to solicit rights to the biography of the master. As events snowballed, the first-ever chance to author a book fell in my lap! It was not until the master acquiesced that I hastened to ready myself for a task that one innuendo after another came filtering through. For years the project was the most sought-after among those who are far more superior to me in learning and writing. But, green as I may be, I happened to be the one with the right causes and conditions.

In the course of the next 600 or so workdays, the master tolerated and commiserated with the worldly, unknowing creature that I am; the inquisitive – at times unrelenting – journalist that I was trained to be, the master accommodated to the fullest and showered with quotable quotes.

In no time did he free me from nagging thoughts of certain restrictions which a biographical project on a living subject might otherwise entail. He showed me trust; he gave me room. I, too, soon found myself in touch with the openness and pureness beneath that towering countenance.

In the following I have shortlisted some of the primary source materials on which I worked:
- Nineteen personal interviews, each lasting two to three hours and resulting in thirty-two ninety-minute cassettes
- Interviews with thirty-eight relatives, teachers, disciples, devotees, friends, Buddhist scholars, Buddhist and non-Buddhist personalities, and members of the media
- Source texts: nineteen of the master's titles; the complete lectures in four volumes; the complete diary, letters, notes, newspaper and journal clippings [of his activities] in Taiwan (since 1968), Hong Kong, Germany, and the United States; *Universal Gate* magazine; *Buddha's Light Newsletter*; *Awakening the World*; and major religious references such as *Biographies of the Eminent Masters, The Buddhist Religion and Buddhist Monas- teries in Taiwan, The Ch'an School and Tao School,* the *Fo Guang Encyclopedia*, and others.

To further capture Master Hsing Yun's life and spirituality, I visited Fo Guang Shan in Kaohsiung, other branch temples, and related organizations many, many times, and traveled to his hometown, Chiangtu, in Chiang-su, Ch'i-hsia Temple, Nanjing, where he was tonsured, Hong Kong, Germany, and the United States. I *hung* around as best I could for his lectures and classes, travels and visits, meetings and conferences, or when he entertained guests and devotees and rejoined loved ones. On one such tour last summer, it seemed that he finally had to say something about my shadowing him. "You sure are getting the *hang* of this!" he laughed.

The illustrious venerable and his phenomenal feats are not for me to affirm. This is not a book about an unreachable legend. I am merely trying to recreate an honest, intact record of this philosopher of life, his words and actions, his thinking and spirit... overall, just as he is. My touch I want to be light, my expression I hope to be open. May readers not only find it a successful story but also benefit from the enormity of his wisdom and intensity of his life force.

Although the protagonist is a Buddhist monastic, I have intended that the religious flavor be somewhat diluted, and, indeed, this is a book for everyone, not just Buddhists. Hoping to interest and inspire, and to ensure readability throughout, a popular approach has been adopted in the general presentation. May readers, too, be led to reflect on their Buddha nature and, ultimately, find the clear, cool source of the river of life.

The text is titled *Handing Down the Light* to represent the Dharma as a light which, when passed onto the hands of Master Hsing Yun, has come to shine across five continents. Further, the light, also representing his aspirations and deeds, shall continue to dispatch messages of compassion, joy, generosity, appreciation, affinity, humility, and gratitude through the defilements both within our minds and without.

The project has, for the past two years, kept me from home and loved ones more often than I would have liked. Gratitude is especially due to my parents, whose love and concern for their daughter, and their grand-daughter, seems boundless. Most of all, I must thank my loving husband, without whose support this task would never have come to such a prompt finish.

Last, may I offer this book for the benefit of all sentient beings.

C.Y.F.

Translator's note

Quintessentially this being the narrative of a many-splendored career in religion, translation has been a cross between literature and journalism, with a dash of sinology.

All Chinese names and terms, for most of the past, have been romanized according to the Wade-Giles system except for a few established in the Pin-yin phonetic system, like the extremely familiar Beijing, Nanjing, and others. Specifically, the less familiar names of places in China and Taiwan follow Wade-Giles.

All proper names, especially those of places and institutions, have been transliterated, with respective translations given in parentheses unless stated otherwise. Efforts have been made to translate these to enhance textual understanding and to convey an atmospheric feel.

Second and ensuing mentions of a place, institution, or publication without official translation, however, are in roman, which is a slight departure from the regular practice of italicizing titles of publications.

Last, all footnotes have been researched and written expressly for this translation.

A.L.M.

A Note on the Revised Edition

The first English edition of *Handing Down the Light*, published in 1996, was eagerly awaited by a growing number of English-speaking readers worldwide who have become increasingly interested in Buddhism and in the inspiring life of Venerable Master Hsing Yun in particular.

However, in the ensuing four years since publication, it has become apparent to us that our task in sharing this portion of Chinese Buddhist history is not yet complete. The English-speaking disciples of Venerable Master Hsing Yun have pointed out many constructive ways in which the text could be improved and thus better communicate with its intended audience. Hence, a new editing and revision team was formed by Venerable Tzu Jung, abbess of Hsi Lai Temple, in the fall of 1999 for just such a task. We would like to make particular note of all their efforts and to thank them for helping us to improve upon the contents of the text. In particular we thank Brenda Bolinger, Lucie Gonzalez-Kitchen, Mason Fries, Scott Herby, Laura Neustaedter, Ching Tay, Madelon Wheeler-Gibb and Corey Bell for their efforts in bringing forth an edition which we hope will both benefit and inspire the reader.

Fo Guang Shan
International Translation Center
Hsi Lai Temple
Los Angeles, 1999.

Preface

"Let your heartbeat resonate with the rhythm of all people! Let your bloodstream flow in oneness with all beings!"

Just what are we reading? An election promise? A bestseller's blurb? A rave review of a rock star's pop-culture appeal? A physician's formula for healing?

The impassioned cry is actually Venerable Master Hsing Yun's socially conscious vision for spreading the Dharma.

In the warming presence of its universal, harmonizing energy and commitment to render faith, joy, convenience, and hope unto others, humanistic Buddhism has opened hearts and transformed lives across the globe.

*   *   *

Discovering a religion that resonates with me has been a life long search. As a result, I have utmost admiration for those whose personal spiritual path has become clear. I am eager for the day when I, too, will be confident about what practice is right for me.

Over the last few years, I have been honored to spend time in Master Hsing Yun's company. Each time we met though, I hesitated to ask him about Buddhist philosophy, encouraging him to speak instead of social trends, relationships, educational systems, media impact politics between Taiwan and the mainland, and much more. Hsing Yun elaborated on these topics within the domain of *humanistic Buddhism and realistic Buddhism,* the forms of Buddhism he advocates. His eloquent arguments and profound connections caused me to consider how students may have benefited from his teachings if he had served as a professor. I learned an incredible amount during each of our lively exchanges.

I first began to admire the master through his column in *Global View Monthly* and his personal reflections in *Universal Gate* magazine. While I saluted his philosophy and concepts, I knew very little about his journey to promote Buddhism.

I yearned to know how he made complex doctrines easy and understandable with such wisdom and compassion:

- How he makes these seemingly complex doctrines concrete and practical
- What underlies the competence to run the multi-dimensional organization of Fo Guang Shan
- What noble and innate qualities enabled him to pass on the abbotship and complete Fo Guang Shan's succession at age fifty-eight, and create a more expansive space for Buddhism
- How he, with the strength of his vows, his causes and conditions, and his virtuous deeds, has projected Buddhism to the corners of the world.

At long last, the story of Master's influence on the world would be told.

*   *   *

In depicting a character of such profound depth and multiple dimensions as Master Hsing Yun, Fu Chi-ying has undoubtedly succeeded.

Using a clear-cut structure, fluid language, delightful illustrations, and information from personal interviews, the author enables those who are both familiar and unfamiliar with master to experience how he created Fo Guang Shan and the dynamic growth of humanistic Buddhism.

The greatness of Master Hsing Yun, as presented in this biography, is threefold. He is
- A religious reformer of remarkable resolve and practice
- A masterly innovator with the compassion and wisdom to popularize the Buddhist teachings, and
- A caring educator who makes religion practical and accessible.

His will to reform stems from his determination, his will to innovate from his creativity, and his will to educate from his compassion. With his determination, creativity and compassion, Hsing Yun is a Buddhist master from whom the world shall benefit, and a social educator whose influence reaches far and wide.

*   *   *

I have always believed that "concepts are capable of redirecting the course of history." Now I believe even more that "religion is capable to redirecting the course of life." What is recorded here about the master are the philosophies and actions which have transformed many lives.

Humanistic Buddhism and *realistic Buddhism*, which the master has spent a lifetime teaching, have not only changed the lives of countless Chinese people but will inarguably alter Chinese and world history in remarkable ways. Of course, his profound teachings have had the most impact on the dynamic and ever-changing island of Taiwan. Surely, the expansion of Buddhism in Taiwan has been a miracle which surmounts even the tremendous growth of their economy.

The author eloquently describes Hsing Yun's journey to

endear Buddhism to the hearts, minds and lives of people in many lands:

> *Every step he takes leaves behind trails of lotuses,*
> *the wind under his robe sweeps clean [the path to]*
> *the Pureland.*

With a heart of devotion and compassion, the monk from Yangchou transcended the limits of time and distance to gracefully create an infinite world of Buddha's Light.

As Buddha's Light International Association (BLIA) rapidly expands worldwide, Master Hsing Yun has many more miles of path to tread and much more Dharma to preach.

Kao Hsi-chun
Taipei
December 1994.

Part One

Many, Many Returns in Buddha Karma

At twenty-five

His birthplace in Chiangtu (Courtesy of Fu Chi-ying)

Ch'i-hsia Temple where Hsing Yun was tonsured
(Courtesy of Fu Chi-ying)

Sharing a private moment with his mother

Venerable Master Chih K'ai (second from left) and teachers at Ch'i-hsia

Chapter 1
To the delight of all Buddhas

*I*n March, Chiangnan¹ is a lush, green region alive with flitting orioles, floating butterflies, and budding peach and plum trees. Yangchou is nestled in this fertile land, a mere three hours from Nanjing, the hub of ancient Chinese culture.

Historically, Yangchou has been well known as a city of political, social and religious significance. It was one of nine provinces of the Hsia dynasty [c 2205 – 1766 B.C.E.], and, with the opening of the Grand Canal during the reign of emperor Yang of the Sui dynasty [589 – 618 C.E.], it was where cultural and economic forces converged. Situated at the estuary of the Yangtze, Yangchou has been a favorite sojourn for the literati throughout the ages. Emperor Ch'ien-lung of the Ch'ing [1644 – 1911 C.E.] dynasty was known to have traveled through Chiangnan six times while he was sovereign. T'ang [618 – 907 C.E.] poet Li Po [701 – 762 C.E.], in bidding his peer Meng Hao-jan [689 – 740 C.E.] farewell, once wrote:

> *Heading west, my old friend*
> *departs from Huang-ho Lou*
> *(Chamber of the Golden Crane)*
> *Amidst the mists and blossoms*

---
¹ The region south of the Yangtze.

> *of the third moon,*
> *he sails for Yangchou.*
> *Into the azure distance*
> *recedes the image of*
> *that lonely sail,*
> *Leaving behind the sight*
> *of the Yangtze flowing toward*
> *the sky above.*

Few other verses convey so simply the boundless beauty of Yangchou. Once tranquil and pristine, Yangchou is now quickly emerging as a dynamic metropolis in a country experiencing great change and reform.

Blessed hometown of Chiangtu

Accessible by a forty-minute drive from Yangchou is the county of Chiangtu, which in its pristine simplicity and serenity, has never been a tourist hot spot or a strategic transport location. But there is a distinct wonder about Chiangtu, for it is where one of this century's most illustrious religious leaders was raised.

There, in a gray-brick courtyard west of Hsien-nu (Goddess) Temple was the homestead of Venerable Master Hsing Yun of Fo Guang Shan (The Mountain of Buddha's Light).

On the twenty-second day of the seventh moon on the lunar calendar, 1927, an infant's cry rang from the abode of the Li family who ran a humble incense business. This child was their second son, with an elder brother and sister preceding his arrival. The birth of the boy, then named Kuo-shen, was anything but ordinary.

The matriarch of the family Mrs. Li[2] [Nee Liu Yu-ying], now a spirited and healthy old lady, still recalls every vivid detail:

"In labor with your master, I had a dream of a little golden figure. He was rummaging through the odds and ends by my bed with quiet determination.

'What are you looking for?' I asked.

'He's looking for stalks of rice [grain],' said a graying old man also present in her dream.

'My bed is stuffed with hay. How can there be any stalks of rice!'

At that moment, the little golden figure performed a miracle, and pulled a stalk of rice from under the bed.

The old man then told me: 'This *tao*[3] shall be fruitful.'"

The prophetic dream was the first of several unusual happenings. The chubby newborn was rosy-cheeked on one side and quite pale on the other. A pair of fine reddish lines painted the space between his nose and upper lip. Neighbors were soon gossiping about the "little monster who was born in to the home of Li Ch'eng-pao."[4] To prevent curious stares from the villagers, his mother loosely tethered him with a sturdy piece of string and kept him indoors most of the time until, inexplicably, these unusual birthmarks vanished by age two or three.

---

[2] Mrs. Li is fondly known as "Grandma Li" to many Chinese people who regard her as a caring and compassionate woman. She passed away in May 1996.
[3] *Tao*, rice, is a pun for *tao*, the way. This is also intimation on the mother's part that her child's life shall be fruitful due to his many accomplishments.
[4] Master Hsing Yun's father.

Plum of the Li family[5]

Hsing Yun has no recollection of these mythical tales. But each time his mother spoke at great lengths about the past, he would smile and listen contentedly as a son should. When others passed on these remarkable stories, his countenance was neutral, with neither pride nor objection to his noteworthy birth.

After nearly fifty years of aging, the Li home in Chiangtu has been renovated. The revived two-story single-family home with a spacious courtyard now houses the youngest brother Kuo-min and his family. A stroll up Li-min (Benefit People) Bridge, near to the Goddess Temple, brings into view the Grand Canal, which was once glorious and pure, but now suffers from devastating pollution and stagnation. Mrs. Li, early on, recognized the unique strength and courage of her son:

"Daily necessities in those days had to be purchased on the opposite bank of the canal. With the nation engulfed in war, nobody would risk their lives ferrying others back and forth for a mere pittance! Your master though, then only ten, would strip to his waist, tie his shirt round his forehead, and plunge right in. The rushing current of the canal daunted many, but he would always bring home the necessities. Everybody thought this second son of ours was special: of all the plums in the Li family, this would be the one to watch for."

Despite abundant praise of his gallantries, Hsing Yun retained an innate and subtle humility.

---

[5] Li, Master Hsing Yun's secular surname, is a pun for *li*, plum or a choice object. It is the same character in the Chinese language.

Grandma, the most beloved

Without reservation, Hsing Yun remembers his maternal grandmother Madam Liu [Nee Wang] with respect and tenderness. Though illiterate, she could chant the *Diamond Sutra* by heart, and had been a vegetarian for over half a century.

Years later in a Buddhist seminar, Master Hsing Yun fondly remembered his grandmother's religious influence on him as a child: "My grandmother became a vegetarian at the age of eighteen. Rising daily at dawn for her morning prayers, she would chant Buddhist texts like the *Amitabha Sutra* or the *Diamond Sutra* despite her illiteracy. My sister and I were raised under her wing, and the two of us would try to outdo each other as strict vegetarians. I was three or four then and quite unaware of the Buddhist teachings underlying vegetarianism. I was merely trying to please Grandma.

"My childhood was spent in her company. Everyday, sometime between midnight and daybreak, she would get up to meditate, fold her legs, rest her shoulders, assume the full lotus position, and control her breath. In the process, her tummy would roar like rushing rivers and swelling seas. As a sleepyhead roused from slumber, I would ask: 'Grandma, why is your tummy crying so!' 'This is called mastership. Mastership from practice,' was her reply."

The devout practice of Hsing Yun's Grandmother gave this inquisitive child and his older sister ample opportunities to accompany her to nearby temples where they paid homage and prayed to the Buddha. Occasionally, she would return home with the altar offerings, such as fruit or rice, which the children gladly consumed. As an eager child trying to imitate his beloved Grandmother, Hsing Yun experienced his first connections with the Buddha.

On occasion, monastics were received into their household. Grandmother was naturally the influence behind these visits. In an era of war and turmoil, the monastics impressed him tremendously with the grace of their robes, the serenity of their demeanor, and the respect they received from villagers. "How nice it is to be a monk!" he began to think.

Hsing Yun held his grandmother up as a consummate role model because of her noble character. She was industrious, frugal, and kind. During his monastic training, he missed her most dearly. When he turned twenty, he returned home to see her. Sewing peacefully under a tree, she began relating to him what she would expect for her own funeral, should the event take place. She hoped that things would be left in the hands of this grandchild, who was now a monk.

Two years later, the communist regime took over the country. That was the last time the two of them were together. When his grandmother passed away, Hsing Yun was already in Taiwan and had no way of tending to her funeral as promised. He had been extremely close to his Grandmother and his remorse was poignant. In a loving gesture to her, he made a regular practice of financially supporting his three uncles at home, hoping to return – if only in the slightest manner – what he had received from his Grandmother.

Buddha nature in the tot

Unable to offer bedazzling riches or a glorious ancestry, Hsing Yun's parents bestowed the gift of great character upon him. He took after his father in moderation and integrity and his mother in gallantry and fairness. His grandmother's compassion added to the wealth of qualities from which he was to benefit for life.

From a very early age, Hsing Yun has shared an exceptionally close and harmonious relationship with his older sister, Su-hua. These affectionate siblings recently reunited after more than forty years of separation. Reflecting on their childhood, Su-hua brimmed over with the same tenderness: "He was so different from the rest of us." She could not remember her kid brother ever fighting with anyone. In fact, a three-year-old Hsing Yun would drag the family candy-can to the courtyard, where its entire contents were given to friends in the neighborhood. Others considered this generous act foolish, and teased the son of the Li family for knowing little else but how to give everything away to others.

In looking back over their childhood, Su-hua realized that her younger brother had reflected characteristics of the Buddha Nature[6] from a very early age. She guessed that his willingness to consider monkhood probably stemmed from causes and conditions of many past lives.

Another time, the five-year-old Hsing Yun spotted a bunch of little chicks huddling together in the rain. He carried them back home, one by one, and placed them before the wood-burning furnace to help them dry off. One made a dash into the fire in panic. When the child snatched it back, he found its lower beak had been burnt quite badly. To help it to eat, he dug a tiny hollow in the earth, put in some rice, and let it feed from there. The chick was tenderly nursed

---

[6] Buddha Nature is the capacity shared by all sentient beings to awaken from ignorance to their true nature.

back to health and eventually grew into a thriving and mature hen.

Su-hua shared yet another episode vivid in her memory. On a deep wintry night during a family gathering for fireside stories, an elder began a narrative about human suffering. The main character was a white-bearded, impoverished, ailing, and hunger-stricken old man living in the mountains. Before the storyteller ended, the little brother had disappeared, only to be found underneath the table, weeping and feeling sorry for the poor old man! Even when comforted that it was just a tale he would not come out, and he rejected dinner altogether because he wanted to give his portion to the suffering old man in the story. His anguish was not appeased until he was allowed to visit his maternal grandfather that evening, to whom he kindly offered his dinner.

Last year, at the knowledge of her brother's homecoming, Su-hua, together with her daughter and two sons, came all the way from Liuchou, Kuanghsi, to Nanjing by way of a forty-eight-hour train ride.

In the courtyard of the brand-new home, which her brother had built for their mother's retirement, a serene Su-hua looked every bit as lovely and genteel as she must have been in her youth. Recent travels have brought her to both Hsi Lai Temple in America and Fo Guang Shan in Taiwan. Of course Su-hua recognizes the influential and admired leader that Hsing Yun is today, but deep down, he will always be her chubby, dimpled kid brother.

Mother, mentor of wisdom

The abundance of homes where "the wind sweeps the floor and the moon lights the house" demonstrated the confining poverty of the northern Chiangsu province where the Li family resided. Manual labor was the main means of livelihood and schooling was only for the privileged few who could afford it. Hsing Yun's folks, though somewhat better off than others, were unable to send him to a private school. With passion and eagerness for learning already in evidence, seven-year-old Hsing Yun found his first mentor in his illiterate mother.

The young Mrs. Li was frequently ill and often bedridden. Her loving second son would read to her from the *ch'i-tzu-tuan*,[7] then popular in Yangchou. She knew the piece by heart and would correct his blunders as he read, helping him build a fine vocabulary, encouraging his enthusiasm for reading, and reinforcing in him the principles of loyalty, honoring one's parents, integrity, and moral virtue. Years later, he still remembers the names of all one hundred and eight characters and their respective characteristics in the classic *Shui-hu Chuan* (Water Margin).[8]

Family resources eventually allowed private schooling during the next two or three years. Unfortunately, this luxury was interrupted by local bandits and the occupation by Japanese troops. Little would he have expected that the passages from Confucian texts absorbed during this brief period

---

[7] Folkloric literature primarily of mythological, historical, and chivalrous themes, written in a prose made up of structured seven-character (or word, as in the Chinese language) sentences.
[8] A masterful fiction set in thirteenth-century China about 108 characters compelled to flee social chaos under the decaying Sung dynasty. It is said to be authored by Shih Nai-an. Many English translations exist.

would remain the only formal education in his entire life.

Strictly speaking, he never spent a single day in a regular school, or earned a graduation diploma, a multitude of which he has handed out in later years. He never attended a university but founded Hsi Lai and Fo Guang universities and has been awarded an honorary doctorate. His devotees, among the most highly educated in the history of Chinese Buddhism, hail from Harvard, University of California, Berkeley, and similar institutions. Countless intellectuals have taken refuge with him. To them, his lack of degrees and diplomas is irrelevant. To them, he is a true teacher and master.

His triumph over the expected illiteracy of northern Chiangsu residents represents a teaching he still propagates today: limitations are merely perceptions, and potential may be realized despite even the worst obstacles.

Half a century separation

Upon entering the monastery, Hsing Yun became a monk who transcended the three realms of desire, form and formlessness.[9] The vast compassion of his true nature has since been offered to all living beings. Still, the innate attachment to loved ones is hard to relinquish. When communication with his family was impossible and he had no way of knowing whether his mother was alive or deceased, he would not celebrate a single birthday. In Buddhist culture, a mother's birthday is an occasion to appreciate and honor her for the suffering she experienced in giving birth. Hsing Yun was deeply saddened that he could not express his respect and

---

[9] Living beings are reborn time and again into these limiting realms.

love to her on this special day, and chose instead to remain solemn and alone.

Each year he would rise early, go before the Buddha, quietly light incense, and chant in solitude. He dedicated this practice to the health and well-being of his mother. Finally in 1986, Venerable Tzu Chuang, then abbess of Hsi Lai Temple, Los Angeles, finally located Mrs. Li, who was indeed alive and well. To honor his mother, on his sixtieth birthday, Hsing Yun held a grand Dharma function to show gratitude and celebrate not only his mother's birthday, but the birthday's of others who shared her generation. Invitations were extended to a thousand lay and sangha community members also in their sixties. At this special gathering, the Buddhist spirit of honoring one's parents would be manifested through treating all parents as one's own, and sharing a sense of community with others in the same generation.

As family visitations from overseas resumed in China, his mother was able to join him on various trips to Japan, the U.S., and Taiwan. At long last, mother and son spent the lunar New Year together at Hsi Lai Temple – their first in fifty years and their first since the beginning of his monkhood. The family reunion was truly an intimate and touching one for both of them.

As much as he missed his mother all those years, she too had suffered. She was condemned to hard labor, eking out a meager living. The family was considered outcasts for having a son who resided out of the country. Hsing Yun was harshly judged for supposedly compromising his loyalty to the nation. His mother was not even allowed to keep a photograph of him. When circumstances worsened, she was repeatedly detained and interrogated, and pressured with a devastating choice: "Leniency if you confess the whereabouts of your son, and punishment if you don't."

Thankfully, this painful and frightening era has now passed. Despite his lengthy and distant travels to spread the Dharma for the benefit of all sentient beings, Hsing Yun is dedicated to the role of a dutiful son. He continues to care for his mother from afar, arranging for neighbors to visit and play a daily game of mahjong with her.

In the spring of 1994, Hsing Yun left Kaohsiung to return home. With a birthday cake, peach-shaped buns, longevity noodles, and flowers in hand, and disciples and devotees tagging along, he went to celebrate his mother's big day. "How I've cried for you! My eyes are failing!" the mother was heard to whisper as she held her son's hand in hers. The gentle master proceeded to sit quietly with his mother, helping her to enjoy her birthday cake.

Her gift to all living beings

Mrs. Li, at ninety-four,[10] is a walking historical text. Having braved storms of epic proportions – the fall of the Ch'ing dynasty, the Hsin-hai Revolution,[11] the rise of modern China, the strife of the warlords, the Sino-Japanese war, the civil war between the nationalists and communists, the Cultural Revolution, and the recent reconnection between Taiwan and the Mainland – her thoughts and actions do not arise without deep contemplation. Once while walking about the

---

[10] In 1994.
[11] The revolution led by Dr. Sun Yat-sen which overthrew the Manchurian Ch'ing regime in 1911.

grounds of Hsi Lai Temple with her son in the moist, cool morning air, they arrived at the slope to the left of the entrance. Hsing Yun, turning the key to a side door, announced, "This door opens to a shortcut leading to the temple." "Main door or side door," responded his mother, "in this world of ours, the best people take the main door, the mediocre wait for another, and the worst choose nothing. There's no shortcut!" With a colorful, and at times turbulent foundation of experience, Mrs. Li embodies strength and perseverance.

Mrs. Li feels that her life's most momentous decision was to offer her son to Buddhism by letting him take the tonsure.[12] Her family seems to have been blessed with exceptional longevity: she and her three brothers together add up to over 350 years of age; her four children, over 280 years; both generations, over 600 years.

On a past visit to Fo Guang Shan, one of the devotees asked if Mrs. Li would like to say something. Contrary to her son's concern over her possible stage fright, she stood at the podium before an audience of twenty thousand and spoke with confidence: "Fo Guang Shan *is* the pure-land; heaven *is* among us. May the Master guide you; may you attain the Way at Fo Guang Shan. You're all so kind. This old grandma has little to offer you: I can only give you the gift of my son."

Afterwards, when they were alone together, Hsing Yun teasingly asked his mother: "How could you give me away so easily? Don't you want me any more?" "So many need

---

[12] The tonsure is a monastic ritual involving the shaving of the head, signifying entrance into the order.

you. How can I keep you all to myself? You're not mine; you belong to everyone," she replied.

It is true that from the instant the tearful Mrs. Li agreed to allow her beloved son to leave home to become a monk, he has been a great offering to all sentient beings.

Chapter 2
Promise on Cloud Dwelling Mountains

The bloodiest chapter in contemporary Chinese history opened with the eruption of Japanese gunfire on Lu-kuo (Rush Waterway) Bridge, Hopei, on July 7, 1937. Thereafter, Japanese militarists proceeded to impose havoc on millions of innocent lives across the land.

On towards destiny via the unknown

It was under these dire circumstances that Hsing Yun's father left home on business. Hsing Yun was never to see his father again and the family never received news of his whereabouts. Financial ruin plagued the family for the next few years. Hoping to locate her husband herself, Mrs. Li decided to take twelve-year-old Hsing Yun with her to look for her husband in Nanjing. The year was nearing its end and the northern winter was harsh and unrelenting. As the delicate young woman and her little boy, who had never in his life crossed the county gate of Chiangtu, began their journey, they had no idea where it would lead.

To the joy of all the hearts he has touched, their extraordinary quest led to the child's destiny – the fruition of many lives of connection with the Buddha.

Hsing Yun recounted what happened: "Midway to Nanjing, we bumped into the newly formed peace corps practicing their drills. As I gazed intently at the scene, I was approached by a monk who was one of the receptionists at the temple on Ch'i-hsia Shan (Cloud-dwelling Mountain). Probably thinking I looked cute with my round cheeks and big ears, he casually asked whether I was willing to become a monk. Simply out of instinct, I quickly replied, 'I'm willing!' Before long a message came from the abbot Venerable Master Chih K'ai: 'I've heard that you want to leave home to become a monk. You may do so under me as your master!'"

But how could his mother let go! In trying to find her husband, she was about to lose her son. How was she going to face those at home! With noble calm, young Hsing Yun insisted that he had given his word and would keep his promise. With sadness and understanding, she tearfully accepted his choice.

Forlornly and alone, his mother headed home, and Hsing Yun stayed at Ch'i-hsia Temple. His father continued to be missing and villagers speculated that he was probably one of 300,000 innocents who perished in the Rape of Nanjing [1937 C.E.]. Although Hsing Yun did not remember much about his father, on his first homecoming he had the ancestral shrine renovated, the memorial tablets of both his maternal grandmother and father put in a place of honor, and asked family members to light incense and pray regularly.

Ch'i-hsia was both a mountain and temple of historic renown. Under Master Chih K'ai, Hsing Yun received the Dharma name Wu Ch'e (Thorough Realization), and the monastic name Chin Chueh (Instantaneous Awakening), and became a disciple of the forty-eighth generation of the Lin-chi division of the Ch'an school. He became the youngest student at Ch'i-hsia Vinaya College, which was open to monastic students from all over the area. The fact that Hsing Yun was tonsured there did not make Ch'i-hsia his ancestral monastery. In accordance with the monasterial propriety of the time, Ta-chueh (Great Awakening) Temple of Yihsing where his master was tonsured became his ancestral monastery instead.

So many monks in northern Chiangsu

As one considers the circumstances of Hsing Yun's decision to become a monastic, one may ponder over the phenomenal number of Buddhist monastics in contemporary China who originated from the northern Chiangsu province. Well-known monastics from this area include Venerable Masters Chih Kuang, T'ai Ts'ang, Nan T'ing, Tung Ch'u, Yen P'ei, Chu Yun, and others. It seems clear that there is something special about this region.

The harsh environment is one unique and influential feature. The lowland of northern Chiangsu is where the hopelessly silted Huai River is redirected by way of the constricted Grand Canal, which floods every year between summer and fall when the Huai swells. Moreover, because it is formed by the continual rise of the sea level, the soil simply contains too much salt to be suitable for agriculture. Residents, lamenting over life's impermanence and toil, are often compelled to turn to spiritual practice for strength.

Next, driven by the region's poverty, there came a shift of the rural population to urban cities like Shanghai. Professional pursuits were mainly limited to manual labor. With respect and admiration, the struggling villagers learned peace and patience from the serene demeanor and tranquil lifestyle of the monastics.

The region was also permeated by the belief that an entire family lineage benefited from the vows and practice of one person committed to the monastic life. When monkhood for fathers and brothers improved the quality of life for those at home, they frequently returned to lead sons and nephews onto the same path.

The supreme monastery of the Six Dynasties

Historic temples abound in the Chenchiang, Chinshan, Chiaoshan, and Yihsing counties of Chiangsu. One of them is Ch'i-hsia Temple, built during the Six Dynasties period [208 – 588 C.E.]. There in the shade of the luxuriantly forested Cloud-dwelling Mountain, where ancient and regal maples spread like evening clouds, the gathering literati used to stand and gaze, awestruck by its beauty.

Passing through the mountain gate, the steps leading to the temple are lined with old trees and new blossoms. A halfmoon-shaped lake beyond shimmers in the sun. A twenty-five cent admission is collected in the garden, and then again at the temple to aid in maintaining its impressive and historic presence.

In the cool April air stands the majestic P'i-lu[1] Shrine. On the lawn surrounding the five-story Sarira Stupa[2] young Hsing Yun spent many pleasant hours after school. Parts of

---

[1] Vairocana, originally the sun, meaning the pervasive Buddha's light upon all living beings or the ultimate enlightenment attained from endless kalpas of practice.
[2] The stupa or pagoda storing the sarira; relics left after the cremation of a Buddha or saint.

the hexagonal stupa have become time worn and crumbled away. Inside the 1,500-year-old stone cave of a thousand Buddhas, figures of the Bodhisattvas and arhats[3] still maintain the full lotus position, but unfortunately without their heads – evidence of violence against them by the ignorant Red Guards. The authority's reconstructive efforts have only minimally helped salvage much of the beauty that once graced the stupa.

Its cloud-dwelling remoteness was probably what kept Ch'i-hsia Temple from total ruin during the siege of the Cultural Revolution. The main shrine and side halls are still intact. But the waft of incense is thin and the presence of devotees, rare. At times an old monk, frail and alone, emerges. The sramaneras (novice monks), in groups of three or five, appear subdued and downcast. Though structurally sound, the Temple has lost much of its vitality and vibrance.

Even the Buddha, in the face of half a century of desolation, is unanimated. One cannot help but wonder about the dawns and dusks Hsing Yun spent among those many splendored maples and within those long, resplendent walls.

Poor as a temple mouse

Naturally, in the scantiness of wartime livelihood, there was a shortage of devotee visitations and donations to the temples. Even though laypersons were aware of the great virtue and merit of making offerings, most were simply too poor to do so. In those early days at Ch'i-hsia Temple, indeed, Hsing Yun was as poor as a temple mouse.

---

[3] A Buddhist saint; one who has attained enlightenment and is no longer subject to death and rebirth.

Each letter he wrote his mother he had to keep for a year because he could not spare the postage. A torn robe he would mend with paper; a worn sole he would fix with some cardboard; a lost sock he would replace with a reject from another pair. He cannot quite recall having ever worn socks of the same shade due to the scarcity of his possessions. He vividly remembers the one bucket of water shared by all for the morning toilette. The act was restricted to the so-called *two times and a half* – first, soaking the towel; second, wiping the face and soaking it again; and wringing the towel the remaining half. The facecloth used for washing often remained dirty. After the ritual, the cleansing water turned to mud. Still, it was carried off to flush the latrine.

Food was in extremely short supply. There was literally too little gruel for too many monks. Hsing Yun remembers that Ch'i-hsia Temple had housed a sangha of over four hundred monastics from all over China. Rice, often mixed with other grains, was served twice a month. Otherwise the daily gruel, more a watery broth than anything else, was accompanied with either beancurd dregs or salted turnips. Leftovers of the dregs, when sun-dried again, were contaminated by droppings of birds who came to feast on them, and the turnips were often infested with maggots. The vegetable soup, quite free from substance, would probably be clean enough for laundry. Sometimes, with little snails and earthworms lining its bottom and afloat with bugs, it started to smell quite badly even during the chanting preceding the meal. With both difficulty and gratitude, Hsing Yun would close his eyes, hold his breath, and gulp it down.

Our human condition renders us prone to sickness and

pain. One time, Hsing Yun came down with a case of skin ulcers so horrendous that each time he removed his garb, his ailing skin was painfully torn. Despite the pain and danger, due to scarcity of resources he was not able to see a doctor.

Another time, he contracted malaria. Monasterial discipline disallowed sick leave and he was compelled to go about the daily routine like the others despite bouts of chills and fever. It was not until weeks later that his master, who headed the Buddhist college, was informed of his condition and sent someone over with half a bowl of salted vegetables. In tears, Hsing Yun ate them and was moved with gratitude for this gift of healing.

To anyone living in the affluent modern world, a half-bowl of salted vegetables would be trivial, but to the stricken Hsing Yun, it was comparable to the most delicious delicacy. The kind gesture gave rise to his determination to spread the Buddhist faith in order to reciprocate his master's graciousness, and it reinforced his view on hunger – no one should go hungry. Today, kitchens in all the branch temples are ready, around the clock, to provide for whoever comes to the gate.

Nonsentient vs. sentient, unreasonable vs. reasonable

There is no end to the suffering of the body; nor do the trials of the spirit seem any easier.

The new kid at Ch'i-hsia Temple often attended lectures for seven or eight hours at a time, palms joined and kneeling on the gravel until his arms were so numb that they no longer felt like his own and the gravel had sunk into his little knees. He was only twelve.

When, at fifteen, he received the complete precepts of

monkhood,[4] he began to realize the depth of their meaning. He vowed to accept the sentient with the nonsentient, and the reasonable with the unreasonable.

"I remember answering in the negative when the preceptor asked if I had ever killed. The next instant a whole bundle of willow twigs came down on my head: 'Not even mosquitoes and ants?' I quickly changed to the affirmative. But down came the willows once again because, regardless of the victim, killing is a sin. Then the preceptor asked: 'Did your master send you?' 'I've come on my own,' I replied as I was whacked a third time. 'So your master didn't send you. In deciding to come yourself, you deserve to be beaten,' the preceptor said. 'Yes, the master sent me,' humbly I corrected myself once more. 'What if you weren't sent? Would you have come just the same?' And I was hit the fourth time."

The willow twigs banished arrogance and obstinacy; the beatings transformed clinging to the ego, to the absence of it. As Hsing Yun's religious sentiments and integrity took form, a personality evolved that "is content with every encounter, lives according to circumstances, is carefree in the mind, and commits for the sake of others."

To the keenly inquisitive youth, that was only the beginning of the training period. It became more difficult in the next fifty-three days. Each time he raised his head, wondering where sounds of the mountain or streams came from,

---

[4] Refering to the Triple Platform Ordination: the first in which the novices receive 10 precepts; the second in which the bhiksus and bhiksunis (monks and nuns) receive 250 and 500 (actually 348) respectively; and the third in which the preceptees aspire to be Bodhisattvas.

the leading master in the preceptoral hall would catch him and the bamboo cane would strike: "What is there to listen to? Close your ears now! Young as you are, what sound can you claim to be yours?" At that, he would hasten to gather mind and spirit and block out the leaves that rustled like waves and rain that beat on the eaves. But again the master's cane found him: "Open your ears to hear! What sound can you say is not yours?" At other times, he would be hit for peeping at the liturgical ceremonies at the preceptoral shrine: "Your eyes are drifting! What is there that is yours?" Then, on exiting the hall, he became aware of the grass that swayed with the breeze and the geese that soared with the clouds and, in panic, shut his eyes to them. "Open your eyes to see! What is there that isn't yours?" He was hit once more.

This form of training, one of inclusion and acceptance of any and all circumstances, laid the groundwork of his practice and preaching, and nurtured a personality that is equally at peace with having and not having, hunger and fullness, day and night, more and less, advancing and retreating, largeness and smallness.

Master Chih K'ai, disciplinarian and reprimander

Venerable Master Chih K'ai treated his disciple with austerity, founded on deep love. At the time of the lunar New Year, everybody else would take time off to go home. Not Hsing Yun. He yearned to be reunited with his family but could not unless the master gave consent: which he did not. In ten years, in fact, he had given his disciple only two sets of clothing. During the occasional tutorial, he treated Hsing Yun the way a traditional master treats his disciple, disciplining and reprimanding to strengthen and ennoble his will.

On one occasion, Hsing Yun was chided in class by another teacher. Master Chih K'ai, hearing the news and thinking he might be wronged, sent for him. After the master asked about his circumstances, he raised the teacup before his student and said: "You thought telling me your woes would get you something from me, didn't you! Listen, even your allowance is less than the spare change I spend on tea. But I'm not even giving you that! Why? You may not understand now, but you will appreciate my intentions someday."

As he grew in years and wisdom, he did come to appreciate the reasons and the profundity of those intentions.

The reason for denying him a visit home was due to his need to deepen and mature in his spiritual practice. Despite the possession of stable roots and a good nature, it was feared that exposure to outside elements might be distracting, and that he might retract and lose the desire for the Truth. Rigorous training was designed to teach him to prevail with mental fortitude. Mastering this skill entailed the endurance of pain and poverty. In the end, he learned to let go of material life and ceased to ask for more or desire different circumstances.

After four decades, Hsing Yun returned to Ch'i-hsia Temple to sweep the burial stone of his master for the first time. He, who rarely sheds a tear prostrated before the memorial tablet of Master Chih K'ai, told of his own struggles to fulfill his master's wishes, prayed, and wept.

Media producer Chou Chih-min who toured with him records what she witnessed:

"The parade to his ancestral monastery was overwhelming. The sound of the bell and drum resounded as a solemn and important pronouncement. The master's gait was weighty and his eyes were brimming with tears. Speechless and with great reverence, he prostrated before the Buddha time after time. When finally he was invited to speak, he broke down in tears before he could begin. Ten minutes passed, and the abbot posed the request once more. The master began again: 'I was tonsured at Ch'i-hsia Temple. Forty-six years I have been away and today I am home to visit my ancestral monastery. How beautiful this sacred place has been kept! With their lives the venerables must have guarded this place, and with their hearts, tended the grounds! How you must have been there for him when Master Chih K'ai suffered, consoled him when he would rather have died! I cannot possibly begin to thank you! ... I thought I would be strong but, here I am in my ancestral monastery, I know not what to feel any more...' At that, he wept again."

Master Chih K'ai died defending the Buddhist faith in the turmoil of the Cultural Revolution. He was buried in his hometown Haian, Chiangsu. In a spirit of service and reverence, Hsing Yun began to financially support his master's family and during every homecoming, chants sutras and prays in gratitude at his master's graveside.

Hsing Yun's family felt the heartache of his extended absence. His mother took advantage of visiting him as often she could. To be near him, brothers Kuo-hua and Kuo-min lived and worked at the temple for a few years. Terribly worried about her brother's badly worn shoes, sister Su-hua learned the special skill of making monastic footwear from a nun who lived miles away. Unsure of his exact size, she made two pairs – one larger and the other smaller – which she asked someone to deliver. It was years later that Su-hua realized that Hsing Yun gave them away to a couple of young novices much poorer than himself, and he continued to make do with the pair that he had.

The young and valiant monastic

The six years on Cloud-dwelling Mountain laid the foundation for Hsing Yun's lifelong commitment in Buddhism. By the time he was admitted to Chiao-shan Buddhist College, Chenchiang, in 1945, he had matured into an astute and compassionate young monk.

Chiao-shan Buddhist College, among the most reputable higher institutions, was home to an outstanding faculty and student population. Its chancellor, Venerable Master Hsueh Fan, is now the abbot of Ch'i-hsia Temple. There, Hsing Yun studied *Abhidharmakosa (Compendium of Abhidharma)* under Master Yuan Chan and early Buddhism under Chih Feng. Master Ming Shan, the vigilant octogenarian abbot of Chiao-shan and Pao-hua temples, coached him on the doctrine of Yogacara[5] for half a year and remembers the young man in his late adolescence as "very focused on his studies, very reticent then, but quite eloquent now." They have taken time to get together a few times these past years and, whenever credited for having been the renowned mentor to a distinguished student, Master Ming Shan smiles and says: "Hsing Yun has done much to revitalize Buddhism. Truly,

---

[5] The Mind-only philosophy that nothing exists apart from the mind.

he is my master now!"

Shih Ming, a classmate from Chiao-shan, takes pride in Hsing Yun and recounts those days they shared: "You were so supportive of my two feature columns, *New Voice* and *Kalavinka*,[6] in the local Chenchiang newspaper. Each time I asked for a piece of your writing, you would always shake your hands first. This was to tell me that you would have it when you gestured to me that you wouldn't. Then you would lower your head in silence, and the conversation and laughter of our mountain stroll would subside. I knew you were organizing your thoughts and beginning to compose a masterpiece. Then at study hall that evening, you would place in my hands the completed work.

"I became a reporter for Nanjing's *Buddhism Monthly*. Once I was packing for another trip when you slipped a bundle of cash into my pocket, saying, 'I know your hard work brings little profit. Be sure to feed yourself!' I smiled, and accepted your gift. When we met again on my return, I lifted my garb and jokingly asked you, 'Can you tell I used your money wisely?' You were pleased with my ample belly and laughed heartily."

Books, the causes and conditions

In the 1930's, China witnessed an increased immersion of Western culture into its own. Without newspapers available in the typically reclusive orthodox Buddhist monastery where Hsing Yun lived, discontent began to stir among the young minds in the sangha, who were eager to keep abreast of

---

[6] Wondrous sounds.

the times. Fortunately, however, an evacuated country school left behind a library. The older monastics were indifferent, but Hsing Yun spent hours in this newly found retreat away from the monotony of the monasterial life. Without hesitation, he flung himself into the sea of Chinese classics and, to this day, admits to savoring history and biographies the most. In perusing translations of Western works, he was first introduced to contemporary Western thought. This opened a window within his heart to the world beyond the monastery, and beyond China.

Today, Fo Guang Shan provides over twenty libraries for its international department, the lay community, students, and children. These facilities can be traced to the circumstances, which first bonded Hsing Yun to a library five decades prior.

Once touched by the joy of books, the potential impact of Hsing Yun's lack of schooling completely disappeared. Every cent he had was invested in new titles; he would miss a meal rather than a book. Since this discovery, a delightful volume is often the gift of choice between the master and his disciples.

In his avid reading, Hsing Yun sharpens his comprehension and clarity, and seeks to draw his own conclusions. He adds commentaries and annotations, makes generous notes, jots down unforgettable lines, and always indicates the sources. Perusing personal notes each time is equivalent to reading the book once again. This practice enables him to tutor the most intellectually gifted scholars among his disciples, and to become a best-selling author and articulate public speaker.

By the time he left Chiao-shan Budhist College in 1947, Hsing Yun had studied in the monastery for nearly ten years. The journey form Ch'i-hsia Vinaya School to the preceptoral hall of Pao-hua Shan, and from Chiao-shan Buddhist College to the meditation hall of T'ien-ning Temple, Chinshan, completed Hsing Yun's training in the Buddhist discipline and doctrine. The blend of masterly training and self-education fully immersed him in the Mahayana[7] spirit of the non-duality of practice and understanding. Afterwards, with youthful ardor, he stepped into a tumultuous and desperate society and found himself embroiled in the survival of both the nation and his faith.

---

[7] Greater Vehicle.   Salvation for all, as all are the Buddha and will attain Budhahood.

Chapter 3
Facing the turbulent times

Graduating from the Chiao-shan Buddhist College, Hsing Yun first became director of Ta-chueh Temple and then principal of Pai-t'a (White Pagoda) Primary School. Stepping beyond his monastic Buddhist background and into the pulse of society, Hsing Yun crossed over the threshold of a great epoch.

It was a maddening time. The belligerence of the warlords, the aggression of the Japanese, the strife between the nationalists and communists, and the suffering of the common folk outraged him as they did thousands of young patriots. Accompanying the outrage toward injustice was a deep sadness arising from his Buddhist compassion. Of critical concern was the Buddhist religion itself, hanging precariously on the brink of extinction. Hsing Yun recognized the crucial need for reform and regeneration. "Buddhism doesn't exist solely for personal wants and desires! Don't ask it for favors. We all must on behalf of Buddhism offer guidance and nurturing. This great responsibility is ours!" That was the birth of a body of thought which would continue to evolve in the years to come.

Buddhism in China, its ups an downs

Indian Buddhism was introduced into China during the

reign of emperor Ming [58 – 75 C.E] of the Eastern Han dynasty and flourished for the next 400 years in the Sui and T'ang dynasties. Mainstream Buddhism during the period was society-oriented. Many eminent monks were active in both political and literary circles. Some were highly regarded in the imperial court, such as T'ien-t'ai (Heavenly Terrace) school's Master Chih I [538 – 597 C.E.] in the court of emperor Yang of the Sui dynasty, Fa-hsiang (Dharma Mark) school's Master Hsuan Tsang [602? – 664 C. E] in the court of emperor T'ai-tzung of the T'ang dynasty, Hua-yen (Garland) school's Master Fa Tsang [643 – 713 C.E.] and Ch'an school's Master Shen Hsiu [605 – 706 C.E.] in the court of empress Wu Tse-t'ien of the T'ang dynasty. Other monks were known to befriend such literary luminaries as Po Chu-I [772 – 846 C.E.], Wang Wei [701 – 761 C.E.], Li Ao [772 – 841 C.E.], and others.

    The Buddhist community attempted to reach the general public by way of literature, drama, and art, and in so doing became responsible for enriching the cultural contents of the era. Through other services, especially financial asisstance and charitable deeds, religion and livelihood were further interwoven. These included the establishments of *the inexhaustible treasury*, which was a banking system offering interest-free and contract-free loans,[1] *clinics* which offered medical services for the sick, and *fields of pity*[2] to help the needy. These efforts to offer convenience to the community were immensely successful during the Sui and T'ang dynasties.

---

[1] In the original text, established by San-chieh Chiao (Three Period Sect).
[2] Regular collections of finanical contributions to aid the needy.

The tide turned drastically by the Sung [960 – 1279 C.E.] and Yuan [1279 – 1368 C.E.] dynasties, however. Political persecution and the rise of *li-hsueh*[3] doomed the prosperity Buddhism had previously enjoyed. The intellectuals drifted away from the monastics, and the monastics themselves from secularity altogether. The founding emperor, Chu yuan-chang [1328 – 1398 C.E.] of the Ming dynasty, had been a novice Buddhist practitioner in his youth. He fully recognized this all-embracing faith[4], its popular appeal, and its valuable influence on society. Concerned that religion might instigate division, instead of cohesion, he took action to control it. To do this, he allocated vast mountain properties to the monasteries and the monastic population was relocated to the designated areas. From that point, Buddhism made a distinct departure from society, and its contact with the general public swiftly declined. Behind the closed mountain gate, Buddhism assumed the format of a conservative, reclusive, and impractical religion. Clearly, its integration with Chinese culture was waning.

Venerable Master Lien Ch'ih [1532 – 1612 C.E.] of the Ming dynasty wrote in the *Leisurely Writings by the Bamboo Window* about corruption in the sangha which so anguished him: "Some act like geomancers, like prognosticators, like

---

[3] A school of learning in Sung which employs the rational approach in the study of the classics.

[4] In the hereditary caste system of ancient India some 3,000 years ago, social distinction was drawn in accordance with the four castes: brahmins (priests), rulers and the military, farmers and traders, and serfs. But Sakyamuni Buddha taught compassion for and equality among all living beings who, he maintained, all possess the characteristics of wisdom and virtue, and will all attain Buddhahood. Such an advocacy invariably illuminated the despairing lower class at the time, who rallied around in zealous support.

physiognomists, like alchemists. ... Some hold their record of donations with arrogance and pride. ... Some posed as fortune tellers, carrying around a mere copper piece, beating it with a bamboo stick to predict the future..." Monastics degraded Buddhism by behaving as roving practitioners of the occult and or simple paupers. "This is the absolute worst of *mo-fa*!"[5] lamented Master Lien Ch'ih, fearing the disintegration of Buddhism.

Without cultural support, the once hearty pulse of Buddhism became faint, and monastics shifted their focus to merely performing funeral services. The religion totally dissociated itself from the general populace and the literati detached themselves from a degraded and stagnant sangha. Ironically, the occasional monastic who expressed concern for worldly affairs or possessed a reputation akin to the literati was criticized as overly secular. Venerable Master T'ai Hsu, who lived at the turn of the century, was among those who were victimized by this common misconception of Buddhism, which is often, unfortunately, still believed to be true.

The initial founding of the Republic of China in Mainland China was accompanied by a movement against Confucianism engineered by young intellectuals who had little knowledge of Western thought. Buddhism also received a public beating during this period. These intellectuals judged the clay buddhas and country monks as feudalistic, misguided, and superstitious hybrids, and they viewed monastic ceremonies with disdain. "Down with the temples and up with

---

[5] The last of the three formal periods of the Buddhist teachings in which its deterioration will lead to its eventual extinction. The first period was *cheng-fa* (period of correct doctrine) and the second was *hsiang-fa* (semblance period).

public education" was a common mindset promoting a means of national salvation. In 1927, warlord Feng Yu-hsiang, nicknamed *the Christian General*, ordered the annihilation of Buddhism in Honan province. At his command, monastics were exiled, or viciously murdered. Likewise, the provincial authorities of Chechiang wanted to eliminate the sangha, and the central government's minister of internal affairs, Hsueh Tu-pi, proposed that monasteries be converted into schools. The entire nation was inflamed by an anti-Buddhist sentiment. This was one of the most painful and devastating eras in the history of Buddhism in China.

Master T'ai Hsu, the legend

Finally, the seemingly defeated young sangha saw flickers of light in the perilous darkness. It rekindled hope in their religion and validated their patriotism. Venerable Master T'ai Hsu [1889 – 1947 C.E.] was the beacon at the forefront who led the way.

Many of Hsing Yun's teachers at Chiao-shan had studied under Master T'ai Hsu. Hsing Yun read his works extensively. The desperate young sangha at the time was particularly impassioned by his call, "Every citizen is accountable for the rise and fall of a nation; the sangha is accountable for the rise and fall of Buddhism." Master T'ai Hsu taught a redirection of Buddhism from the passivity of reclusion to the potential of humanity. In spearheading massive reforms in the Buddhist hierarchy, monasterial assets, and doctrinal teachings, he urged that "worldly matters be viewed through a spiritual leans and tended to accordingly."

In restructuring the Buddhist hierarchy, Master T'ai Hsu

urged that the dormant sangha be revitalized, training every monk to be a skilled instructor and every nun a qualified teacher and nurse. In reforming doctrinal teachings, he encouraged people to substitute the fatalistic belief that "life is suffering" with a positive attitude which affirms that life is valuable. He envisioned reliance on the monastery replaced by self-sufficiency that is attained through individual efforts and cultivation.

Master T'ai Hsu also designed the contemporary format of Buddhist education. In 1918, the groundbreaking of Minnan Buddhist College caused a uneasiness across the nation. Unfortunately, the relationship between the school and the monastery where it was housed was plagued by conflict that they had difficulty resolving. After ten years of irreconcilable tension, the partnership dissolved. Several attempts were made to eliminate the friction and reconnect, but these endeavors were never successful.

With astute observation and analysis, Master T'ai Hsu knew that Buddhism could not exist without a united China. In the pursuit of national unity, he called for monastic participation in anti-Japanese activities in the divided and desperate country. "The nation, society, and all living beings are one," he advocated.

Despite condemnation and accusations of betrayal from the senior sangha, the younger monastics rallied to support him and hailed him as the savior of Buddhism in modern China. At the end of the war, Hsing Yun found himself in the master's Personnel Training Class in Chinese Buddhist Affairs. A classmate demonstrated his loyalty, saying, "Should Master T'ai Hsu ask me to tread boiling water and prance on fire, I would not ask why."

Language, the tool of reform

While stationed at White Pagoda Primary School as principal, Hsing Yun cared for the young and spent long hours pondering how to carry out Master T'ai Hsu's ideal of a new Buddhist faith. Like Hu Shih-chih [1891 – 1962 C.E.][6] who maintained that "China's doom was poverty and ignorance," he realized language was the tool of reform and bridge to the public. He soon embarked on a number of literary creations: *Raging Billows*, a monthly publication he founded with classmate Master Chih Yung that ran for more than twenty issues; *Hsia-kuang* (Splendid Light) *fu-k'an*, a supplementary he edited for the newspaper *Hsu pao*; and extensive essay contributions to local papers in Chiangsu. His writings generated a considerable readership among the young. Barely twenty himself, Hsing Yun was ready to bring Buddhism to a new height by urging that service conventions be revised and monasterial management be reorganized. While writing profusely, he read literature of the 1930s with voracity, absorbing mountains of knowledge.

After Japan surrendered, China struggled to gain stability and momentum once again. However, before stability was completely attained, the nation became embroiled in yet another civil war. Hsing Yun was compelled to cease his endeavors, delaying the process and progress of change. With Master T'ai Hsu's passing away in 1947, his call for reform was silenced. In this bleak moment, he never imagined that

---

[6] Educator and philosopher.

years later, his ideal would be launched from Taiwan by the renewed efforts of a young monk whom he had only met a few times.

Nanjing fell into the hands of the communists in 1949, and the nationalists were about to lose Chiangnan. Daily, the wounded multiplied and the country agonized. Members of the sangha, under Venerable Master Le Kuan, began to organize medical relief groups. In honor of their vow, they strove to provide services for all living beings.

The Dharma lineage is preserved

Hsing Yun's close friend, Master Chih Yung, had tried for approximately two months to bring a 600-member medical relief force to Taiwan. On the tacit agreement not to perish together, Chih Yung decided to stay behind and defend Buddhism, while Hsing Yun lead the relief group to Taiwan.

Heavy at heart, Hsing Yun returned to Ch'i-hsia Temple to bid farewell to Master Chih K'ai. His plan to spread the Dharma in Taiwan delighted Master Chih K'ai, who gave his immediate approval. The night before Hsing Yun's departure, the master prepared a sumptuous meal in the refectory to honor his beloved disciple. But when dinnertime came, neither had the heart to raise his chopsticks. Speechless, their eyes were riveted on each other. Both men were moved to tears.

Back in Nanjing, Hsing Yun learned that a Taiwan-bound vessel was soon leaving Shanghai. Without delay, he took the night train to Ch'angchou. In the silent darkness of the Buddhist college, schoolmates he knew – and some he did not – were roused and invited to accompany him to the brave new world of Taiwan.

Over a hundred had pledged to follow Hsing Yun but only seventy – including Masters Yin Hai and Hao Lin who now reside in U.S.A. – actually boarded in Shanghai. With the vow to preserve the lineage of the Dharma, he and the others sailed the vast sea. The voyage would chart a new course in Hsing Yun's life. It would also draft the next chapter in the history of Buddhism in China.

Part Two

Crossing the Nighted Sea, Light in Hand

In his thirties

Enjoying a quiet moment in Ilan

At a charity sale of Buddhist memorabilia in support of the Tibetan Buddhist movement in the late 1950s

First Dharma lecture at Lei-yin Temple, Ilan, 1953

Promoting the reprint of the Buddhist Canon in Changhua, 1955

Getting a send-off from a young devotee at Sungshan Airport, Taipei, in 1960

Chapter 4
The T'ang monk[1] sets sail

*I*mmigrants from Fuchien and Kuangtung provinces[2] carried their Buddhist faith with them as they set sail for Taiwan, then under Dutch rule, near the end of the Ming dynasty. Due to the efforts of the immigrants who established their faith in Taiwan, Buddhism began to prosper when Cheng Ch'eng-kung[3] [1624 – 1662 C.E.] assumed leadership. The Mi-t'o (Amitabha) Temple was erected by his son Cheng Ching, a devout Buddhist, and K'ai-yuan Temple by his mother, who invited the sangha to care for the place.

By the Ch'ing dynasty, more of the sangha followed the same route as the early immigrants from Fuchien and Kuangtung. Taiwan witnessed the birth of numerous Buddhist temples throughout the country. Many temples over 100 years old are still standing, including Chu-hsi, Fa-hua, Ch'ao-feng, Ling-yun and Ling-ch'uan.

The occupying Japanese practiced a form of Buddhism in which the precepts and rules of discipline were less strict. This influence resulted in many monastics abandoning celi-

---

[1] Referring to Hsing Yun here. *T'ang Shan seng* in the original text, indicating that the monk hailed from China, referred to as T'ang Shan (mountain of T'ang). The Chinese people are commonly known as *T'ang jen* (people of T'ang) after the mighty T'ang dynasty. Hence, this coinage
[2] In southern China.
[3] Leader of resistance against the Manchu invaders at the fall of Ming. He later regained Taiwan from the Dutch.

bacy and vegetarianism. Some monastics altered their practice by wearing their cassocks only within the temple walls. Together, with practitioners from minor sects such as Lunghua and Hsien-t'ien who were not required to take the tonsure, it was often difficult to distinguish who were the monastics and who were not. The irregularity and non-uniformity of monastic lifestyle and appearance caused many misconceptions about Buddhism.

Just a shirt on his back

The civil war ended in 1949. Shortly thereafter, a million more Chinese followed in their forefathers' footsteps and crossed over to the enchanting isle of Taiwan. The youthful Hsing Yun was among them. The notion of spreading the Dharma in Taiwan was a new prospect to him. He had heard little of the land, which remained as outlandish to him as depicted in archaic texts. He had been told tales of the rich and powerful who fled China, and ended destitute and homeless.

Like the other passengers from T'ang Shan scurrying east, Hsing Yun began life in Taiwan with no more than straw sandals on his feet and a shirt on his back. The only baggage he had was misplaced, and he offered his robe to his fellow monastic, Venerable Chu Yun. Locals saw his sandaled feet and stared with astonishment – a monk with shoes! Embarrassed, he went barefoot like everyone else.

His group of followers were quickly disbanded. Like the others, Hsing Yun, then twenty-three, was on his own. While seeking shelter in Taipei for two days, he was repeatedly told that the monasteries there were either "full" or not prepared to accommodate travelers from outside the province.

At one point, a venerable monk spoke with un-characteristic coldness, "How are you qualified to be here?" The night was cold, a storm was raging, and Hsing Yun was hungry. He stumbled into the knee-deep rain water and soaked his only clothing. Finally, under the big bell at Shan-tao (Good Guidance) Temple, he curled up for the night.

The stranger in the strange land did not even speak a word of the dialect. However, the next day he decided to look up an old classmate at a monastery in Keelung. By the time he arrived, it was past one in the afternoon. Asked if he had eaten, a visibly embarrassed Hsing Yun replied: "No, I haven't eaten or drunk anything. Not since noon yesterday!" Just when his classmate was about to show him into the kitchen, a desperate and sorrowful voice cried, "We can barely feed ourselves. I'm sorry, we simply cannot help you. Please seek help elsewhere." Everybody had difficulty just surviving, and lending others a hand was a terrible hardship. Hsing Yun understood their plight, looked around, and realized he must keep traveling. He turned to go, but was stopped by his friend. A pot of porridge had been cooked for him. His friend had paid for the rice from his own meager earnings. As Hsing Yun held the bowl that day, his hands could not stop trembling from hunger, and his heart, from gratitude.

After finishing the meal, he thanked his host and bade him good-bye. He intended on going up Ch'eng-tz'u Liao in Kuan-yin Mountain, but rain flooded the road, leaving him stranded at the station, famished and shivering. Only someone who has experienced incredible hardship and helplessness can identify with the plight of this lonely young monk.

At long last, Yuan-kuang Temple

Ultimately, it was the compassionate Venerable Master Miao Kuo of Yuan-kuang (Perfect Light) Temple in Chungli who gave Hsing Yun a place to stay. With utmost gratitude, he toiled hard to reciprocate the kindness. Daily, he drew 600 pails of water out of the bottomless well for over 80 inhabitants of the monastery. Before daybreak, he tread the shadows on the moonlit dirt road, pushing a handcart, and traveling five miles to the market. Amidst breezes through the boughs, and idyllic peace over the land, barking dogs from afar, and the clatter of his own wooden clogs, he would silently recite the name of Avalokitesvara Bodhisattva. When he reached the market, the vendors were still asleep. He would knock on their doors, make his daily purchases for the monastery, and take the same dirt road back, chanting "Avalokitesvara Bodhisattva, Avalokitesvara Bodhisattva."

In the monastery, few were as young and robust as Hsing Yun. He performed each task with energy and attention, including cleaning the latrines and helping to wrap and bury the bodies of the deceased.

Despite the enormous amount of chores, Hsing Yun never deserted his reading and writing. Once, he earned a small sum helping out in a chanting service. With the money, he hastened to buy himself new stationery. He was elated! Many times, fellow monastics and devotees found him writing and thought he was ignoring more important tasks. He still recalls the concerned reaction of an elderly devotee, "Master, you must go and work, or else you'll starve!" During the same period, he took three months off to tend the woods around Fa-yun (Dharma Cloud) Temple in

Miaoli. There on the grass he crafted *Singing in Silence*, edited a monthly magazine, *Life*, and wrote radio scripts.

Hard to tell the Buddhas and deities apart

A daily routine of physical labor and basic chores was a natural way of life. Most people dared not venture beyond dreams of domestic well-being and a simple livelihood. As a visionary, however, Hsing Yun knew there was much more beyond complacent living. His dynamic and devoted will to advocate Master T'ai Hsu's humanistic Buddhism in Taiwan never subsided. He remained persistently enthusiastic in spreading the Dharma. This great vow was not easy though, especially in the volatile cultural context of Taiwan forty years ago!

Scholars of Taiwan's religious evolution have long maintained that polytheism was the natural answer to a life at the mercy of the elements: typhoons, earthquakes, and threats of similar magnitude. There was simply nowhere to hide. Except, maybe, in the asylum of the Taoist temples that were rapidly being built. Many of these temples had their eaves bedecked with ornate figures from mythology. Deities such as Matsu,[5] Lu Tung-pin,[6] the earth gods, rock gods, and tree gods were depicted, along with Buddhist motifs and symbols. In blending images and architecture from both Taoist and Buddhist traditions, it was often difficult to distinguish a Taoist temple from a Buddhist one.

In some respects, Buddhist monasteries in Taiwan differed significantly from the land-owning, self-sufficient es-

---

[5] Goddess of the sea.
[6] Taoist immortal.

tablishments of Mainland China. Within the Taiwanese system, temples were constructed and sustained by donations from devotees and contributions to the monastics. However, because Taiwan was experiencing an economic plight, substantial monetary gifts were nearly impossible. For an extended period, meager finances in the Buddhist community dictated a daily struggle to simply stay afloat. Any idea of progress had to wait.

In addition, the monastics in those days were not well educated. Most were competent in chanting the sutras and performing services to deliver the dead from hell, but preaching the Dharma was an advanced skill not yet possessed by many. During this era, misconceptions abounded that Buddhism's only social impact involved tending to the deceased. There appeared to be very little intellectual value in the religion, and many were apathetic.

With devastating impact, a wealthy and overbearing American presence in postwar Taiwan brought Catholic and Protestant influences to the cities and villages. President Chiang Kai-shek and his wife became converts, as did social leaders and other famous public figures. While Christianity was blossoming, Buddhism was wilting. Many people vividly recall terrible events that spiraled into disaster: the violation of temple sanctity, the transformation of Taipei's Shan-tao Temple into military recruiting offices and the degradation of the main shrine of Yuan Shan's Lin-chi (Gracious Regard) Temple when it was turned into Chung-shan T'ang.[7] A similar invasion of Buddhist sacred space occurred when the

---

[7] Memorial hall for Dr. Sun Yat-sen, founder of modern China.

100 year old Tung Pen-yuan (East Original Vow) Temple in Taipei almost became a mosque. This intrusive plan was the authorities' attempt to welcome their imperial friends from the Middle East. However, the temple was saved from demolition when a sizeable mosque was erected elsewhere, with government funding.

Incarcerated three times

The [nationalist] government had barely gained any stability in Taiwan. Uncertainty was in the air. Newcomers from the mainland were viewed with suspicion. Intelligence gathering and security measures were of high priority. Many people including monastics, suffered great persecution.

Hsing Yun has been incarcerated three times during his lifetime. The first happened when he was directing White Pagoda Primary School. Continually trading positions of pursuer and victim, the nationalist military hunted for communist guerillas during the day, and the communists assaulted the nationalists after dark. Hsing Yun was nabbed by both parties and subsequently pressed for *enemy* intelligence from both sides.

In 1949, rumors circulated that 300 monastics were sent to infiltrate Taiwan. Hsing Yun, along with Venerable Master Tz'u Hang – who later founded Maitreya[8] Inner Court in Hsichih – and other monastics from the Mainland, were jailed for alleged espionage. For twenty-three days they were bound and shackled and mercilessly shoved around. There

---

[8] Friendly, benevolent. The next Buddha, now in the Tusita heaven, who is to come after Sakyamuni Buddha.

was not even room in the cell to lie down. Eventually the group was rescued from confinement by devotees Sun-Chang Ch'ing-yang, Wu Ching-hsiung, and others.

Shortly after the imprisonment, the police acted on anonymous reports alleging that Hsing Yun was receiving radio broadcasts from the mainland in the day and disseminating procommunist literature at night. He was under surveillance around the clock. However, a year passed and suspicion dissolved. Those sent to follow him were affected by his teaching and actions, and soon became his followers.

Amidst the white terror in 1952,[9] Hsing Yun accepted a teaching appointment offered to him by Venerable Master Ta Hsing at Ch'ing-ts'ao (Green Grass) Lake Buddhist College in Hsinchu. He found himself having to apply for leave of absence with the local sheriff whenever he left the college property. Years later in Kaohsiung, Fo Guang Shan was again faced with the allegation of storing over 200 rifles. By then, Hsing Yun possessed a clearer understanding of the times, enabling him to successfully communicate and negotiate with those in power.

A rising star

Taiwan began to benefit from the eminent presence of Buddhist monastics arriving from China. The true splendor of Buddhist doctrine was unveiling before society. Indeed, Buddhism was gaining strength. While all this was happening, Hsing Yun emerged from his ordeals quite unscathed. With increasing clarity, he understood the depth and impor-

---

[9] Terror happened in the daytime.

tance of the thought that "Buddhism depends on me." The young monk, noble in heart and disciplined in mind, would soon shine his light to the far corners of Taiwan, and beyond.

Hsing Yun developed a tremendous number of affinities[10] during his two-year stint at Yuan-kuang Temple. He was Master Miao Kuo's true protégé. His earnestness and diligence endeared him to many. Grass-roots support was mounting. He still talks about a gracious elderly lady who used to sneak him a bowl of noodles: "Each time I saw her deeply wrinkled hands reaching through my study window with the steaming bowl of noodle soup, broth spilling on the sill, I was touched beyond words!"

As the pulse of Buddhism gained strength, Master Miao Kuo's knowing hand guided Hsing Yun further down the path. He stepped deeper into society and began to walk alongside the public. With keen and compassionate observation, he nurtured a profound knowledge of the place and its people, sensing what he must do to help them.

---

[10] The Chinese word is "yuen," meaning profound spiritual relationships that prevail and deepen through many lifetimes.

Chapter 5

Ilan, the cradle

The Buddhist community in Taiwan resembled a dry and desperate plain, where the foundation for spreading the Dharma and cultivating living beings necessitated the right circumstances, courage, wisdom, and perseverance. Settling into his position in Ilan, northeastern Taiwan, Hsing Yun was equipped with all four attributes.

Going to the mountain city
The next chapter of Hsing Yun's life began in 1952. He encountered layman Li Chueh-ho during an executive election of the Chinese Buddhist Association. Li was anxious to find a monastic willing to teach Buddhist doctrines in his hometown, Ilan. But Ilan was a poor and remote city. The Taipei-Ilan highway was sharp and winding, with perils at every turn. The train ride from Taipei included five hours of uncomfortable, dangerous travel through numerous sooty tunnels. A few teachers of the Dharma would visit distant Ilan only once, opting never to brave the filthy and dangerous journey again.

Undaunted by the potential problems, Hsing Yun eagerly volunteered his service. He boarded the train, set foot in Ilan and never spoke of leaving. The community's immediate appreciation of Hsing Yun quickly blossomed into reverence and the will to be wholehearted followers.

In those days, going to a place like Ilan took great courage. Hsing Yun's calm bravery was born from a fiery determination to spread the Dharma, accompanied by a peaceful acceptance of life's conditions – even when they were as dreadful as in Ilan.

Geographically, Ilan is situated on a delta. Overlooking the Pacific at one end, the city is blockaded from the vast plain in the northwest by mountains at the opposing end. Life was insulated and the people were introverted. Hsing Yun's destination was Lei-yin (Sound of Thunder) Temple in Peimen (North Gate). Built during the reign of Tao-kuang [1821 – 1850 C.E.] of the Ch'ing dynasty, the former residential structure with the traditional courtyard was wrecked by a typhoon in 1963. Locals, headed by Hsing Yun, endeavored to rebuild it and construction was completed in 1978. It was here that Hsing Yun's career as an influential leader and teacher truly took flight and began to soar.

Treading the premises of Lei-yin Temple for the first time, Hsing Yun discerned why the place failed to retain other teachers of the Dharma.

He remembers leaving Taipei early that day and reaching Ilan shortly past noon. Crossing the temple threshold, he first saw three military families squatting inside. The shrine was there; the cushions for worship were not – they had been turned into pillows for sleeping. Clothes and footwear were scattered all over. A stove blocking the latrine was still smoking; it had to be removed to gain entrance into the latter.

Hsing Yun let his eyes roam awhile until they alighted on an elderly bhiksuni, Venerable Abbess Miao Chuan, who was chanting the sutras to relieve devotees' suffering. When finished, she emerged with the query: "Are you the monk coming to lecture?" "Yes," he responded. Another half-hour passed before she returned with a cup half filled with tea that had already turned cold.

Finding a niche in the shrine

Without delay, Hsing Yun embarked on his life's work. Devotees were receptive to his teachings. He found a niche in the main shrine. It was windowless and the ceiling was low. Once inside, he could not stand up straight, but he was content.

People who were there in those days might still remember that they had to pay for the installation of every light bulb in the household. To minimize expenses, he hung the bulb before the Buddha in the day and dragged in to his nearby quarters to read at night. The cord was short, so he read and wrote at the threshold – the buzz of the mosquitoes kept him company until daybreak.

His soupspoon was of scrap lead so light that he found himself chasing it after the wind picked it up for a fluttering dance. For the first six months, he slept on the floor. Finally, the devotees chipped in for a prison-manufactured bamboo bed and chair. The bed squeaked with every toss and turn. But still, Hsing Yun was content.

The entire community was poor, and Hsing Yun was not excluded from such hardship. However, life's limitations never concerned him nearly as much as the obstacles surrounding the development of Buddhism as a whole.

The conditions of the time were not very conducive to

spreading the Dharma. Taiwan was still reeling from half a century of Japanese rule. For its socially suppressed and educationally deprived people, a focus on religion would be a difficult leap. Also, in its reclusivity and independence, Ilan was paranoid about anyone and anything from outside its boundaries. Needless to say, the arrival of this young monk caused quite a reaction from the intensely private and suspicious inhabitants. Some even challenged his wit and endurance with a few rude tests.

Master of North Gate

Buddhist lectures at Lei-yin Temple were often disturbed by clamor outside. Quick-witted, Hsing Yun turned off the light, illuminating only the spark of incense before the Buddha. The rowdy gatherers, shocked by the sudden darkness, saw the magnificent sitting posture of Hsing Yun, and heard the lectures clearly. By means of "silence," many hostile people were transformed from arrogance to friendliness.

Another time, Hsing Yun was nearly assaulted before a huge congregation. He was in the middle of an evening lecture in downtown Ilan where seven avenues converged. The violent disruption was instigated by a group of Christian zealots. Amongst his own followers, attitudes got a little explosive, too. Many locals still objected to his presence. The radicals even threatened to remove him altogether.

Hsing Yun remained peaceful amidst the continual threats. The people of Ilan were eyewitnesses to his energy and bearing, his maturity and wit and his knowledge and charm. They did not know his name, but to them he was the master of North Gate. The older devotees certainly remember how he used to look. A-yao Ku, now over 80 years old, is among Hsing Yun's earliest followers. "He was so cute!" she grins, showing her gold teeth.

Naturally, the young and handsome monk with the commanding presence was an item of enormous interest to the girls. *Shih-ku*[1] Hsiao Pi-hsia, who has followed the master for almost four decades, recounts the time he went over to the office where she worked to make a phone call. In the next moment, Ilan was literally incommunicado because all operators – their supervisor included – were out to size him up! Today, most employees in the office are Hsing Yun's followers.

First site for humanistic Buddhism

Life may be tough for the folks of Ilan. But once they had experienced the benefits of their Buddhist faith, Hsing Yun realized, they would in turn become the support structure of Buddhism. He was prepared to help Ilan become the first site in which to practice humanistic Buddhism.

To combat the prevalence of illiteracy in the 1950s, he decided the most beneficial method of practice would be to call on the name of the Buddha and to chant the sutras. *Nien-Fo hui* (sutra-chanting sessions) were formed in which devotees would learn to recite the Buddhist texts. These sessions were a legitimate and effective form of public education. A formal lecture hall was added to Lei-yin Temple to accommodate the needs of the increasing attendees in 1956.

---

[1] A female layperson who lives in accordance to vows similar to monastics but does not shave the head or wear monastic robes. *Shih-ku* are included in the decision making process in Fo Guang Shan.

At its inauguration, many highly cultivated masters, including master Lcan-skya, came to offer their congratulations.

The chanting sessions were his first triumphant venture into the genre of regular lectures. To announce a forthcoming lecture, a devotee would carry a board with the inscription "Please heed the sutras" through the streets, and another would be the crier tapping a hand-drum. The site of the chanting sessions was virtually the birthplace of Buddhism in Ilan. North Gate's bus stop still reads "Nien-Fo hui".

Sower of Bodhi seeds

Inspiring and cultivating the interests of the youthful Buddhists would be next. Although not a natural singer, Hsing Yun formed a group of gregarious song-birds – the first-ever Buddhist choir. His lyrics were set to music by Yang Yung-p'u. The kids flocked in. They brought their own chairs and poured tea for one another. Next, he offered a creative writing workshop. He treated every submission with the utmost attention and respect. The young intellectuals were enthralled. Venerable Tzu Hui, a first-generation disciple reputed for her literary talents, was candid about her initial intention: "I went to the master to learn writing, not Buddhism!"

In one article, Venerable Tzu Hui reflected on the mood shared among her peers at the time: "The chanting sessions in Ilan included a range of projects to compassionately and creatively guide the young. ... I have no words for the grace in his demeanor, the depth of his thought, the extent of his knowledge. I was simply touched. ... We used to place our writings in a drawer beneath the altar in Lei-yin Temple. We would retrieve them the next morning when we turned in another batch. Our papers were always meticulously critiqued. We could not wait to exchange them. Everybody was so excited. After a while, the master would round us up for an overall critique, and we would be taught the techniques of composing."

Bodhi seeds – morsels of Buddhist teachings – were sown among the little ones, too. Specialized groups were formed for those attending junior and senior high schools. Teachers among the followers provided subject tutorials for the under-privileged. To the disbelief and delight of many parents, these young people became living proof that "children of the Dharma never go astray."

Cheng Shih-yen, educator and best-selling author on Ch'an studies, was a student in one of the tutorials. He recalls how the master went to great lengths in devising the most attractive projects for the kids, how well he understood them and how he would pat them on the shoulder and sit them down to chat. The children would eagerly fly to his side after school. Members of the student body walked with confidence and pride, Cheng remembers. Years later at Fo Guang Shan's first international Ch'an conference, Hsing Yun ran into the child from the tutorial, now an adult, and he said, fondly, "O the willow seed carelessly planted is actually turning into a shade tree now! I'm so glad to see you again!"

Roots of compassion

Viewed from the standpoint of modern marketing, Hsing Yun possessed a keen sense of what activities would be most appealing, and therefore most successful, for the general public. Through his rich understanding of humanity, he cultivated opportunities that would benefit and please a diverse range of people. Early training in Buddhism brings out innate insight and compassion, he believed. Preschool and primary level classes soon expanded into Sunday schools complete with all kinds of contests in the arts. Bodhi seeds, indeed, must be sown in the young.

Venerable Yi Kung, who holds a master's degree in Indian philosophy from Tokyo University, attended one such class for children. She took the tonsure two years after university graduation and has followed the master for two decades. She tells of frequenting Lei-yin Temple with her two sisters at age four or five, and being drawn solely to the delicious snacks – Buddha or no Buddha! For the promise of a gift, like a steamed bun, a peach-shaped longevity bun, candied crispies, or a "Buddha's Hand" made of flour, the bouncy little girl would settle down to chant the sutras for the length of a burning incense. "In sharing the Dharma with people, we must be sensitive to their physical needs as well as their spiritual needs!" In time she began to resonate with the Dharma. "A lot of us were probably transformed while munching a little 'Buddha's Hand!'" Venerable Yi Kung laughs heartily.

Hsing Yun touched the average devotees with his sincerity and diligent, humble service. He conducted seven-day chanting sessions, set up the lecture hall, cooked the vegetarian meals, and waited on tables. Of course he played all the Dharma instruments during chanting. And, whenever the pet monkey in a nearby kindergarten scampered off, somebody would invariably yell, "Master! The monkey's gone! Please fetch him back!" He would lay down whatever he had in hand to retrieve the mischievous creature.

Ilan, this is forever

There seemed to be no limit to master's generosity and energy. He would buy several hundred issues of the *Life* magazine he edited and then gave them away. For *Awakening the World*, he actually went out soliciting subscribers. Income from his writing was channeled into the purchase of silver chains with sauvastika[2] pendants which he hoped young devotees would wear with pride, and notebooks and pencils for the students and children's classes.

In 1958, a lantern parade was held to honor and celebrate the growth of Buddhism. It was the Buddha's birthday. Tibetan buddhists under the Dalai Lama were rising against communist oppression. Hsing Yun decided to echo their cry, and gather all the followers for a special event. Every district in Ilan was represented by a float. The parade of lights ran forty-eight kilometers (thirty miles). Three fifths of the populace attended the celebration. With bright colors and countless participants, the parade demonstrated the power of unity. Buddhists had their first taste of solidarity.

Throughout the course of twelve years, the alien monk and the city among the hills had become inseparable. "Coming, no one is there to greet me; going, no need to bid goodbye. That's the feel of home," he says. No matter how far he roams, or how much time passes, his heart is always in

---

[2] A sign on the Buddha's chest. A symbol of the sun or lightning; a sign of blessing and of good prevailing over evil.

Ilan.

Truly, Hsing Yun reserves a special affection for Ilan. At Yuan-ming (Perfect Light) Temple by Chiao Hsi (Rocky Brook) he finished *Biography of Sakyamuni Buddha's Ten Great Disciples* at the speed of 10,000 characters per day. The quietude and comfort of Ilan enabled him to work with great focus and dedication. Even now, he misses the restful walk along the brook at the end of each day!

In Ilan, Hsing Yun reared almost all of his first-generation disciples: Hsin Ping, Tzu Chuang, Tzu Chia, Tzu Hui, Tzu Jung, and other venerables who form the nucleus of Fo Guang Shan.

The most engaged devotees of Fo Guang Shan also come from Ilan. One such follower is Weng Sung-shan, founder of the China Buddhist Art Center. The former paint- ing apprentice reciprocated Hsing Yun's support in helping him learn to carve Buddha statues thirty years ago by a gene- rous donation to the Fo Guang University foundation. He also thanked the master for the chance to offer his gift.

Lei-yin Temple, the beginning

Without Lei-yin Temple, Fo Guang Shan would not exist; without Fo Guang Shan, there would not be over one hundred branch temples around the globe, the thousand disciples, and the million devotees. Enshrined in the temple is Vairocana Buddha. Lei-yin Temple was the spark that ignited the fire of Humanistic Buddhism.

The source of one of the century's supreme masters and the impetus to Fo Guang Shan's impressive flourishing – that is Ilan. To call Ilan the cradle for the modernization of Buddhism in Taiwan would not be an overstatement.

Chapter 6
Master of innovation

By age thirty, Hsing Yun stood at the threshold of his mission to modernize the spread of Buddhism and had positioned himself to take some creative risks.

Although subtlety in Chinese thought was admired, it made for passive Buddhists when it came to the spread of the Dharma. And though devotees were welcomed, they were not actively sought. Generally, Buddhist monastaries kept a low profile. But times were changing and the age-old relious experience had to change, too. Hsing Yun considered how technology, politics, the economy, society as a whole, and even the makeup of the congregation could be integrated. How could orthodox Buddhist doctrine and this developing state of affairs connect? And who should help Buddhists awaken to the causes and conditions of this new age? The difficulty with Buddhism does not lie in abstract semantics, Hsing Yun realized, but in adapting the spread of the Dharma to the times and in following causes and conditions to explain them.

No stranger to the dynamics of the modern media, Hsing Yun decided to systematically employ it to propagate the Buddha's teachings in Taiwan.

Language, his beloved medium

Throughout his career, Hsing Yun has never ceased to call upon the wisdom of language as a vehicle for the joy of the Dharma. Language is his beloved medium. Early in his days at Chiao-shan Buddhist College, he collaborated with classmate Master Chih Yung in founding a monthly newsletter, *Raging Billows*, and edited *Splendid Light*, a supplement to the newspaper *Hsu pao*. He also wrote for local papers in Chiangsu. In Taiwan, he quickly assumed publishing commitments with the magazines *Awakening to Life* and *Life*. During 1957-58, he took over one journal and started another, *Awakening the World* and *Buddhism Today*, respectively. In 1979, he founded *Universal Gate* magazine. The original fifty-eight page black-and-white production has evolved into a 200-page glossy magazine of high quality in content, design, production and distribution, and is read by Buddhists and non-Buddhists, alike.

Though never schooled in writing, Hsing Yun has fared well as an author and maintains an unbridled passion for the printed word. To him, the pen is the duster with which he clears away the mind's defilements and obstructions. His first work, *Discourse on Avalokitesvara's Universal Gate Chapter*, took form at Yuan-kuang Temple. Then came *Singing in Silence*, composed in the woods at Fa-yun Temple. Special mention must be make of *National Master Yu Lin*, a bestseller that turned into a big-screen feature and TV series.

This story came about while Hsing Yun was traveling across Taiwan on speaking commitments. He and his friend, Venerable Master Chu Yun, spent one night at a farm in Yu-chih, Nantou. Given the courtesy of a spot closest to the toilet in the farmer's room, the pair found the stench of the nearby commode unbearable. But not wishing to be ungrateful for their host's thoughtfulness, they resolved to stay-out the night. "Hey, Chu Yun, tell a story. I can't sleep," confessed Hsing Yun. Master Chu Yun was a consummate story-teller.

"Let me tell you about Master Yu Lin then." By the time he finished, morning had broken. "I won't let your efforts go to waste, Chu Yun!" promised Hsing Yun.

Returning to Lei-yin Temple, he painstakingly wrote down the story.

Writing under the pen-name Mo-chia, he was soon recognized as an emerging new talent. Once a friend offered the suggestion that he consider becoming a professional writer: "With that pen of yours, why don't you just go and be a journalist!" In some sense, that is actually what happened.

Hsing Yun's brain-child, Fo Guang Publishing House, has been energetic in publishing Buddhism-related titles. Genres range from biographies and literary pieces to articles on doctrine and etiquette. Recently, cassettes and videos have been produced. Most important are the *Fo Guang Tripitaka*, the award-winning *Fo Guang Encyclopedia*, and English translations of sutras. Hsing Yun's monthly journals, which appeared in *Universal Gate* magazine over a four-year period, have been published in a set of twenty volumes. They are thought to be an excellent way to connect with his disciples and followers worldwide, as well as an effective means of spreading the Dharma. Fo Guang is collaborating with UC Berkeley to computerize the Buddhist canon.

In his own words: "By means of the prajna[1] of language, not only are those of us here and now able to connect with the thoughts of the Buddha, but also beings living millennia from now and light-years from here shall be helped to understand the wondrous wisdom of absolute reality!"

Going the electronic way

In keeping with modern advancement, new electronic technology has become a tool of Dharma propagation. As early as the days in Ilan, there was the Buddhist choir. Then came the radio programs, *Voice of Buddhism, Sound of Awakening the World, Gate of Faith, The Wondrous Use of Ch'an,* and *Wisdom of Life*. The latest addition to the list is the programming for Chinese-speaking audiences in Los Angeles, California.

The following works have also been made into television broadcasts: *Sakyamuni Buddha,* 1972; *Sweet Dew,* 1979; *Gate of Faith,* 1980; the award-winning *Venerable Master Hsing Yun's Buddhist Lectures,* 1983; *The Sixth Patriarch's Platform Sutra,* 1985; *Hsing Yun's Ch'an Talk,* 1987; *A Verse Per Day,* 1989; the award-winning *Hsing Yun's Dharma Words,* 1991; *Hsing Yun Speaks a Verse,* 1991; and *Hsing Yun Says,* 1994. These programs are on all three channels in Taiwan – often simultaneously.

Music from the heavens

The original Buddhist music was *fan-pei*: *fan* being the

---

[1] Wisdom.

music of Mahabrahma,[2] and *pei* being clearness and pureness. *Fan-pei* is truly music from the heavens. In quiet moments, the heavenly music can expand and elevate people's minds. Important in early preaching, *fan-pei* was later employed in the praise of the Buddha. Musical instruments that the Buddhist devas are depicted, include the p`i-p`a (Chinese lute), cheng and ch`in,[3] all of which Chinese music has adopted.

Hsing Yun cut the first-ever Buddhist ten-inch records in 1957. Six in all, they included some twenty numbers. Wu Chu-che, who was teaching at the polytechnic college in Taipei, was offered a key role in producing them despite the fact that he and Hsing Yun had not even met before the project. The two had no dispute whatsoever about popularizing and humanizing this time-honored faith. Wu applauded Hsing Yun's originality and offered his help without reservation. The half-dozen records which resulted struck a chord with wide audiences in Taiwan and all over Southeast Asia.

Three decades later, a 200-member choir from Fo Guang Shan Buddhist College gave a historic Buddhist chanting performance at the national music hall in Taipei. The event helped lift Buddhist music to an unprecedented status.

The growing popularity of karaoke and KTV has sparked notions of putting the various Buddhist praises in a similar format. Hsing Yun wants Buddhist chanting to fill every household. From radio to TV programs and records to karaoke, Hsing Yun has emerged as a modern master of

---

[2] The third heaven of the first dhyana (literally meditation), the self-existing origin of all living beings. Its ruler is infinitely protective of the Buddhist doctrine.
[3] Both string instruments.

Dharma propagation.

Alongside the simple folk

In 1954, Hsing Yun began to lecture systematically on the Tripitaka (Buddhist Canon) in Taiwan.

Tzu En, then a teacher at the polytechnic college in Ilan, tells of his experience in following the master into the countryside: "We would bike when the distance was manageable. As the youthful monk crisscrossed the countryside, his thirty or so equally youthful followers tagged along. In the evening breeze, we would race against the setting sun. The master would either lead or follow behind everyone. When bikes broke down or there was an uphill ride, we would all dismount to walk our bikes together. When a typhoon struck, we would just *bask in the Dharma rain*! On our return we would sing aloud the master's *Song of the Dharma Preacher* and make our way back to Lei-yin Temple."

"We would take the train when the destination was far off. We had to scramble somewhat for the train, which ran infrequently in those days. Later on, however, the people manning the various stations along the Ilan route became so touched by us that they made sure all of us were on board before the whistle blew."

As the day of a Dharma function approached, locals would parade through the streets sounding a gong and announce: "The Dharma is coming!" When the day finally came, there would be parades of the deities and the celestial beings leading the way. One such event drew a crowd of 5,000 in the tiny town of Yuli, Hualien. Whether it was out in the open, inside the small town theater, or on the grain-drying ground, Hsing Yun and his young friends busied themselves setting up the microphone, extending wires, screwing in light bulbs, putting up posters, arranging the seats, and ushering in the audience. The young preachers then took the podium. Simultaneously, in both Mandarin and the Taiwanese dialect, aided by a slide show, they would read from the scripts their master had perfected for them. By the end, the crowd was overjoyed.

For the next thirty years, Hsing Yun lectured in towns and villages, schools and factories, national museums and memorial halls, art centers and sports stadiums. Time stood witness to how the compassion and wisdom of the Buddha could reach far and wide.

Across the oceans

Hsing Yun began moving his stage across the oceans about a decade ago. He visibly stepped-up his teaching, especially in Hong Kong. Late in the summer of 1993, he made his way into a jam-packed Hunghom Coliseum, which seats 20,000. For three consecutive days, he spoke on topics from the *Diamond Sutra* to *Research on the Prajna of the Nature of the Immaterial*. Media coverage was overwhelming. Each evening the coliseum filled well before the lecture was to start. On hearing that some people could not get into the coliseum, Hsing Yun arranged with Venerable Tzu Jung and the stadium officials to have a mega screen set up for those unable to gain entrance. For two hours [the minds of] those who attended 'seated or otherwise' took a refreshing shower in the ambrosial rain.[4]

Similar to Catholic and Protestant preachers, Hsing Yun has for years been speaking in prisons. His lectures in Taiwan prisons are by formal appointment from the legal department. A few disciples and followers do the same on a regular basis.

When he was last in Hong Kong, he spoke in the Stanley Prison for the third time. With compassion, he talked to murderers, robbers, and drug dealers who were serving time in isolation. "These walls are nothing. Real incarceration is within the mind," he told them. That day the Buddha must have seen the thirty or so incarcerated men as the living beings that they were, not the deadly menace perceived through the eyes of others. Quietly the group listened to Hsing Yun's counsel to seek the Dharma for an end to their violent ways. Many were brought to tears when, during the refuge ceremony, the master sprinkled their heads with sweet dew to dispel calamities and to bring about repentance.

Hsing Yun has an unwavering dedication to the revival of Buddhism, and a sensitive touch upon the pulse of Taiwanese society. The construction of Taipei's P'u-men temple in 1978 launched another series of Dharma functions; namely, "The Gathering of Bright Lanterns", "The Gathering To Reciprocate Parents' Kindness," Dharma meetings for women, and Ch'an and Pureland practice. The cross-island alms-round's function, a contemporary version of a time-honored monastic tradition, and home visits, called 'lighting up the homes,' are regarded by some as a form of direct

---

[4] *Kan-lu fa-yu* in the original text. The Buddha Truth.

marketing in the spread of the Dharma.

Following the Master

Hsing Yun's projects have received their share of support and criticism. He has been condemned as garish and revolting, and feared because of his charisma and popularity. But as time has passed, his strategies have not only proved effective but have also been borrowed by monastics of other monasteries. Though some have tried, no longer can anyone deny that he is a significant modern Buddhist leader.

Once a student marveling at Hsing Yun's eloquence questioned him with, "Master, how come you always have so much to say?" It was not always the case. During his early years in the monastery he had never crossed paths with a stranger and, if he had, would not know how to talk with one. Ten years of his life revolved wholly around teachers and peers, and the first public lecture at Lei-yin Temple was a petrifying experience for him. The whole time he had to hold the edge of the table in front of him to hide his shaking knees. Off-stage, he found himself drenched with sweat. As appearances increased, though, so did his confidence and carriage.

In the beginning, his lectures were not all sellouts. To disciples he confesses his life's most embarrassing moment—when, forty years ago in Ilan, he went on-stage to find not a single soul below. "The time and date were correct, I mumbled to myself. I waited and waited. Finally a handful of latecomers sauntered in. I began somehow. By the end of the lecture, the crowd hadn't gotten any bigger."

Now, he speaks eloquently. Guests at Fo Guang Shan

wanting to hear him speak, need only allow him the benefit of composing his thoughts during the five-minute walk from Hsi Ling (West Range) to Pao Ch'iao (Treasure Bridge) to hear wonderful words. For over ten years he has needed only to look over television scripts thirty minutes before shooting. The record of 100 episodes shot in a single day without a retake still amazes people.

Giving society what it needs

Sometimes, people leave traditional Dharma lectures saying how wonderful they were while others admit to being perplexed. It is much easier to speak on the Dharma in ways that few can understand rather than with a clarity that all can perceive. What good is a lecture if the audience does not leave with new insight, asks Hsing Yun.

To explain Hsing Yun's popularity, Academia Sinica social researcher Sung Kuang-yu gave this analysis: "Conventional wisdom states that all a Dharma lecture needs is a building big enough to house a few rows of seats. Hsing Yun moves out of this static thinking. He sees the needs of people and makes Dharma accessible to them."

Those who have been to one of his lectures praise how the sound and stage designs are employed for religious expression: "The curtain rises to reveal five Buddha images set on a crimson carpet with an azure backdrop. Four groups of attendants bearing flowers, candles, fruits, and tea walk solely through a mist created by dry ice. The deep resonance of a single drum marks the procession. The lighting turns magical. Fifty cassock-clad monastics appear with Dharma instruments in hand. It's all so arresting."

With the mood established, Hsing Yun takes center stage and delivers his speech. It is said that folks were so moved during one of his thirty-minute lectures, they broke into applause seventy-two times.

Monastics usually teach one sutra at a time and expound on each word and phrase. This may take months. Venerable Master Chih I of the T'en-tai school, teaching the *Sutra of the Wondrous Truth of the Lotus*, spent ninety days on the character "*wondrous*" in the title alone. Modern life is too filled with work and social obligations to allow for such expansive analysis. Yet bits and pieces of lectures here and there serve us no better as Buddhists.

Aware of the tension between society's desire for thoroughness on the one hand and the pressures of time constraints on the other, Hsing Yun's lectures represent his mastery of innovation. In terms of a single topic, listeners course through the Dharma within hours. Topics always pertain to some aspect of everyday life and human psychology. Examples of his topics include the nature of emotions, the maintenance of one's well-being, the role of religion, and a top-ten list about life.

Greatness of wisdom and completeness of harmony

Though Hsing Yun still speaks with a slight country-boy Yangchou accent, his charisma is undeniable. Whatever the issue, his skillful discourse - which might include historical incidents or contemporary anecdotes, ancient poetry or modern theory - leaves few to walk away untouched or unconvinced.

Longtime follower Chang P'ei-keng of the Chinese-

Tibetan Cultural Association of the Republic of China looks at his teacher as a walking Buddhist lexicon and a human compendium of modern humanities and sciences: "The master's realm is the realm of prajnaparamita, that of the greatness of wisdom and completeness of harmony. He weaves an array of knowledge seemlessly in conversation; he cross-references without deserting the theme; he always sets off from the Dharma, traverses an ocean of knowledge, and returns home to the Dharma. With such ease he maneuvers through a field of information and knowledge!"

Some years ago in Japan, after finishing a talk, "*The Message of the Twenty-first Century*," a middle-aged lady came up to Hsing Yun and expressed utter amazement at her sudden comprehension of the Dharma. She told him that after attending more than 200 lectures and spending years reading through Buddhist literature, his speech finally opened her mind. A seemingly astounded academic noted the complete absence of any mention of the Buddha. The manner in which Hsing Yun spelled-out ways to purify the mind so helped his audiences, they were ready to regard him as a living Buddha.

Adapting to conditions

Hsing Yun skillfully adapts the contents of his lectures to meet the hearts of his audience. Once while visiting a dance troupe, he brimmed over with stories about devas dancing about, scattering flowers, flying thorough the heavens, and making offerings to the Buddhas. Then he focused on Buddhist chanting and songs of praise. To the spellbound musicians and dancers, he presented song and dance as another vehicle of the Dharma.

Another time, Hsing Yun spoke on *Buddhism and Chinese Literature*. He took an assembly of literati through an entire course in the translation of Buddhist texts: how Buddhism came to China, how Buddhist textual translation enhanced the Chinese literary vocabulary, how many literary works came to have the imprint of Buddhist thought. His audience came to realize that the master had treaded the same path as they.

He even discussed *"Religion and Strategy"* with strategist general Chiang Wei-kuo. Citing personal experience in the understanding of the Dharma and the living of life, he spoke in depth about various types of contingencies in life and war. His listeners became his captives.

With scientists he debates the scientific viewpoint of Buddhism; with economists, how material value is explained from a Buddhist conception; with engineers, monasterial architecture. His methods of teaching and inspiring are such that people from all walks of life are led to the Dharma.

Like Master T'ai Hsu's blackboard, which was once feared as a form of wizardry, Hsing Yun's innovations and reforms have been called wondrous, even spellbinding.

Unfazed, he says: "Modernization is a form of exploration. It entails betterment, anticipation, adaptability, and promotion. As nations, societies, and religions evolve, they must seek progress. That quest for progress, and the will to be in agreement with Buddhist doctrine, combined with teaching skills, will result in timely and versatile representations of the Dharma, which will facilitate an understanding of Buddhist teaching. In fact, since the days of

Sakyamuni Buddha, this is what Buddhist preaching has always sought. During the Buddha's lifetime, Dharma was passed on through speech. Then there were pattra[5] sutras, engraved sutras, and printed sutras after his paranirvana. Now there is the computerized Tripitaka!"

The new generation of Buddhists is totally at home with markers and whiteboards, slides and projectors, and huge cinematic screens. Few have any qualms about the Buddhas enshrined in the halls of government, or the soundings of drum and bell in the city or the countryside. Hsing Yun's innovation and foresight have helped make possible the modernization of Buddhism and the spread of Buddhist teachings throughout the world.

---

[5] Palm leaves used as a writing material.

Part Three

'Tis with Him Perpetual Buddha Truth

With Venerables Tzu Hui and Hsin Ping (left) at the construction site of Fo Guang Shan, after overgrowths of jute and bamboo were cleared

Though not born a surveyor, the master was involved in every aspect of Fo Guang Shan's construction

Listening intently as the then Taiwan's Internal Affairs Minister, Hsu Ch'ing-chung, gave a speech at the opening of Fo Guang Shan's Great Compassion Hall

With Hao Po-ts'un, Republic of China's presidential advisor, at Hsi Lai Temple, 1993

With Chen Lian, head of Fo Guang Shan's supervisory council

With Chiang Ching-kuo, head of R.O.C.'s executive council, in Fo Guang Shan, 1972

Receiving an honorary doctorate degree from
the University of Oriental Studies, U.S.A., 1978

With friends in the media industry (*l-r*), publisher Kao Hsi-chun,
editor Wang Li-hsing, and media executive Wu Shih-sung

Presiding over the Triple Gem Refuge and Five Precepts Ceremony for all races at Hsi Lai Temple

Officiating a wedding in Malaysia.

Always happy to see young ones taking part in Buddhist activities, Sangha Day

The master handing out envelopes of money to the poor in Bodhgaya, India

Chapter 7

Heading south

A good walker walks far; a good swimmer swims further. Though Ilan was lovely and cherished, Hsing Yun realized the need for a great and resourceful expansion. He chose an unlikely tract of hilly and scrub-covered land on the outskirts of Kaohsiung. According to Buddhist doctrine, all things arise from causes and conditions. Hsing Yun began by exploring one aspect of Kaohsiung's potential and ended up with a multifaceted endeavor dependent upon conditions of all forms. The most important cause was the determined and courageous Hsing Yun himself.

His relationship with Kaohsiung took root when he was excused from his commitments at Lei-yin Temple to make frequent excursions there to preach the Dharma. He soon generated adequate support for plans to construct a temple. He was twenty-six at the time. A place of worship and a cultural service center were constructed, followed by Shou-shan (Longevity Mountain) Temple in the heart of Shou-shan Park. He then found himself commuting regularly between the north and south, Ilan and Kaohsiung.

Monastics are instructed

Hsing Yun knew temples and monasteries alone could not revive Buddhism, purify minds, or transform personal tendencies. But education could. "It must always be a priority in nurturing new leaders in the Buddhist lineage, for then one can start projecting into the future without end," he thought.

The class of '64 was the first to attend Shou-shan Buddhist College inside the temple. From the small group of twenty or so, annual admissions quickly mounted until the temple became overcrowded. To Venerable Tzu Chia, a graduate and director of Fo Guang Shan's cultural department, it seems like yesterday when she and her peers studied in the evenings within the confines of the hall of relics, and it is almost unbelievable how wonderfully it has all grown. Meanwhile, in making plans for a modern institution of multiple functions - educational, cultural, and religious, following the monasterial pattern in which he matured - Hsing Yun positioned the college for the anticipated enrollment boost.

Many people rallied in support of his aspiration. Cheng Ching (Pure and Clear) Lake, where the Grand Hotel now stands, was the choice site. Purchase of the property was made possibly by the sale of the building, which housed the Buddhist cultural service center.

Maybe it was Hsing Yun's sense of independence that was at stake, but as the contract to buy the land was readied for signing, a disciple's words changed everything. The history of Fo Guang Shan would tell a different story if not for Venerable Yi Yen's observation: "The lake is a tourist hot spot. For sure our temple is going to share that trend. People are going to stream in, sightseeing while paying homage to the Buddha. President Chiang Kai-shek might even be an occasional guest."

That statement bothered Hsing Yun. He did not want the temple to become an addition to the lake. He hoped visitors from far and near would come with joined palms and a heart full of devotion to the Buddha. He dropped the plan. The decision was not nearly as appreciated then as it is now. Through the years, Fo Guang Shan has attracted thousand of people from Taiwan and abroad to come and pay homage. Some people have even developed scenic spots in the vicinity. The president did not come, but one of his sons came three times and at least once while he was president himself.

While Hsing Yun pondered the next move, a debt-laden Chinese couple from Vietnam let Hsing Yun know that their vast, hilly property in Machu Yuan (Bamboo Grove), Tashu Hsiang (Big Tree Village), Kaohsiung, was up for sale. They pleaded for his help without which, they said, suicide would be their only recourse.

Hsing Yun was deeply moved by their plight. And in considering the terrain, he reflected on how the most extolled Buddhist monasteries in China are deep in the mountains. As the saying goes, of all the celebrated mountains under heaven, most have caretakers that are monastics. Mountains like E-mei (Lofty), Wu-t'ai (Five-terrace), P'u-t'o (Potala), Chiu-hua (Nine-flower), are all in China. It was time to pick-up the torch and found another monastery in the mountains of Taiwan.

Looking divine as he advances

Hsing Yun was firm. He wanted to see the land firsthand. More than thirty years have since passed but he still recalls what he did that day. A hired bus took Hsing Yun and a few devotees for an hour's journey along a rugged road. Upon arrival, they found a treacherous thicket-covered land stretched as far as the eye could see. They were stunned. No one would even leave the bus—except Hsing Yun.

"Forget it master! Who would bother to come up here to pray? Except you, that is," mumbled the group.

"Fine, fine," he replied, losing none of the enthusiasm. " I'll go myself."

He took his cane and vanished into the thorny grove.

Some were awed by his determination, while others clearly thought the whole episode a waste of time.

An hour elapsed. Finally, he emerged - weeds and red dirt on his collar, and a broad grin on his face.

"My apologies! I've made you wait too long!" He said as he wiped the sweat off his forehead.

He still teases some of the older devotees who went along that day: "You said that no one would care to climb this mountain. Haven't you been doing exactly that all these years?"

When asked about his intentions, he answers that the raw, untamed mountain offered opportunity. The monasteries existing in Taipei were run by monastics many years his senior. Hsing Yun, then in his thirties, virtually had nowhere to go to be on his own. Furthermore, the location allowed more liberty from the distractions of politics and socializing which might keep him from his true task of education and preaching. There was no strife up on the mountain. It would be right for starting from scratch.

The pioneering days

Those were pioneering days. Only a few devotees supported his decision. A follower who joined Hsing Yun at Shou-shan Temple and one of the key figures in construction of Fo Guang Shan, Hsiao Ting-shun says that no other experience in his lifetime would mean as much to him. Hsiao used to ride a motorcycle 'with the master clinging to his back' up the untraveled path, traverse three hills, and go on foot for another two hours before making it to the construction site (where the Buddhist college now sits).

"There was little we could do but stick to the geographical contours," recounts the shy former carpenter. We would snatch a piece of bamboo and sketch in the dirt. The two of us would think hard, and plan where to dig and where to build.

We'll be drenched with sweat one moment and dry another. Discussion went nonstop. Often we didn't sleep until the wee hours and would rise to work again at the break of day.

The land was far from flat. I've lost count of the thousands of truck-loads of dirt that it took to level it."

"Resources were limited. When they ran out, work would halt. Truthfully, all we wanted was a small place. We would be satisfied with a few parking spots before the mountain gate. That was good enough to start."

Decades of southern sunshine have tanned Hsiao and seem to have energized him. The rapport shared between Hsiao and the master is like no other. With his latest project, the Triple Gem Shrine behind him, Hsiao, who is unassuming and short on words but delivers where it counts, sums up his experience this way, "We didn't make a lot of money working with Fo Guang Shan, but I have received a lot of joy. Each time somebody speaks well of Fo Guang Shan, I feel this life of mine has been very worthwhile."

Consider the ways of the ant, and be wise

Abbot and Director-in-chief of the Committee of Religious Affairs[1] Venerable Hsin Ping was the first among the monks to join the construction. He was stationed in a shack in the bamboo grove with no electricity. To fetch water, he had to descend to a brook half an hour away. At night, he had to patrol the grounds in pitch-darkness. The hills were so steep the bulldozer could not climb by itself, so the students in the second and third classes at the Buddhist College had to literally push it along. The hourly rate of the machine was exorbitant considering living costs at the time and their own financial circumstances, so Venerable Hsing Ping's most pressing charge was to ensure that the machine was put to full use. "Not a dollar from the devotees shall go to waste," he used to say.

Venerable Tzu Jung had come to Kaohsiung from Ilan with Master. The roof of Dragon Pavilion on East Hill was being laid when midway through the process, the worker mixing the cement left for the day. "We didn't want the pouring suspended for fear that the roof might crack and leak in the future," relates Tzu Jung. "The master and the bunch of us knew the importance of completing the job, so we picked up where the man left off. Into the night we worked

---

[1] The highest policy-making body of Fo Guang Shan.

with two motorcycles' headlights on us. Venerable Yi Yen was up on the steep roof to smooth the cement, which kept sliding down. She exerted herself so much pushing the cement back up again that her hands started to bleed."

The most frenzied time was when a typhoon caused a tremendous downpour, which washed away the upper dam of the Release Pool[2]. Hsing Yun plunged into the clay-red rapids, and the others followed. First rocks, then their own bed quilts were passed along to block the opening and blanket the earth. They struggled together until the storm mercifully gave out, and light appeared behind the clouds.

Hsing Yun looks out from the balcony of Founder's Quarter and remembers: "We were like ants moving T'ai Shan."[3]

From nonbeing, being springs

Chronologically, the first-phase construction of the Fo Guang Shan complex included Tung-fang (Eastern) Buddhist College, Ta-pei Tien (Great Compassion Hall), Kuan-yin Release Pool, Dragon Pavilion, and the image of Maitreya Buddha.

The second phase saw the completion of Ta-tz'u (Great Compassion) Nursery, Ch'ao-shan Hui-kuan (Pilgrim's Lodge), Chieh-yin Ta-Fo (Great Welcoming Buddha), Fo Guang Vihara, and Ta-chueh Temple.

During the third phase the Main Shrine, Ching-t'u Tung-k'u (Pureland Cave), P'u-men High school, Wan-shou Yuan [Longevity Park, a cemetery], and an exhibition hall

---

[2] Pool for the release of living creatures.
[3] The eastern sacred mountain in Shantung, China, about which folklore abounds.

were finished.

In the fourth phase, Machu Yuan [a guest house], Ksitigarbha[4] Hall, E-mei Chin-tin (Lofty Gold-roofed) Samantabhadra[5] Hall, Ta-tz'u An [named Great Compassion, a living quarter for nuns], and a service center for devotees where built.

The latest additions have been T'an-hsin Lou [Devotee's Chamber, an activities center for devotees], Chin-yu Fo Lou (chambers of Gold and Jade Buddhas), and Ju-lai Tien (Tathagata[6] Hall).

The Great Welcoming Buddha, standing a lofty 32-meters (104 foot), beckons those on their way to Fo Guang Shan. It is the sixth largest Buddha image in the World.

Literally with his bare hands, Hsing Yun created a Buddhist holy site of world renown. Truly, from nonbeing being springs.

Seen from any viewpoint, Fo Guang Shan looks to have been sculpted out of the hillside. There is a precision and harmony about every element: the grandeur of the architecture and openness of the temples, the moving artistry of the Buddha images and layout of the courts and gardens, even the decorative touches of the halls and chambers. It all reminds one of the saying, "There is a world in each bloom, and a Buddha on every leaf."[7]

With his ideas sketched on paper, Hsing Yun met with Hsiao who transferred the plan onto the dirt with his bamboo

---

[4] Earth Treasure. Deliverer from hell.
[5] Universal Sagacity. Bodhisattva of the great practice.
[6] One of the titles of the Buddha.
[7] Buddhist truth can be manifested in our daily life.

stick. Thus, Hsing Yun irrigated a wilderness and raised a sacred dwelling place. In building Fo Guang Shan, architectural expertise and construction committees were never a factor. Just how did he do it? "I'm certainly unlearned in architecture," he says. "From the mainland to Taiwan to the rest of the world, I've walked many miles and seen many structures. In each and every case I observe and contemplate. I ask myself, would I have executed a design for a property differently if I were in the architect's shoes? By the time conditions are ripe for a temple or a school, construction plans have long been in place. That practically eliminates the prospect of complications." The answer to his success is a simple one: "One must pay attention."

Many-splendored land

The exterior design of Fo Guang Shan is modeled after classical Chinese place architecture with numerous Buddhist motifs added. Its interior provides for the technological sophistication needed for a variety of functions. The complex has a state-of-the-art multimedia audio-visual center, a conference hall with simultaneous interpretation equipment at every seat, a lecture hall with a capacity for 2,200, and a first-rate internal and external communications network. Fo Guang Shan is the first-ever computer-managed monastery.

Devotees and visitors may savor a relaxing cup of Fo Guang tea, take pleasure in a restful moment in the shady pavilion, enjoy the amenities of the guest house, drop by the service center for a tour, or consult the monastics on various issues.

Traditionally, monasteries have been known to be dark

and gloomy. The bright and airy Fo Guang Shan has turned all that around. It is the expression of its leader's disposition and personality traits, and an embodiment of his concepts and reasoning. Critics have called Fo Guang Shan wealth-oriented. Indeed, there are business people who would like to know its secret to success. There isn't one. It is simply thirty years of earnest devotees and visitors gathering every weekend to partake and contribute to the Dharma. They come from the ten directions.

Fifty lasting *firsts*

The achievement of nurturing a million or so devotees and one hundred or so branch temples aside, Fo Guang Shan has fifty lasting *firsts* in Buddhism within Hsing Yun's comprehensive vision.

These first time achievements include: the first Buddhist choir, Dharma radio programs, music recordings, television appearances, Dharma lectures in the halls of government, monthly sutra-printing, public discussion session, children's class, Sunday Class, ten-thousand Buddha hall, pre- school education workshops, bright lanterns[8], slide shows, weddings, Indian cultural research, college-level summer camps, city college, mobile clinic, public library, home for the terminally ill and lodging for their families, hard-bound texts, devotee's uniforms, monastic hierarchy, cross-country preach- ing, religious souvenirs, student body, devotee study pro- grams, Sangha Day, temple housed in a highrise, alms-round Dharma functions, Dharma passing ceremonies, short-

---

[8] Lit for a year's blessing at Fo Guang Shan.

term monastic retreats, preaching to the militia, devotee service center, thanksgiving Dharma functions, and annual meetings for devotees. Also within the list of firsts are: International Buddhist examinations,[9] triple practice sessions in the Ch'an, Pureland, and Tantric schools, *Return to the Epoch of the Buddha* functions, museum and exhibition hall, home visits and service, art gallery, the *Fo Guang Tripitaka*, the *Fo Guang Encyclopedia*, preaching on the outer islands [of Taiwan], a world organization (Buddha's Light International Association), and a 200-member pilgrimage to India.

To Hsing Yun, the creation of organizations and functions is the result of decades of collaborative efforts. Fo Guang Shan being what it is today, its creator wants the 'glory to the Buddha, achievement to be for all, benefits to the monastery, merits to the devotees.'

Rather that the ready made success offered by the beautiful reflections of lake Cheng Ching, Hsing Yun picked an unlikely spot in Kaohsiung county, which now enjoys the beautiful rays of Buddha's light. Not surprisingly, real estate values in the vicinity have soared; public utilities have been updated; highways added; employment has multiplied; and schools built. Neighborhood and village get-togethers and festivals are now a regular attraction. Each year opens to an endless string of community activities which take advantage of the amenities of Fo Guang Shan. To Kaohsiung, it is not only a religious landmark. It is also the basic promoter of community spirit and a dynamic cultural

---

[9] This is voluntary exam taken by Fo Guang devotees which familiarizes them with the history of Buddhism as well as its teachings and practices.

institution.

The view of Fo Guang Shan is awe-inspiring: the five peaks undulating like the petals of an orchid, the tidal sea of lush green woods, the statue of the heaven-touching Buddha, the parade of halls, the overpowering heights of the structures, the juxtaposing eaves. It is a place of beauty which presents twentieth-century Buddhism not only as a religion but also as a culture, an educational opportunity, and a charitable endeavor.

Chapter 8
Epoch of Buddha's Light

*L*ooking toward the Great Welcoming Buddha at Fo Guang Shan, one sees the picturesque backdrop of shimmering Kaohsiung-Pingtung Brook. Since its inception in 1967, Fo Guang Shan has come a long way to become southern Taiwan's most unique landmark and one of Asia's foremost Buddhist sacred sites. Yet, based on the Buddhist concept of matter coming into existence, dwelling, deteriorating, and returning to non-existence, Fo Guang Shan must no be measured by the splendor of its form alone. Fo Guang Shan's reason for being is in the principle and practice of Humanistic Buddhism.

Coming out of the mountain gate

Humanistic Buddhism is central to Hsing Yun's sharing of the Dharma. From Master T'ai Hsu, he learned that monastics must come out of the mountain gate. Fo Guang Shan became a testing ground for this principle.

He defines this theme in one of his lectures; "To have the Dharma isolated from daily life is the worst failing of Buddhism today. The most seasoned believer can't seem to get rid of greed, anger, and ignorance, and the most learned in the doctrine are still bothered by gossiping about people's ideas of right and wrong.

Once Buddhism breaks away from real life, the Dharma stops serving our needs and ceases to be our guide; once it fails to enrich the content of our lives, its existence becomes meaningless. The Buddha's teachings are for the improvement of life, purification of mind, and uplifting of character. It is a Buddhism which is pertinent to life and living that I want to spread.

The vitality of Buddhism depends on how well one corresponds with the Buddha's teaching while sleeping, talking, walking, or any form of activity. The Buddha spoke about resolve of the mind. To apply that teaching, we resolve our mind in the way we conduct our daily lives, in the way we give, and, overall, in the way we practice Buddhism. Sleep done with intent becomes more restful; food eaten with attention becomes especially tasty; a road walked with resolve becomes smooth before our eyes; a problem tackled with determination turns into a delightful challenge.

The resolve of the mind is an aspect of Dharma teaching useful in harmonizing all levels of human relation. It is not simply philosophical rhetoric. The Dharma is to be exercised and fulfilled as thoroughly as possible. There is no way that life and the Dharma can part company."

Carrying the Buddha's light

"Give others confidence; give others joy; give others convenience; give others hope" – those of Fo Guang Shan live their faith under this code of ethics. What many business people hold as a maxim, "create the future" and "develop consensus", Hsing Yun has long put into practice. Many times he has spoken on what it means to be a Fo Guang

Buddhist while explaining these concepts.

Above all, a Fo Guang Buddhist is fully engaged in daily matters. Dismissed as passive and out of date, Buddhism has been declining for many decades. In looking for deliverance from existence, it habitually overlooked issues arising from existence. How can Buddhism be accepted by a society if it departs from the realities of family life, the work place, and local and national concerns? The Fo Guang Buddhist seeks to master living within the mundane world while spiritually transcending it.

Secondly, a Fo Guang Buddhist assists first the living and then the dead. One of the greatest misconceptions about Buddhism is that it is primarily a religion in which to chant for and deliver the dead. Having no misgivings whatever about Buddhist services for the purpose of gathering merits, the Fo Guang Buddhist believes the living, much more than the dead, need Buddhism, and will therefore carry it from the temple into homes and communities.

Living with deep understanding of and attention to the cycles of cause and effect, life and death, is the practice of a Fo Guang Buddhist. To merely have a yearning for a good, clean life of spiritual practice tucked in the mountains safely away from the distractions of modernity is unrealistic. Virtuous and eminent masters of the past all began with the re solve to serve all sentient beings. Some promised to shoulder people's burdens like an ox throughout many lives; others vowed to serve and suffer through endless years. Ch'an master Huai Hai of Paichang [720-814 C.E.] initiated a rule of productivity at his monastery – no food without work. Today, a similar rule may guide one's life: prepare appropriately and live well. Then one may talk of extinguishing the cycle of rebirth.

Finally, a Fo Guang Buddhist is as a humble pine who withstands the tests of time for a thousand years or as a plum tree who gracefully bears the weight of winter's snow and ice. Only the patient shall know success; only the humble shall be truly great.

Culture is the vehicle of the Dharma

Fo Guang Shan is built upon four aspirations "to spread the Dharma through culture, to nurture talent through education, to benefit society with charity, and to purify minds through cultivation." Fo Guang Shan is no longer just a reputable temple in Tashu, Kaohsiung. It represents thirty years of unstinting effort by a thousand-member sangha and a million-devotee populace around the world.

Alms-round donations commemorating its twentieth anniversary have funded the Fo Guang Cultural and Educational Foundation in underwriting national and international Buddhist scholarly conferences. It also financed the publication of the Buddhist journals *Benevolent Teachers, Blessing*, and the weekly *Buddhist News*, as well as gifts of books to libraries, schools, and prisons. A decade was spent in researching, annotating, and indexing the *Fo Guang Tripi-taka*. In 1989, the *Fo Guang Encyclopedia* was awarded publishing's Golden Cauldron Award in Taiwan. The *Buddhist Historical Chronology* was named the most distinguished textual reference volume. The three monumental works of the Tripitaka Editorial Committee are collectively heralded as the triple gems of Buddhist scholarly research.

Awakening the World[1] is provided free to a readership of 100,000 in forty-two regions and nations. Published three times monthly since 1957, the publication continues to function as an information circuit for Buddhists worldwide. *Universal Gate*, which offers a mix of popular articles and literary pieces, has a global circulation of approximately 30,000. Launched in 1979, this polished Buddhist magazine is the only advertising-based product with financial self-sufficiency, using computerized management, and distribution networking.

Hsing Yun is an accomplished and dedicated author, editor and speaker who has ensured that his disciples, like himself, are properly groomed for literary endeavors. Venerable Tzu Hui, Tzu Chia, Yi Kung, Yi Yu, Yi Sheng, Yi Chun, Yung Chuang, Yung Yun, and Man Kuo represent three generations of published writers. Sales of Hsing Yun's four-volume lectures have never slumped; nor have the sales of other titles: *Biography of Sakyamuni Buddha, National Master Yu Lin, Hsing Yun's Ch'an Talk, Hsing Yun's Dharma Words*, and *Hsing Yun's Verses*, among others.

Fo Guang publishing House has, during four decades, put out hundreds of serial titles, encompassing sutras and discourses, scholarly journals, literary anthologies, biographies and doctrinal commentaries. The latest ventures are children's books, comics, cassettes, and videos – all attempts at giving orthodox Buddhism a contemporary appeal. The publishing house, together with *Fo Guang Scholarly Journal* and Fo Guang bookstores, form a diversified vehicle for teaching dharma.

---

[1] It was changed to a monthly publication in Aug. 1995.

Together with the Buddhist exhibition hall, art gallery, and exhibits of Tunhuang[2] paintings and Buddhist art, these vehicles demonstrate Fo Guang Shan's awareness of cultural importance and the many ways in which Buddhist faith can be expressed.

Education is the nursery of talent

From Shou-shan Buddhist College, to the current three-year sangha education program (see also Chapter 9), applications for admission have been on a continual rise, as have the credentials of the candidates – about one third of which show a university education. Many candidates with years of professional work experience return to school with aspirations to learn the Dharma.

Ilan's Compassionate and Nurturing Kindergarten was the first-ever Buddhist Kindergarten, with graduates totaling over 30,000. Three more schools have followed, Tainan's Compassionate Vehicle, Shanhua's Wisdom and Compassion, and Fo Guang Shan's P'u-men. Chih-Kuang (Wisdom Light) is a secondary-level business school. Last but certainly not least, P'u-men High School, located at Fo Guang Shan, went from 91 students in 1972 to 1,600 today, and has emerged as one of the most outstanding private institutions in Taiwan. Hsi Lai (Coming West) University in Los Angeles, California, is a small institution of higher learning with a brilliant faculty and an international student population. It is also positioned as a future hub for international Buddhist academic

---

[2] City in Gansu, China, near which cave temples of a thousand Buddhas were unearthed in the early 1900s. Invaluable finds include 5th – to 10th – century manuscripts and other block prints and paintings.

exchange. To top off Hsing Yun's passionate dedication to education, the new Fo Guang University is scheduled to accept applications for its graduate school in 1995.

The establishment of a city college at P'u-hsien Temple, Kaohsiung, in 1983, sparked similar projects in continuing education at other branch temples. It offers three-month courses in Buddhist studies in response to the need of working folks to use free time for academic and professional advancement. This format remains both in-depth and broad-based and takes the Dharma further into society.

A variety of specialty classes also have been arranged in response to increasing social diversity and devotees' requests. These include courses in vegetarian cooking, calligraphy, T'ai-chi, as well as choirs and orchestras.

Charity is the vehicle of benefit

Few are familiar with the history of Fo Guang Shan's charitable activities, which though long-standing and encompassing, are internationally downplayed out of respect for recipients.

The Compassion Foundation, working to "benefit society through charity" conducts charitable and social welfare activities that span the length of a human life. They include the Great Compassion Nursery for orphans, Fo Guang Retirement Home, Ilan Graciousness Home for the Needy, Fo Guang Walk-In Clinic, mobile clinics, foundation fund for the sangha, home visit and service plan, regular functions to release live creatures, winter collections of food and clothing for the poor, and disaster relief. Fo Guang Shan has also allotted 2,000 cemetary niches for ashes to house those selected by Kaohsiung's County Social Welfare Department at no cost to the families.

One recipient of these compassionate efforts was Wang Hsiao-min, who, thirty years ago, was hospitalized in a vegetative state following a traffic accident. When her treatment exhausted family resources, Fo Guang Shan took her mother and sister under its care.

Ilan Graciousness Home is an example of the tenacity required when undertaking charitable ventures. It was formerly a Christian-owned charity, which later experienced financial strain. Hsing Yun took over the operation together with the fate of its occupants. The newly graduated Venerable Shao Chueh and Yi Jung volunteered their services and thereby consummated the Bodhisattva Way by devoting half of their lives to washing, feeding, nursing, and, eventually, laying to rest those frail, lonely folks. Both of them have received awards from the government for their exemplary deeds.

Fo Guang Shan has also contributed to natural disaster relief funds around the world, be it in response to flooding by the Yangtze River in Mainland China or catastrophic typhoons across Taiwan. Fo Guang Shan has undertaken to fundraising and relief efforts of enormous proportions.

Behind its low profile in charity is a profound consideration for the self-esteem of the recipients. The hundred or so children in Great Compassion Nursery are sheltered as much as cared for in life. Hsing Yun calls them his princes and princesses and insists they be fed and clothed like any other, and cherished like gems by those who attend them. He wants them to feel respected, and that they belong with him. To those who came without a surname he gives his own secular name, Li. The nursery is off-limits to tourists. The children are raised out of the spotlight, intending that they not be hurt a second time. Amidst the sense of peace and security that prevails in the impeccable classrooms and dormitory, director Hsiao Pi-Liang's tone is soft yet firm: "This is a home. You don't showcase it. The kids call me Mom. For that alone I must give them a safe, cozy place they can call home, too."

Some rough statistics indicate that over 30,000 low-income patients visit Fo Guang Shan's clinic annually. The mobile clinic's thirty-three ambulances travel through twenty-eight cities, more than fifty towns, and over one hundred villages to serve the sick in outlying areas. And six affiliated temporary lodgings in Longevity Park provide a form of consolation for the families of the terminally ill. Burials, provisions, and medical relief are commonly provided.

Community cultivation, a means to purify minds

Thoughtfully organized Dharma functions, community cultivation, practice, chanting, and Ch'an meditation together form the mature religious composite into which Fo Guang Shan has evolved. Devotees from around the globe attend repentance services, solitary retreats, sangha-lay person joint practice, Eight Precepts and seven-day cultivation retreats, pilgrimages to the temple[3], pilgrimages to India, tours through various branch temples, and annual meetings for devotees.

---

[3] A pilgrimage event in which the monastics and devotees walk from the main gate to the Buddha Hall while chanting a Buddha's name and making a full prostration on every third step.

Led in the direction of the Buddha gate by causes and conditions of their own, those who aspire to let their good roots flourish discover a dwelling for their minds and a support for their faith.

Fo Guang Shan ranks high in devotee popularity, positive social impact, and national reputation. When any monastic is asked casually by a Taiwanese citizen: "Are you from Fo Guang Shan?" it is because Buddhism, monasticism and Fo Guang Shan are synonymous for most. The leader of this Buddhist order, which has growing international importance, is Master Hsing Yun.

Prayer beads worn around the pulse of time[4]

Hsing Yun has no intention or desire to be pedestaled as the founder of yet another school in the history of Chinese Buddhism (perhaps it could be called Fo Guang, like some supporters hope will happen someday). Hsing Yun takes comfort in a good career, and plans that Fo Guang Shan, will be:

1. a contemporary religious body and system including
    a. gender equality in career advancement
    b. harmony between monastics & lay people
    c. solidity in the foundation of religious undertakings
    d. notable cultural and educational achievements
2. an international Buddhist body and network which includes
    a. Buddha's Light International Association
    b. global branch temples

---

[4] As in the original text. It refers to the tremendous historical sense of time Hsing Yun has maintained throughout his career.

c. international conferences
   d. non-sectarian communication and exchange
3. a society founded on humanistic Buddhism, which is characterized by
   a. Dharma teaching in contemporary language for contemporary needs
   b. the practice of Buddhism within the family
   c. social application
   d. a variety of activities
4. a bridge between mainland China and Taiwan which encompasses
   a. joint Buddhist Association as the foundation
   b. culture and education as the primary objective
   c. cultural undertakings
   d. educational endeavors

It began from nothingness; it will end in endlessness. Hsing Yun's prayer beads are worn around the pulse of time. As he, with his transcendent spirit, strides the path of worldly affairs, so too strides Fo Guang Shan. With the footprints of Fo Guang Shan there will certainly be evidence of an important influence within the development of Buddhism in China.

Chapter 9
An outstanding disciple of Buddhism

Ascend the realm of purity
to seek the Truth.
Enter the mountain of treasure
to learn the Dharma.

What propels Fo Guang Shan is the energy of those whom Hsing Yun took four decades to nurture.

His conviction that the future of Buddhism depends upon the cultivation of the young – to whom he will be handing down the light someday – stems from the integrity of his orthodox Buddhist background. Early during his teaching career in Taiwan, he came face to face with a low standard of education among the sangha. Memories of the semi-illiterate chanting by rote still haunt him. So bad had the reputation of monastics become that the taking of tonsure by high school graduates was greeted with dismay by the general public. Many monastics sought earnings from services conducted for the dead and rarely lifted a text or sutra to glance at, much less read. All were regarded as "withered buds and rotten seeds." Properly educated monastics were a rare breed.

Revival begins with the right people

As the revival of a nation begins with the right people, rejuvenation of Buddhism, Hsing Yun knew, would have to start from the beginning - the creation of a pool of talent. In fact, when some of the young followers in Ilan had requested to be tonsured, he declined because he had no school for them. Not until the Buddhist College at Shou Shan, Kaohsiung, was built, were young talents able to stay. Many then were tonsured.

The class of '68 from Tung-fang (Eastern) Buddhist College (formerly Shou-shan Buddhist College) was to Hsing Yun an unprecedented yield from years of labor in Buddhist education. This graduation in particular symbolized the crossing of Buddhism over the Taiwan Strait. This group of locals would take leading roles in the future development of Buddhism.

Hsing Yun saw in Tung-fang Buddhist College a fertile ground in which to nurture the new buds in Buddhism. A mix of traditional spirit and modern information and methodologies was a concept that became the backbone of Fo Guang Shan's education body. It was also later referred to and adopted by other Buddhist colleges.

The credit system was employed in Tung-fang Buddhist College's three-year-program. Members of its prominent faculty included Fang Lun, who was a specialist in the Buddhist Canon, T'ang I-Hsuan, Venerable Hui Hsing, Venerable Chu Yun, among others. The array of courses offered included introduction to natural science, introduction to social sciences, introduction to philosophy, Chinese history, Western history, Chinese literature, western philosophy, basic teaching in Chinese culture, foreign languages, administrative affairs writing, and sutra-chanting.

The first group of graduates – twenty in all, are now heading monasteries, assuming teaching positions in other Buddhist colleges, lecturing on the Dharma, or researching Buddhist classics. The second and third classes totaled approximately seventy graduates. By then Hsing Yun was concerned about the lack of usable space and began to look elsewhere. That, indeed, was the underlying cause for Fo Guang Shan.

Young intellectuals are received and guided

There is a saying that goes: "Better to lead an army garrison than a sangha." Such is the formidable task of Buddhist education.

Hsing Yun worked feverishly to provide for everyone who attended the Buddhist College - free tuition and books, room and board, clothing and other necessities. "You and your students are going to starve," some warned him with kind intentions. "Left with nothing, you'll end up losing your devotees altogether." Hsing Yun believed in what he was doing and braved on. The first structure to be put up on the once thicketed land was the Buddhist College, west of Treasure Bridge. With this structure, the building of Fo Guang Shan began.

To keep the institution going, he, who never favored specializing in services for the dead, would do so, sometimes through the night, to raise funds. At one point, the young woman in charge of academic affairs resolved to take the tonsure and joined him in those chanting sessions. That was

Venerable Tzu Chuang. The teacher, who managed student affairs and worked part-time in a bakery to acquire extra sponsorships, was Venerable Tzu Hui. The kindergarten teaching staff, Venerable Tzu Jung, Wu Pao-ch'in, Yang Tz'u-man, and others gave up their salaries. Devotee Hsiao Pi-hsia sold her properties to finance the cultural and educational foundation. Venerable Tzu Jung would later direct the charities of Fo Guang Shan and spearhead Buddha's Light International Association; Tzu Chuang would pioneer Hsi Lai Temple; and Tzu Hui would found two universities: Hsi Lai and Fo Guang.

The college-level Buddhist summer camp in 1969 was designed to bring young intellectuals out of the ivory tower and down to earth to tackle life's issues. There ensued a growth in Buddhism in academia years later, and the top students included Fo Guang Shan's own Venerable Yi Kung, and Yi Fa, together with the gallant Venerable Chao Hui - now all pillars of the Buddhist community. Thus the summer camp fostered a challenging environment where young minds responded to the call for a life of commitment and service.

Strength of the mind, a very present constituent

Hsing Yun invested most heavily in cultivating the talents of the young, both in financial terms and, especially, in strength of mind. The odds against him were unimaginable. Just prior to launching the second college-level Buddhist summer camp for 600 participants, the water tower broke down. Anxiously, Hsing Yun supervised the emergency repairs during the day and stood guard, ear against the tower wall all night, until the rumblings of motor and water began at three in the morning.

Had the motor not started up, he confided to disciples later, he vowed that his blood would turn into pure water for the consumption of the young people about to swarm in.

In fundraising for the research department of the Chinese Buddhist Research Institute, Hsing Yun and his students rolled up their sleeves and put on their aprons to cook for devotees, hoping they would be pleased with the rice and noodles and would be generous in their support.

His determination and sincerity struck a chord with many that lent a hand. Venerable Tzu Chuang remembers an extraordinary experience, with a hint of the presence of the Buddha.

It was the eve of another summer camp, and funds were drained, with delivery of provisions still up in the air. Just when she was beginning to wring her hands with concern, she saw an elderly figure coming up the arched entrance. It was a peasant woman, straw hat on her head and shoeless, who requested specifically to see the director. Venerable Tzu Chuang received her and treated her to soup and rice noodles, which she clearly enjoyed. Then, quite unexpectedly, she produced a paper-wrapped package and said: "Give this to the grand master. You may do whatever you please with it." Then, she turned and was gone. Inside was a neat bunch of notes amounting to NT$50,000 (US$1,868) in the then new currency in Taiwan. The emergency lifted, and to this day, no one has the slightest inkling of who she was or where she was from.

The sangha takes on a new look

Rather than a moldy picture of frailty and boredom, Hsing Yun contends that Buddhism is contemporary, progressive, and vibrant. " Buddhism needs the young, but the young need Buddhism more," he says. The Buddhist College at Fo Guang Shan is now peopled by youthful, amicable, confident, and disciplined pursuers of the Dharma. Hsing Yun has given Chinese Buddhist monastics a brand-new air. If Shou-Shan Buddhist College was a delicate, budding plant in Buddhist education, Fo Guang Shan is a luxuriant, fruit-bearing tree.

At the summit of Fo Guang Shan's three-tier structure is the Chinese Buddhist Research Institute, which encompasses three-year research programs in Dharma propagation, sangha education, fundamental doctrine and systematic etiquette, and monasterial management. Research fellows with master's degrees and graduate students with bachelor's degrees produce, on completion, a thesis in Buddhist studies no shorter than 60,000 words in length. Acceptance of the thesis by the examination panel leads to the conferring of a master's degree in Buddhist studies.

Fo Guang Shan Ts'ung-lin College is divided into two branches of study. One branch is a center for global scholarly exchange, and it produces a constellation of international teachers of the Dharma. The other branch is a four-year program with departments in sutra and doctrinal studies, management of ceremonial services, social application, and preaching within a cultural context.

Tung-fang Buddhist College administers both a men's and women's two-year school. The curriculum is a blend of tradition and modernity, of practice and comprehension. From fundamental Buddhism to higher research, the educational programs form an integrated whole. And, in answer to demands raised in recent international lecturing, attention has been paid to foreign languages and computer studies.

With 11 departments, 28 classes, a faculty of 200, and a student population of close to 800, this Buddhist College system has made history in renewing the Buddhist academy that flourished centuries ago. From this point on, Hsing Yun will be looking in the direction of Nalanda's[1] record population of 30,000.

Equaling the Confucian sages

To cite statistics from 1994, Fo Guang Shan's sangha had surpassed 1,100. Of this number 225 are bhiksus (monks), 937 are bhiksunis (nuns), and 30 are of the *shih-ku* status. Annual increase averages 100. The majority are between 21-40, with a good 70 percent being graduates of college-level education. Also, 35 hold master's degrees and 3 have doctorates. Most are from Taiwan. About 10 percent are from France, Hong Kong, Indonesia, Malaysia, Nepal, Singapore, Thailand, Vietnam, the United States, and elsewhere.

The monastics of Fo Guang Shan pride themselves on their record of having many members of the same family tonsured under the same master. Venerable Tzu Chuang, her father Hui Ho, and nephews Hui Lung and Hui Chuan all follow Ven. Master Hsing Yun in the monastic life. There

---

[1] Unwearying Benefactor. Name of a historically renowned monastery and Buddhist institute of higher education in India.

are sisters, like Venerable Tzu Jung and Yi Lai, and other siblings, mothers and children, all of whom come to address one another as Dharma brother.

Hsing Yun was alone when he landed in Taiwan. Now, the sangha of Fo Guang Shan holds three generations, including himself. After the founder, the succeeding generations of bhiksus are named, in order of tonsure: Hsin (mind), Hui (wisdom), and Cheng (vehicle). The second generations of bhiksunis are named as follows: Tzu (compassion), Yi (Accordance), Yung (Constancy), Man (Completion), Chueh (Awakening), and Miao (Wondrousness). The most recent third generation is named Tao (Way). Historian Orient Lee compares this lineage with the seventy-two Confucian sages.

3,000 splendid rules, 80,000 minute details

Hsing Yun has created a unique system with a capacity to minimize internal strife. The monastics of Fo Guang Shan, according to the master's rule, do not take disciples or build temples of their own. All disciples follow the discipline of Fo Guang Shan, and no one has a personal following. Venerable Tzu Chuang is the master of tonsure to the third-generation bhiksunis, and Venerable Hsin Ping [now Venerable Hsin Ting], to the third-generation bhiksus. Hsing Yun is the master to the second-generation monastics, and grandmaster to the third generation.

Observers think this system, with its protective measures against internal division and even possible corruption, and its family-oriented sense of justice, is a worthwhile reference for similar institutions.

Producer Chou Chih-min of the television program *Ai-*

hsin (Loving Heart) is among those of the media who have become great admirers of Hsing Yun's management methods. She relates an episode in her career that illustrates the strength of the sangha under Hsing Yun.

"Late 1979, I was working on an episode entitled *Buddha's Light Throughout the Universe*. It was the sixth day of the Chinese New Year holidays. Holiday revelries were still going strong when I, along with four colleagues, went to Fo Guang Shan. What transpired within the first half-hour we were there was absolutely eye-opening. I first showed Venerable Tzu Hui an outline of our needs. Without much ado, and after only fifteen minutes, Ven. Tzu Hui presented me with a detailed schedule indicating where to work, with whom, and how. Even a theme was included for our convenience. We couldn't find a flaw even if we had tried. The next two days we adhered to the timetable presented to us and the shooting was smooth sailing all the way."

This incident mirrors Hsing Yun's personal style. Planning, open discussion, delegation of responsibilities, monitoring of progress, reflection on the process, projection into the future – a complete and totalistic approach in which not a step is skipped or an effort wasted.

Observers are inclined to share the observation that the branch temples of Fo Guang Shan, and its monastics for that matter, engender a different feeling than most Buddhist establishments. They have about them a composure and propriety which are uniquely Fo Guang Shan's. Indeed, every move or gesture they make reflects "the 3,000 splendid rules, 80,000 minute details." These bhiksus and bhiksunis are not only well versed in the multiple chores and skills of a conventional monastery but are also equipped with the knowledge and capacities needed for writing and theorizing, monasterial management and accounting, social work and teaching, computers and mechanics. For the Buddha's way is of joyful transcendence, and the mundane way is of practical necessity. Together, the two combine to become the consummate method for the deliverance of all living beings.

Ingenuity regenerating itself

Hsing Yun thinks that ingenuity regenerates itself. Therefore Tzu Chuang, Tzu Hui, Tzu Jung, Tzu Chia, Tzu Yi, and others were sent to Japan, despite the shortage of funds. Many asked him to think twice: "What a loss of brain power if they don't return! And if they do, what will you do with the superiority attitude that often accompanies higher learning?" "Even though it will be difficult financially," Hsing Yun replied, "It will not be a problem. They are going to be back to do a lot for Buddhism."

As their master anticipated, Venerable Tzu Hui, an Education major, took over Fo Guang Shan's educational body in its entirety; Venerables Tzu Chia and Tzu Yi headed the compilation of the *Fo Guang Tripitaka* and the *Fo Guang Encyclopedia*; Venerable Tzu Chuang specializing in architecture, masterminded one branch temple after another; and Venerable Tzu Jung, a major in Social Work, specialized in organizing, executing, and supervising large-scale functions.

Hsing Yun could now rest assured that his torch was passing into the right hands. He was able to step down, and he did. He has since been roving among the clouds and across the four seas sharing the Dharma. In the meantime,

Fo Guang Shan continues to thrive.

The selection of disciples with the ability and promise for further study also continues to thrive. Presently in Japan are Tzu Yi, a doctoral candidate, together with Yi Yu, Yi Hsin, Yung Chuan, Man Ting, and others. Hui Kai is pursuing his doctorate at Temple University, and so is Yi Fa at Yale University in the United States, Man Guan, Chueh Mu, and quite a few others, too, are attending universities and colleges across California. Yung Hsien and Chueh Hang are in France; Yung Yu and Yi Yi at Oxford University, England; Chueh Cheng at Sao Paulo University, Brazil; Yi Hua at International University, India; Yi En in Korea. Over one hundred in number, they each know why they are there and what they must do.[2]

These disciples of Hsing Yun's are probably the most qualified ever in the history of Chinese Buddhism. Many of them are accomplished in the foreign languages needed to disseminate the Buddhist faith around the globe.

Life's greatest blessing would be the opportunity to read thousand of books, travel thousands of miles, do thousands of tasks, and deliver thousands of living beings. In dispatching disciples to go abroad and preach, Hsing Yun wants them to realize that "Fo Guang Shan is but a preparatory station, not a terminal, in the spread of the Dharma." Based on individual seniority, dedication, ability, and contribution, he maps out for them ways to further their studies and their lives. Practically everyone has at some point been out of Taiwan. These monastics are a far cry from those

---

[2] The students identified above have graduated and are serving in positions worldwide.

who used to have only the oil lamp and w*ooden fish*[3] for company and died keeping watch over a lonesome temple in the mountains.

Knowing a gem when seeing it

The sight of a youthful monastic in the old days would invariably invite a lament or two: "What a pity! To have renounced the world at such a young age!" There is nothing *pitiful* about joining Fo Guang Shan, where much is invested in training and the trained are allowed plenty of space. For, "being good at discerning the nature of all living beings and not ever being discriminative," Hsing Yun steers his disciples in their development based on their strengths and inclinations. In "accommodating them, shaping them, and employing them," he ensures that they become the best they possibly can be.

Among many others, the eloquent Tzu Hui, Tzu Jung, Hsin Ting, Yi Kung, and Hui Chuan have been sent to preach the Dharma; the literary Yi Sheng, Yung Chuang, Yung Yun, and Man Kuang keep publishing; the academic Tzu Chia, Yi Chun, Hsin Ju, Yung Ming, Yung Chin, and Man Kuo compile the Canon; the compassionate Hui Lung, Yi Jen, Yi Pin, and Yi Lai champion charitable causes; the serene Yi Yen, Hui Jih, and Chien Kuan concentrate on their practice; the stu- dious Tzu Yi and Chueh San further their studies; and drafting specialists Tzu Chuang, Yi Min, and Hui Li build temples and undertake managerial duties.

---

[3] Wooden fish. Two kinds exist, one for keeping time in chanting and the other for announcing meals. One version of its origin is that it serves as a reminder of alertness to the monastics, the fish with its eyes open at all times.

Hsing Yun is like a miner and sculptor in the discovery of talents. "He knows us better than we know ourselves," disciples say, brimming over with gratitude and admiration. Once he was discussing the issue of examination and certification with a jeweler. "He knows gems; I know people," Hsing Yun beamed.

The young monastics of Fo Guang Shan did not take the tonsure out of despair in love or in life; they did so with perfect willingness. With compassion – the love for all, not for one – they have come to serve living beings. While so doing, they radiate joy, drive, wholesomeness, and grace. In meeting these monastics, the rest of the world will have an opportunity to think differently about Buddhism.

Some years ago parents were still heard insisting that their newly tonsured sons and daughters return home with them. These days, however, students of the Buddhist College arrive with their folks' blessings and take the tonsure in their presence. The old way of "grieving for the son relinquished to the gate of the void" has given way to modern parents "cheerily walking their child to the gate of the Buddha."

Author Hsiao Hung sees Hsing Yun in every one of his disciples. "They are so affable – like their master. Passing by, they close their palms in greeting; if the path is narrow, they step aside to let others pass. One has to possess devotion within to display it without. It is not a mere act. It is simply the master's virtues finding expression through his disciples."

Born to be an educator

Learned educator Cheng Shih-yen finds in Hsing Yun a

natural educator with many concepts and theories that should be widely adopted in the educational field. In the past, Hsing Yun witnessed classmates who acted out of line at Ch'i-hsia Temple being ordered to pay homage to the Buddha or kneel before the shrine for the length of lit incense. Thinking to himself that paying homage to the Buddha is such a thing of beauty, he could not believe it should take the form of a penalty. Today at Fo Guang Shan, serious misbehavior is punishable by "being sent to your room and disallowed to pay homage to the Buddha." Cooped up in their rooms with a chance to reflect, usually students have little problem recognizing their own follies. Permitted in the presence of the Buddha again, many prostrate in tears and kneel for a long, long time.

He emphasizes education of the mind. He replaces condemnation with encouragement and chiding with caring. A personal favorite for teachers is the story of Ch'an master Hsien Yai. There was a novice monk who was prone to succumbing to diversions beyond the confines of the monastery. Nightly he would jump over the wall to venture out. One night Master Hsien Yai was on his rounds about the temple when he came upon a stool by the corner of the wall – evidence of an attempt to sneak outside. He removed the stool and stood himself in its place, waiting as the night wore on. At last, the novice returned from his merriment. Not knowing about the absence of the stool, he alighted squarely on the master's head, and tumbled to the ground. When he stood to dust himself off, he found, to his consternation, he was face to face with the master.

"The night is deep and the dew is heavy," the gracious

Master Hsien Yai said, as if nothing had gone awry. "Take good care of your body. Don't let it catch a cold. Run on home and get yourself more clothing."

Not another word was uttered about the incident. No one even knew it ever occurred. Thereafter, though, among the hundred or so novices there were no more nocturnal excursions.

Like the cultivation of orchids, disciples have to be strengthened by the accumulation of learning and nourished by the accumulation of virtue, stimulated by the resonance of the Way and reached by the passing on of the Dharma. Nothing bonds sangha members more than such a connection between the master and his disciples. Yi Kung feels that Hsing Yun is like a parent, "with whom we can pour our hearts out." Likened to Sariputra[4], with his bright intellect and erudition, she says: "The master is the Buddha. I would not have become a monastic if not for him." Even the most obstinate have been touched by his compassion and attained wisdom; even the most incorrigible have been nurtured by his tender care and attained a virtuous way of life. Yi Kung recalls the time she was to relocate to other quarters. The master made sure she was given a larger room "because Yi Kung has tons of books," and a table light "because Yi Kung has a lot of reading to do."

Venerable Hsin Cheng, too, has his share of reflections: "That year in Changhua I was hospitalized after a car crash. The master came to see me. With sweat beading on his forehead, he stood there, as if rooted beside me, looking with great concern at my bandaged leg and toothless mouth. I

---

[4] A principal disciple of Sakyamuni Buddha.

was so ashamed to have him hurting for me like that!"

Inevitable are the occasional disagreements and discontentment among disciples, and they have this thought to count on: "The master treats me like no other. He'll understand!"

Like friend, like teacher, like parent

Disciples eagerly look for ways to reciprocate the master's tender concern. They often follow him in a friendly group as he makes his rounds within the temple complex abroad on lecture tours. It is evident that the feelings between master and disciples are mutual. Whenever he appears fatigued or is delayed at mealtime, they kindly offer him a cup of tea, a meal, or a hot towel.

Hsing Yun has for years been under treatment for diabetes. Disciples will not leave until he is seen to have taken his medication at the end of a meal. Each time the statuesque master boards or exits a vehicle, one of them will lay a hand on the doorway, making sure he does not injure himself by bumping his head.

To the older disciples, he is both master and companion in the Dharma. To the younger ones, he is a parent. "The master is as colossal as a mountain yet endearing," they say. "He is rather like the air we breathe, spontaneous and vital. We cannot be without it. But then again, the pressure is never there."

On the subject of respect towards parents or the elderly, Hsing Yun's sigh is clearly audible. "When most parents are young and useful," he comments, "their service is eagerly sought after – like a basketball. As their effectiveness dwindles with age, they are batted away – like a volleyball. Finally, old and incapacitated, they are kicked around – like a soccer ball."

"I left home to become a monk at twelve. I have no children of my own. Yet my disciples are more loyal and dutiful to me than any children I would have had. One day I shall be old. Yet it is obvious that they are going to hold me and not let me go – like an American football."

In his bid to create inexhaustible brainpower for the Buddhist faith, Hsing Yun has broken out of the limitations of Fo Guang Shan. Projects such as the Chinese Buddhist Research Institute, regular international Buddhist conferences and seminars, the annual international Buddhist examination, Fo Guang Shan Cultural and Educational Foundation, and diverse sponsorships for international Buddhist scholarly research, all serve the same end.

"When rearing the young, they should not fear growth and independence," he has said many times. Trained and matured, he vows they will be as gifts to society, to the nation, and to all living beings.

Modern pioneers for the Buddhist faith

Hsing Yun is fully aware of the widening gap between Fo Guang Shan's incredible growth and the training of its forces. But he has every reason to believe that experiences shall be updated and wrongs righted. It is a path for the next hundred years, and they will get there.

Such a self-assured openness has created modern pioneers for Buddhism. On the shoulders of the thousand or so dragons and elephants at the Buddha gate shall rest the future of the Tathagata. While his contemporaries are piqued by imminent concerns over posterity, Hsing Yun knows that "twenty years from now, Fo Guang Shan shall stand as one of the most powerful religious bodies in Taiwan."

Chapter 10
Traditional monastery, modern visions

*I*f we were to consider Fo Guang Shan as an enterprise, it would be among the top one hundred organizations in Taiwan. Fo Guang Shan functions as a well-organized entity energized by human and financial resources. It inherited its spirit of antiquity from the traditional monastery of the T'ang dynasty and combined this with the ideals of modern management. Overall, Fo Guang Shan embodies modern Chinese Buddhism while also providing a valuable model for business management.

A product of teamwork

Organizational masterpieces are typically the brainchild of their founders. Fo Guang Shan is no exception. The development and operation of Fo Guang Shan arose from Hsing Yun's vision.

In Hsing Yun's world view Buddhism is the enterprise of all living beings. Thus, he sees Fo Guang Shan as a product of teamwork. The Committee of Religious Affairs is vested with decision-making in developmental directions and interdepartmental communication and coordination. The eleven committee members each serve a term of six years. A director-in-chief is elected from the committee to serve a term of six years as well. Presently holding the position is abbot

Venerable Hsin Ping.[1]

Branching out from the above in equal proportion is the abbot's office and the executive director's office. Both of these offices oversee ten management departments governing monasterial affairs, devotees' affairs, charity, social welfare, construction and maintenance services, financial matters, human resources and systematic functions. The director's office also handles departments of education, cultural affairs, monastic elders, Fo Guang Lineage Transmission Committee,[2] Fo Guang Shan Cultural and Educational Foundation, Fo Guang Shan Pureland Foundation, Compassion Foundation, Fo Guang University Fundraising Committee, Buddha's Light International Association and others – totaling over 180 units.

Headquartered in Kaohsiung, Fo Guang Shan has a vast network of over 100 branch establishments. A majority of these were founded by Hsing Yun himself. A handful of these temples voluntarily merged with Fo Guang Shan due to financial strain, internal strife or the absence of a master.

Chi-le (Utmost Joy) Temple, Keelung, newly renovated last year, was one such temple. The causes and conditions that bound the temple and Hsing Yun together through four decades date back to the day he set foot in Keelung. After leaving his ship, he passed an old weathered temple. When Hsing Yun glanced inside the temple a monastic returned his glance. No words were ever exchanged. The temple was Chi-le. Thirty-two years later, the director of the Keelung

---

[1] Venerable Hsin Ping passed away in April, 1995. The new abbot is Venerable Hsin Ting.
[2] The committee takes charge in looking after all monastics at Fo Guang Shan pertaining to education, welfare, reward & punishment, medication, etc., and even the welfare of the monastics' parents.

Buddhist Association and abbess Hsiu Hui of Chi-le Temple – whom Hsing Yun had met only fleetingly at that point in time – invited him to conduct a three-day seminar. Hsing Yun was told that Venerable Hsiu Hui had read his works and readily identified with the concept of humanistic Buddhism. Within three years Venerable Hsiu Hui made a gift of Chi-le Temple and its surrounding properties to Fo Guang Shan.

Yuan-ming Temple in suburban Ilan, where Hsing Yun completed his *Biography of Sakyamuni Buddha's Ten Great Disciples* and his work on the *Sutra on the Eight Realizations of the Great Beings*, was another gift to Fo Guang Shan. In 1982, abbot Chueh Yi entrusted Fo Guang Shan with the temple just prior to his passing away. Yuan-fu (Perfect Fortune) Temple, Chiayi, erected at the turn of the twentieth century, was also entrusted to Fo Guang Shan.

Expansion, both inward and outward

Considering the hundred or so branches stemming from the nucleus of Fo Guang Shan there is certainly a need for an intricate organizational structure. The first level of branch temples is under the direction of headquarters, and includes major temples such as Taipei's P'u-men Temple, Kaohsiung's P'u-hsien Temple, Los Angeles' Hsi Lai Temple and Tokyo's branch temple. Each is organized by its location in a metropolis containing a million or more inhabitants, its ability to hold Dharma Functions for 1,000 or more persons and its 8 or more resident sangha members.

At the second level are the branch temples that maintain the outward appearance of traditional lecture halls and temples, yet are nestled within the structure of modern buildings. Again, each is categorized by its location in a city of half a million or more in population, its ability to hold Dharma functions for 500 or more and its four to eight resident sangha members.

At the third level are the Ch'an and Pureland centers. Each is categorized for its suburban location, its ability to hold Dharma functions for 200 or more and its two to four resident sangha members.

Lastly, the preaching centers in more rural areas are run in an itinerant fashion by visiting monastics.

Financial independence of all branch establishments is required. Financial assistance, however, is often sought from headquarters in cases requiring a major construction project.

The global setup of Fo Guang Shan is unprecedented in the history of Buddhism. Similar to the Vatican, it is especially unique in the centralized training and delegation of its members. No matter how vast the peripheral expansion, resource assignments always come from Fo Guang Shan.

The organization

Two subsystems exist within the organization of Fo Guang Shan, the stages of seniority and administrative appointments.

The stages of seniority fall into five classes and fifteen grades. The first stage is the class of ethical practitioner which includes six levels lasting one year each. The next three stages are; learning practitioner which spans another six grades or levels lasting three or five years each, cultivating practitioner in three levels lasting four years a piece, and teaching practitioner in three grades spanning five years each. The culmination of the sequence is the stage or class of master. The administrative appointment pertains to the delegation of duties at Fo Guang Shan.

Hsing Yun has designed a management scheme of tremendous flexibility and versatility in which human resources are delegated in accordance with academic credentials from both within Fo Guang Shan Buddhist College and from outside the order's educational system. In addition, accomplished study of the Buddhist Canon, character, conduct, practice, contribution and seniority are considerations. This system is capable of promoting outstanding junior members to vital positions as well as bestowing recognition on senior and responsible members.

Undoubtedly, corporate executives are well acquainted with a system which maintains an orderly business by preserving seasoned workers, while igniting innovation by boosting promising newcomers.

Most monastics or sangha transfers come once every three years, usually during the first and seventh month of the lunar calendar. Before the transfer, individual preferences are submitted to the Committee of Religious Affairs who then evaluates them. Implementation of transfers corresponds to the demand by the relevant departments and units. Objections are rescheduled for further discussion. In tackling the enormity of a personnel structure such as Fo Guang Shan's, the order strives for placement of "the right person in the right place."

Regulated transfers result in managerial fluidity. Nobody hangs onto a position or grows powerful enough to abuse it. Promotion and transfer are as defined as awards and penalties. Supply from a pool of talent is always ready, always fresh. The division of labor is best illustrated in large-scale functions, Fo Guang Shan style. Called "humanizing management," these are spectacular human undertakings from an initial delegation of authority through the ultimate execution of a project.

Devotees learn to "abide by the Dharma, not the person teaching it." This protects and maintains each temple. Exposure to constantly renewed leadership substitutes personal sentiment with an open and free system.

Economics

Hsing Yun is an example of a monastic who has never maintained his own personal temple, raised his own funds or pocketed his own savings. Every penny, in terms of income and donations, is channeled to the individual temples for maintenance and other expenses. Financial and administrative authority are distinctly separate within Fo Guang Shan; in the hands of junior executives lies the former, and the senior executives handle the latter. Everyone collects a monthly stipend on the basis of seniority and position: teaching practitioner, NT$400 (US$14); temple head, NT$300-350 (US$11-13); director, NT$300 (US$11); secretaries, NT$200 (US$7); cook for the guest house, NT$150 (US$5) and so on. Daily necessities, room and board, and transportation are paid by Fo Guang Shan. Salaried lay workers receive a monthly average of NT$3,000 (US$112).

Hsing Yun thinks the feasibility of this relative scarcity is empowered by the principle of selflessness upheld at Fo

Guang Shan. In the agricultural spirit of Ch'an practice, advocated by Venerable Master Huai Hai of Paichang during the T'ang dynasty, "no food without work" is alive and well.

Critics have cautioned young people against seeking academic advancement at Fo Guang Shan in what is considered a labor intensive program. "The monastics are made to do drudgery work instead of being encouraged to cultivate their true nature," some say. To Hsing Yun, who was raised performing diverse chores, manual labor is natural. Once separated from fetching water and chopping wood, wearing clothes and eating food, the expression of the Dharma is lost. The essence of Ch'an, or meditation, is reflected in work. Without exception, the eminent masters throughout the ages built their character through devoted labor. The sixth patriarch, Hui Neng, carried rocks and pounded grain, Master Huai Hai of Paichang hauled firewood and fetched water, and, wearing a cloak of straw, Master P'u Yuan of Nanch'uan drove cattle. In his first ten years of monastic life, Hsing Yun spent six serving meals, two years fetching water and a year and a half tending the shrine and working in the kitchen.

Even those attending the Buddhist colleges have obligations in addition to privileges. At Fo Guang Shan, the traditional monasterial daily routine complete with the punctuating bell, drum and board is still intact. Wake-up signal is sounded at 4.20 a.m., followed by morning liturgy and then breakfast. Classes are conducted for three hours each in the morning and afternoon, and self-study is mandatory for two hours in the evening. The day closes with the evening liturgy, meditation and then rest. Chores such as cleaning and cooking are included. For cooking, old-fashioned wood-burning stoves are still ablaze because they are deemed indispensable devices in the training of patience and concentration.

Finances

In supporting its community of monastics and lay people, and initiating diverse projects in education, charity and construction, Fo Guang Shan's financial burden is understandably cumbersome. To maintain self-sufficiency, Fo Guang Shan has established kindergartens and schools, published books and magazines and produced memorabilia and souvenirs. Though assailed for "multifaceted commercialism," Hsing Yun is at peace with his intentions.

"Buddhists are not social deserters," he says. "Nor is there any call to feed on society. It is appropriate for us to trade our labor for our livelihood. In both personal practice and in spreading the Dharma, we have to be self-sufficient before we can serve the public. Most of all, Buddhism, having received donations from society, must give in return. This is the basic reasoning behind the business ventures of Fo Guang Shan."

Indeed, the monastery needs donations to continue providing expanded services to people all over the globe. The two main sources of income in a traditional temple come from conducting repentance ceremonies and services for the dead, and from generous patrons. Hsing Yun believes the funds raised from repentance ceremonies and services for the dead to be a result of a mutually beneficial relationship. While devotees give to the temple, it is only right for the sangha to provide for devotee needs. Therefore, repentance ceremonies and services for the dead at Fo Guang Shan and its branch temples are organized and discreet.

Hsing Yun does not favor the practice of receiving donations from merely a few patrons with hefty checkbooks. Unfortunately, lavish givers may also pose oversized ego problems and end up doing more harm than good to the general harmony that permeates a temple. That is why Hsing Yun prizes small sums from countless humble donors, over huge sums from a handful of generous patrons. Small donations offered with loving kindness engenders kinship among followers far and wide.

"These days most people don't mind small sums," he adds. "When they do give, they certainly have no intention of seeking control of temple affairs in return. Abundant visitors at Fo Guang Shan means more cherished friends and affinities that permeate lifetime after lifetime."

Drops in the ocean

Just how are good affinities from far and wide accumulated? First of all, those who contribute to the temple receive gifts "from the Buddha." In a way, the mammoth Fo Guang Shan has been built from offering little souvenirs to its devotees year after year.

In addition, weekly pilgrimage tours, though not exactly profitable, have become greatly attractive to devotees as well as non-devotees who spend two days and a night at Fo Guang Shan. The tours are one of the most effective means of igniting interest in Buddhism. Among others, Venerables Yung Ping and Yun Wen came into contact with Buddhism and, ultimately, their own destiny in the sangha when they joined a pilgrimage tour.

On the conviction that a great ocean begins with small drops, Hsing Yun had the "City of Buddha Multitudes," a series of indoor and outdoor statuaries, and "The Chambers of Gold and Jade," a multi-functional building erected. These dazzling features were made possible by a collaboration of donors. Along with 480 golden Buddhas surrounding the Great Welcoming Buddha, 8,000 images of Avalokitesvara Bodhisattva in the Hall of Great Compassion, 14,800 images of Sakyamuni Buddha in their respective niches in the Main Shrine, pillars, Chinese roofing tiles, and relief sculptures; these artistic masterpieces allow for devotees to pledge their donations. Each donor leaves Fo Guang Shan having deepened their affinity with the Buddha.

Other Dharma functions such as Lanterns of Light Festival, Chinese New Year's Lanterns of Peace Festival, and thousands of affiliate functions bring in tens of thousands of devotees and their contributions.

In the red

Despite an appearance to the contrary, Fo Guang Shan is not an entity of great wealth. In the words of a temple spokesperson: "Fo Guang Shan is not wealthy, but it knows how to utilize financial resources – even those of next year, and the year after that." It is a center where resources are effectively and efficiently directed to the necessary departments.

Hsing Yun himself does not speak on money matters unless compelled to do so, and often tells disciples to refrain from being overly concerned about them, saying: "You're going to lose sleep knowing too much! This very moment is enough to know."

Supported by neither a nation nor any financial consortium, Fo Guang Shan is accomplished in handling resources. However, it must be noted that, estimated at NT $150 billion (US$5 billion) in assets, Fo Guang Shan is far below the top-ten list of Taiwan's wealthiest religious corporations.

Both a giver and receiver

Hsing Yun is a monk who is unafraid of wealth, unafraid to create the conditions necessary to build wealth, and unafraid to utilize wealth. "I'm both a giver and receiver of wealth," he says, candidly discussing the prevalent view in the Buddhist circle that poverty symbolizes cultivation and wealth is interpreted as a vulgarity.

"Catholics and Protestants are lauded for their financial strength. Why should Buddhists alone shy away from money matters!"

"Wealth is a requisite unless one doesn't want to achieve anything. How best to put to use the devotees' good, ethical and sacred wealth for the benefit of all living beings – that is the question."

For years, the media has lost no time in painting the following picture of Fo Guang Shan: bustling, not the least tranquil; retailing soft drinks and profiteering from souvenir sales; air-conditioned and carpeted guest houses; monastics riding in sedans and making phone calls. Their conclusion: Fo Guang Shan is far too worldly, and Hsing Yun is just an enterprising monk.

Despite the criticism, many visitors to Fo Guang Shan have come away with something far more scared and profound. Apart from areas open to the public where modern comforts are provided for the convenience of devotees and tourists, restricted areas exist where practice and cultivation are conducted. Wood-burning stoves are still in operation. Sleeping quarters, neither air-conditioned nor carpeted, are lined with boards in the traditional sparse manner. Monastics rise at 4.30 a.m. and retire at 10 p.m.. They do not enjoy weekends or holidays, are never paid overtime and wear the same clothing and two pairs of shoes year-round. Fo Guang Shan monastics live a simple life. They do take occasional automobile rides or make periodic phone calls. But then again, in an age of electronics and telecommunications, insisting that monastics should always travel by foot and remain incommunicado at all times would be ludicrous!

Hsing Yun admits he is powerless against the distorted rumors circulating about Fo Guang Shan. He feels deeply for his disciples and followers. He urges them to continue to receive devotees and visitors with kindness and compassion, diligence and service, hoping that with a meal and friendship more resources shall be gathered for the care of the old and young, the running of schools and the preaching of the Dharma.

The system

Many believe that Taiwan has been faithful in propagating the tradition of Chinese Mahayana Buddhism. Moreover, under Hsing Yun's orthodox discipline and etiquette kept intact at Fo Guang Shan, Mahayana Buddhism has been modernized and attuned in accordance with the times. Writing about the hope of a revival, Hsing Yun describes what he feels is a healthy system:

"In the past, the Buddhist sangha maintained a healthy system. The precepts and rules, for instance, were instrumental in ensuring monasterial peace. Similarly, the six points of reverent unity[3] guaranteed monastic harmony. There was monasterial order in Mainland China because there was a system. However, the same was not true in Taiwan; we had no system and we each went our own way."

Hsing Yun grew up in a traditional monastery and later traveled to various places in order to spread the Dharma. Through this practice, he cultivated both his personal temperament and spiritual insight. The Fo Guang Shan that he created is a current version of a traditional monastery in Taiwan. "A temple has to be like a temple; a monk has to be like a monk." The tonsure has to follow a system and so does the passing of the precepts. In 1991, Fo Guang Shan conducted a three-month Ten-thousand Buddhas Triple Platform Ordination. The reception of the complete triple platform precepts – the sramanera or sramanerika precepts, bhiksu or bhiksuni precepts, and the Bodhisattva precepts – qualifies a monastic in the Mahayana tradition. Five hundred recipients attended the most systematically and meticulously executed ordination in Taiwan to date. Every single detail went by the book; work and rest, morning and evening liturgies, explication of the precepts, meditation, rehearsal and

---

[3] Bodily unity as in worship; verbal unity as in chanting; mental unity as in faith; moral unity as in observing precepts and rules; doctrinal unity as in views and interpretations; economic unity as in community of deeds, study, or charity.

labor.   Abbot K'ai Cheng of Hung-fa (Spreading the Dharma) Temple called the event the most accurate and accomplished monastic ordination in Taiwan within the past four decades.   Retired abbot P'u Ch'eng of Song Kwan Sa (Vast Pines Temple) of Korea found the sights and sounds to be invaluable references for Buddhist practitioners.

From propriety to professionalism

Everyone, though burdened with chores and duties, must adhere to the morning and evening liturgies, and never stop learning.   Hsing Yun established Passing on the Light College for the specific purpose of continuing education and in-service training for monastics.   Attendees take four courses per quarter for four years.   In addition, a monthly letter comes from the master himself inquiring about their progress.   Typically, the letters are accompanied by doctrinal themes, textual research, case studies, preaching methods or learning experiences.   Students are required to delve into these materials and submit reports on them.   Examinations are held twice a year, and diplomas are awarded to those who pass.   Failing an exam is not an unusual occurrence.

Fo Guang Shan's welfare system is about the most thorough there is, tending to everything from medical care, leave of absence, continued education and traveling, to family visits, loans and burials for parents.

There even exists a dining system called *kuo-t'ang*.   For each meal, everybody is required to line up, join palms, chant the Buddha's name and wait for the sounding of the board before entering the dining hall.   Seated, everybody begins with the five contemplations and ends with the offering mantra before starting to consume the two bowls (of soup and rice) and one plate (of vegetables) set in front of them. Eating in the deliberate manner of "a dragon swallowing a pearl and a phoenix nodding its head," no one is to glance around or talk. Everyone must completely finish his or her share – a sign of cherishing one's blessings. At the end of the meal, the entire group leaves in single file while tables are quickly cleared.

Life on the mountain can be aptly described as flowing with conditions while remaining disciplined. No one will dispute the professionalism with which Fo Guang Shan conducts itself. It is Hsing Yun's influence at work.

Chapter 11

Dharma should not be separated from worldly awakening

*H*e lives on the mountain but thinks of those below. Feet on the ground, he eyes the universe. From the temples, goodness overflows for the benefit of all living beings. Heavens are fine, but this world is finer.

Hsing Yun's lectures, writings, temples, disciples, his very person and his devotees are all manifestations of the concept of humanistic and living Buddhism.

Some researchers of Taiwanese Buddhism think that Hsing Yun has set up a separate "Fo Guang School" in addition to the eight traditional Buddhist schools.

Though Hsing Yun does not intend to set up another Buddhist school, through tracing his ideas and accomplishments over the past five decades, we can discover a coherent system.

The Buddha was human

The founder of Buddhism, Sakyamuni Buddha, was not a fleeting, ornamental deity. Nor was he a pedestaled savior. He was a real living human being.

Sakyamuni Buddha, originally named Siddhartha, was born on the eighth day of the fourth month of the lunar calendar, 544 B.C.E., in Lumbini, Kapilavastu, India. His parents were Suddhodana, head of the Sakya clan, and his wife Maya.

Siddharta's mother died seven days after his birth, leaving him to be raised by her sister Prajapati. Amidst the adoration of his people, Siddhartha grew up the peerless leader his father groomed him to be. At seventeen he married Yasodhara, who in the ensuing year bore him a son, Rahula.[1]

In neither his nobility nor the affection of loved ones could Sakyamuni find the answers to his questions about the true nature of life and the meaning of the universe. Eventually, he left his palace and went on a quest for truth. He became an ascetic, and for years practiced austerities. Finally, at age thirty-five, Sakyamuni seated himself on the diamond throne[2] beneath a Bodhi tree, gazed at the stars above and in deep and profound meditation became enlightened. Subsequently he began to turn the wheel of the Dharma[3] and founded a sangha. After preaching for forty-five years he entered nirvana in a grove of Sal trees[4] near Kusinagara. Most Buddhist literature that exists is a record of Sakyamuni Buddha's teachings compiled by his disciples after he passed away.

Sakyamuni Buddha, as evidenced in history, was born and raised in this world, attained enlightenment in this world and entered nirvana in this world. He tasted life's joy, anger, misery, and happiness. He experienced human birth, aging, sickness and death. *Buddha* in Sanskrit means the "enlightened one" – Sakyamuni *is* the Enlightened One. We are

---

[1] The Buddha's story here is based on the Fo Guang Encyclopedia and the Chronology of Buddhist History, both published by Fo Guang Publishing House.
[2] *Chin-kang tso* in the original text. The Buddha's seat upon attaining enlightenment.
[3] *Fa-lun* in the original text. The Wheel of the Dharma which crushes all evil, and which rolls on from person to person, place to place and age to age.
[4] Teak trees.

humans yet to be enlightened.

The Dharma as the Buddha taught it in his time, was primarily geared for traveling, living, sitting, resting, thinking and behaving in life. The result of his teachings is a human-oriented Buddhism. Hsing Yun applies the Buddha's teachings of 2,500 years ago to modern life, and in the process, he furthers the development of humanistic Buddhism.

The Five Precepts, cornerstone of worldly peace

When once asked at a military academy about the tangible contributions Buddhism has for a nation and its society, Hsing Yun replied: "The Tripitaka along with its twelve divisions of sacred sutras are all beneficial to the nation and society. But simply the Five Precepts alone will suffice to govern a country and rule the world."

Specifically, freedom in the contemporary sense is that which does not interfere with the freedom of others. That is exactly what the Five Precepts teach. The precept against killing prevents [us] from assailing the safety of others and encourages a respect for life. The precept against stealing keeps [us] from plundering the property of others and creates a respect for the rights of others. The precept against adultery stops [us] from violating others and thus is a respect for virtue. The precept against lying holds [us] from ruining the name of others and thus is a respect for morals. The precept against intoxication prevents us from losing our clarity and keeps us from becoming a danger to others. Should we abide by the Five Precepts, respect one another and fully enjoy freedom within legal bounds, the nation and society will, no doubt, be safe, harmonious, happy and beneficial.

Though six decades have passed since the day he started school, Hsing Yun will always cherish the very first character that he was taught – "jen" meaning people. Throughout his life, Hsing Yun's respect for people has never diminished. Fo Guang Shan exists for the practice of humanistic Buddhism. Those who join its sangha must share the consensus of awakening oneself and others, and benefiting oneself and others. Journalist Wu Ling-chiao once wrote: "Whoever seeks liberation solely for oneself[5] must not seek Fo Guang Shan."

Worldly life is affirmed

In humanistic Buddhism the idealistic and realistic Hsing Yun sees an absolute affirmation of the value of worldly life. He also insists that joyful practice is actually more important than asceticism.

Hsing Yun does not think it realistic to be obsessed with the idea of liberation from birth and death, or to engage solely in solitary practice, turn one's back on worldly affairs and to live off others' support. That, he says, would be a parasitic existence. "Practice, practice – that is all I ever hear about! *Practice* is becoming another word for laziness," once lamented Master Yin Shun. For indeed practice is neither a slogan nor a ritual. Practice is the real life application of the Dharma in the form of service and offering, diligence and patience.

"To tackle life is more important than to tackle death,"

---

[5] *Tzu-liao-han* in the original text. The proper title is arhat, or lohan, the enlightened saint in Theravada Buddhism, who seeks eradication of body and mind and attainment of nirvana.

Master T'ai Hsu once said. Living must be understood before seeking liberation from birth and death. Buddhism is to be applied to daily life because it is a living religion.

Venerable Master Hui Neng of the Ch'an school spoke this verse in *The Sixth Patriarch's Platform Sutra*:

> *The worldly existence of the Dharma*
> *is connected to the world's awakening.*
> *Abandoning the world to seek the Bodhi[6]*
> *is like seeking the horn of the hare.*

In a nutshell, "the Dharma is but the innate goodness of human nature." There lies within every aspect of daily life the potential realization of true wisdom. The following verse gives a metaphorical depiction of such a state:

> *Exhausting the days in quest of spring,*
> *nowhere is it to be found;*
> *Treading the clouds along the mountain range*
> *with [my] sandals of straw.*
> *Returning, in [my] hands [I] chance*
> *to hold the plum blossoms to [my] nose;*
> *Only to be told that, already,*
> *spring is on each and every bough.*

The teaching of Ch'an masters is such that those practitioners who are in business follow a code of ethics, and neither swindle nor evade taxes. Those in the military are valiant and guard the land. Those in office are loyal and

---

[6] Perfect wisdom; enlightenment.

accountable, and serve their hometown. Those in academia are called to focus on their studies and teaching. In other words, when all fulfill their roles with devotion and integrity, the Dharma will be in the air.

A religion of blessings

To Hsing Yun, modern humanistic Buddhism is comprised of sounds, colors, actions and humor. "What I mean by humanistic Buddhism is a life of joy and interest, of gratitude and well-being, of compassion and virtue. Such is the salvation for all as taught by the Mahayana and the way as learned from the Pureland."

The *Amitabha Sutra* speaks about a world of utmost happiness in the West where the ground is resplendent with gold chambers and ceilings are adorned with the seven gems, where water is of the eight virtues, colorful birds speak the Dharma and gorgeous flowers never wither. It is an indication that Buddhist practice does not necessarily mean eating poorly, clothing oneself in rags or being forever deprived of daily necessities.

If joy after death should be sought after, why shouldn't the fortune of living be treasured first? Buddhism is not a religion of suffering but one of blessing. Hsing Yun wishes the beautiful and good side of this world to be cherished with positivity, and defines the Pureland on earth as:

> *Courteous and respectful,*
> *let kind words be uttered.*
> *Hopeful and content,*
> *let happiness spring.*

*Considerate and harmonious,
let freedom come forth and be utilized.
Compassionate and accepting,
let peace and wholeness be celebrated.*

Hsing Yun is probably one of the most listened to storytellers alive. His capacity to elucidate the profound and wondrous teachings of humanistic Buddhism by means of social concerns and familiar, everyday circumstances is deemed magnetic.

On wealth

Since many human beings are particularly attracted to money, Hsing Yun speaks often on the Buddhist view of wealth.

"Buddhism does not deny wealth," he says. Many Buddhists absolutely refuse to discuss the subject, stigmatizing "gold" as a "viper". Practitioners certainly do not recognize *gold* as absolutely necessary to sustaining practice or to spreading the Dharma for the benefit of all living beings. The truth is, however, that the wise cherish wealth and know the correct way to acquire and use it. For when wealth comes in a proper way, abundance should be celebrated. Buddhists have no cause for resistance towards wealth.

Hsing Yun tells a story of a man who took great pains to store gold bars in his cellar. For thirty-odd years the gold bars sat untouched. Then one day the man opened his cellar door only to discover that the gold had vanished. The shock of the empty cellar nearly killed the old man. Attempting to console him, a neighbor asked, "Have you ever spent any of the gold?"

"Absolutely not!" the man retorted.

"So you've never even touched any of the gold in all these years?"

"No, never!" responded the old man.

"Well, don't worry then," said the neighbor. "Let me get some bricks, wrap them up and put them back in your cellar. The bricks can take the place of your missing gold! Why bother to mourn for something you never intended to use in the first place?"

Hsing Yun's story reveals an understanding that "wealth is a blessing, and knowing how to expend wealth is wisdom." Neither one who devalues wealth nor a miser is called wise. *Possessing* wealth is a pleasure, but to be able to utilize it for the benefit of others is the *true joy* of wealth. Most of all, wealth appears in various forms in our life; stamina and health, thankfulness and contentment, a meaningful existence, peace and security for loved ones, a wholesome spirit... all are forms of wealth worth cherishing and cultivating.

On fate

Life is a transient experience. Some moments seem to take a person to the constellations while others plummet one into the fathoms of disgrace and destitution. Seeking an answer to what the next moment might hold, people often resort to all kinds of old-fashioned fortune-telling practices in order to predict their future moments. A favorable prediction will send some off walking on air; an unfavorable one will shroud others with fear. Humanistic Buddhism is empty of such predictions. Fatalism is not the view adopted in Buddhism. Destiny is in our own hands and fate, far from being a fixed entity, can be altered.

Here is Hsing Yun's illustration of how providence is depicted in humanistic Buddhism:

A master who had attained arhatship realized in meditation that his favorite disciple was left with only seven days to live.

"Why does this lovely child have only seven days left of his life?" he thought. "What a misfortune! I cannot honestly tell him the truth. So young, how is he going to take such a news?"

At dawn the master laid aside his heartbreak and summoned the little disciple, to whom he said: "My good boy, you haven't seen your folks for so long. Why don't you pack your things and go home for a visit!"

Innocently, the disciple took leave of his master and went home. One day went by, then another. A total of seven days passed but nothing was heard or seen of him. Just when the master was mourning the loss of his disciple, the little one showed up in his presence quite safe and sound.

The incredulous master took his hand, looked him up and down and quizzed him, "How did you return? What happened in the last seven days?"

Perplexed about the master's concern, the disciple responded, "Nothing, master. Why do you ask?"

Again the master quizzed him, "Try to remember! Did you see anything? Did you do anything?"

"Oh, I came upon a pond on my way home and saw a group of ants caught in the water. So I picked a leaf and helped them back ashore."

The child's compassion at that moment – the master was relieved to learn – had sown such bountiful goodness that in saving the ants' lives he amended his own fate.

Though merely another parable, it once again shows how exhaustible fortune really is. Like a mountain of wealth stacked away, if abused, all the blessings in life may disappear. On the contrary, regular contributions to a savings account will in time amount to a substantial balance. That is also how a life of misfortune may turn around. In humanistic Buddhism we are encouraged to rejoice in life, accept the future, clear our minds, change our ways and create our des- tinies.

On politics

Politics is an ultra-sensitive topic especially in politically sensitive Taiwan. Yet Hsing Yun, with unmistakable integrity as to what he will do and not do has long been speaking publicly on Buddhist political views. When cautioned by followers against the taboo – which most masters and monastics would rather avoid – he replies that politics is a public issue. As gregarious as humans are, no one is an island, and therefore no one can live above and beyond politics. The Buddhists of modern society vote, pay taxes, serve the military when drafted and live a life closely connected with the implications of politics. Since our lives are intertwined with political issues, a proper view of politics is indeed necessary.

"I have renounced the life of a householder, but not the country," Hsing Yun often explains. He means that in accord with the concept of humanistic Buddhism, monastics too, are concerned about the affairs of the state. Chanted monthly on the first and fifteenth days, *In Praise of the Precious Caul- dron* is "done so with deep respect, wishing for longevity for the republic, as long as heaven and earth shall last..."

Ch'an master Ch'ang Lu once prayed for "all countries to be at peace and all frontiers stilled; all arms dismantled and forces dismissed; all winds gentle and rains kind; all men safe and women joyous." Records of politically influential monastics are ample. Venerable Master Hsuan Wan of T'ang, an imperial tutor, coached the heir to the throne in ways to rule his country and love his people. Hsuan Wan instructed the heir to practice charity, eliminate killing, respect nature and observe vegetarianism. In yet another example, Master T'ai Hsu countered Japan's accusation that China was corrupting Buddhism during the Sino-Japanese war by visiting with the Buddhist countries of Burma, Ceylon[7] and others, and winning support in the process. Master Le Kuan called for a rally of the monastics in resistance to the war as well.

Hsing Yun believes that Master T'ai Hsu's moderate and objective standpoint of "questioning politics without intervening" is the attitude for modern Buddhists. He suggests caring about the well-being of the country, but not pursuing the glory and fortune of public office. Politicians may be advised to emulate the Buddha's wisdom as recorded in the *Ekottara-agama;* refraining from corruption, anger, evasion, isolation, trespassing, selfishness and so forth.

---

[7] Sri Lanka

On relationship

Relationships are high on the list of modern difficulties. Too many lives spiral into tragedy because an ego is inflated, a battle of wills seems necessary, or cheating and bullying appear easier then dealing with the problems of relationships. Hsing Yun has lived long enough to recognize even the most subtle causes and effects. He views one's existence as the result of causes and conditions binding one to another. The affairs of the world are plagued with pain, sorrow and anxiety stemming from our common incapacity to treat one another with kindness and cultivate *ourselves* with dedication. Indeed, the strife between *them* and *us* is an epidemic even between loved ones.

In the *Hundred-parable Sutra* there is a story about a couple squabbling over a piece of cake.

A man bickering with his wife over a baked cake thought to himself: "Women just can't hold their tongues. I can beat her at that game!" He proceeded to suggest that the two of them should battle in complete silence, and if either of them uttered a sound, the other would get the treat. His wife acquiesced. In a mute stalemate the pair sat, with the cake placed between them.

Then came a burglar upon the scene. Naturally he had no way of making sense of the two rigid silent householders. Taking advantage of the situation, he began to prowl about the premises looking for valuables. Still the two remained in silent combat. This so emboldened the intruder that he began advancing toward the lady of the house. A moment later, he was laying his hands on her. Remarkably, the husband was utterly unmoved by what transpired before his own eyes.

Unable to contain herself any longer the wife rose to her feet screaming, "Are you blind or something? Can't you see I'm being assaulted?"

Incredible as it might sound, her husband sprang from his seat, snatched the fried cake and started munching it. "Hah, you've lost," he said laughingly. "The treat is finally all mine!"

To be as cold and calculating as the husband in this story – bearing a grudge when there is triumph, and disdain when there is loss, and allowing for boundless ignorance which triggers ceaseless defilements, is the source of strife and hostility in every form.

To resolve a multitude of relational issues whether marital, friendship, sibling or collaborative, humanistic Buddhism offers an obvious and feasible solution "You be big and I'll be small; you have much and I'll have little; you be praised and I'll be scorned; you rejoice and I'll suffer." To illustrate this, Hsing Yun has another story.

There were two neighboring families; the Changs, who were incessantly quarrelsome, and the Lis, who appeared to be forever basking in peacefulness. In time, the Changs felt compelled to ask for advice from their neighbors.

"Why are we bickering from day to day while you seem so at peace with one another?" queried the Changs.

"You fight because you're all outstanding people," replied the Lis. "And we're not even good enough to start a fight."

"That sounds like nonsense! But what do you mean?" asked the Changs.

"Well, take the breaking of a vase for example. You

each think you should be the last to be blamed and that somebody else should be held accountable. The finger-pointing becomes perpetually vicious because you all insist you're in the right and everybody else is wrong," said the Lis.

"As for us, we would rather admit guilt than have another's feelings hurt. Thus, the apology of the one who made the blunder is met with apologies from others who say, 'Surely it's not your fault, no, not at all. I was careless to have left the vase in that spot.' We always start by thinking we're in the wrong and holding ourselves responsible. We do not evade any issues. Harmony, therefore, is a matter of course."

On responding to the times

"An effective writer is capable of responding wholly to the times," humorist Lin Yu-t'ang once said. Likewise, humanistic Buddhism, which is not only a concept but a practice, is sociologically significant. Hsing Yun *is* a religious master "capable of responding wholly to the times." Moreover, he acts in the moment with astuteness and intelligence, charting his own course.

To assuage the agony Taiwan suffered from the severence of diplomatic ties with the U.S. in 1979, Hsing Yun conducted a Buddhist chanting concert to raise funds for a patriotic foundation. To elevate social values above existing trends, he organized a series of campaigns in 1992 which were designed to purify minds by means of the seven precepts. The seven precepts, alongside the basic Five Precepts, are the seven means of self-discipline in modern society; no smoking or drugs, no violence, no stealing, no gambling, no drinking, no indecency, and no quarreling.

To respond to the organ donation drive at Longevity Memorial Hospital some years back, the gracious monk led many others to follow suit by pledging to give his own organs. To play a role in preserving the environment, Hsing Yun rallied public support by speaking up for the reforesting of Kaohsiung, saving the country's water resources, recycling used paper and protecting wildlife.

Perfecting a person, becoming a Buddha

Unlike some reclusive monastics, Hsing Yun adheres to the conviction that "the Dharma is for solving all issues in life," and that a Buddhist should exercise, without fail, every awareness and concern for various social changes. Whatever new phenomenon, trend or social problem that arises, Hsing Yun responds with these questions: "What instructions exist within the principles of the Dharma? How is the contemporary Buddhist to respond?"

Consider the controversy over abortion which many Catholics have persisted in perpetuating to this day. Where, then, do the Buddhists stand? Terminating a pregnancy is a violation of the precept against killing, Hsing Yun asserts, and retribution is an inevitability. However, he points to circumstances such as medically confirmed fetal abnormality or pregnancy caused by sexual assault under which childbirth will, in all likelihood, encumber the society enormously and sink the mother hopelessly into a life of torment. He maintains that as long as the mother is ready to shoulder the retribution for killing, the ultimate decision to end the pregnancy is hers and hers alone. By the same token, Hsing Yun makes it clear that he believes the crucial decision- making which pertains to euthanasia lies with those closest to the patient and must only be rendered with love and compassion.

Hsing Yun does not avoid touchy social issues such as divorce and domestic violence either. On such topics he comments, "The Dharma has it all. I'm merely applying it to our times." Buddhism failing to keep abreast of modern concerns and provide viable solutions to its problems resembles "a grown person stuck in children's clothing." He does not see how much an empty practice can last.

Hsing Yun braved insufferable misunderstanding and mortification through four decades advocating humanistic Buddhism. Time has honored his vision. Master T'ai Hsu prepared an outline for humanistic Buddhism at the turn of the century, and Hsing Yun has succeeded in continuing the momentum. He has paved the smoothest and broadest way for contemporary Buddhism with his lifelong alignment with the idea that "the perfecting of Buddhahood comes by means of perfecting the human."

Chapter 12
Good affinities around the world

*F*o Guang Shan's morning and evening liturgies always open with a passage in praise of the incense-offering:

> *Incense in the burner is lit now*
> *to permeate the dharma realms;*
> *from afar, the assembly of Buddhas have heard.*
> *How promising are the clouds forming above*
> *and how intense is the devotion about;*
> *the Buddhas appear wholly before all.*
> *Let us take refuge with the Bodhisattvas,*
> *[let us take refuge with the Bodhisattvas,*
> *let us take refuge with the Bodhisattvas.]*

This passage tells how the Buddhas, moved by pervading devotion, are glad to protect and guide the chanting and praying, and ensure that blessings are shared with all living beings in the ten directions.

Surrounded by good affinities

People-oriented from an early age, Hsing Yun has acquired countless affinities with friends and devotees. As visible as the promising clouds [depicted in the praise for incense offering], these affinities have been significant catalysts in the creation of Fo Guang Shan.

Statistics from the Taiwan department of civil affairs indicate an average of about one temple or church per 2.47 km^2 (1.54 miles^2). Buddhist temples total 1,560 in Taiwan today. The department of internal affairs estimates 4.85 million Buddhists, 3.63 million Taoists, 0.91 million devotees of I-kuan Tao, 0.42 million Protestants and 0.29 million Catholics in Taiwan.

Statistics from Fo Guang Shan show that over 1 million people have formally taken refuge within Fo Guang Shan's Taiwan temples. This means that one out of five Buddhists in Taiwan is a Fo Guang Buddhist. Notably, in the first half of 1994, within the precincts of Fo Guang Shan, the Taipei temples and Hsi Lai Temple in Los Angeles, over 10,000 devotees took refuge. Over 200,000 donors have contributed to the newly erected Chambers of Gold and Jade Buddhas, the Triple Gem Shrine, and over 200,000 free subscriptions of *Awakening the World* are regularly distributed. Overseas Fo Guang Buddhists number around 200,000.

It is a small wonder that with grassroots support and subsequent social impact, Hsing Yun and Fo Guang Shan have become a sparkle in the eyes of political enthusiasts. Once Hsing Yun was appointed consultant to party affairs by Taiwan's current majority party, the Chinese Nationalist Party (Kuomintang), and another time he was honored with the title of Member of the Central Committee on which he remarked: "As committee member, I honestly don't know what I can do for the party and, in that regard, I certainly don't know what the party will want me to do!" The laurels are for the Buddhist circle as a whole, he insisted, not for himself only.

In fact, all that he has accepted from politicians are gifts of tea for mid-autumn festival and the lunar New Year.

Of course, some politicians appear more sincere than others. Most of the time, they display little affinity with the Buddha, yet close to election time, they begin streaming through the mountain gate. Invariably, they are for headlines in the media: "Hsing Yun Pledges Support for...". On occasion, political luminaries are seen at the head tables at Fo Guang Shan's functions. "There is no need for worry or headaches over the acquiring of needed locations," Hsing Yun says. "Just ask a mayor or county supervisor to come and address the crowd."

Political monk no more

Being dubbed a political monk was certainly not a pleasure. Hsing Yun probes his heart and still remains nonpartisan among political circles. In fact, the government has had little or no part at all in the growth of Fo Guang Shan. Except, perhaps, for ten years of delay in matters of official registration. Hsing Yun was a great sport about the delay saying: "Mayors serve terms of three or five years; this monk serves for life. The permit will come someday."

Actually, it was the dissidents who opted for name-calling to vent their wrath over Hsing Yun's friendliness with the nationalists.

Those who have walked the path of [contemporary Chinese] history with Hsing Yun will never forget how the nationalists fled the mainland only to exercise another thirty years of despotism in Taiwan. Under those circumstances, no one would dare to befriend the dissidents. Lacking in social support, Buddhist groups were vulnerable back then. Like the rest of the population, the Buddhists, together with other religious bodies, had only the Chiang government to support and the nationalist party to vote for. That was the political environment and psychological milieu of that era. Why should Hsing Yun be singled out?

Presently, political conditions and personal values are different. When the Nationalist-backed Venerable Ming Kuang ran for a seat in the national assembly several years ago, not one person called him overly political or anything slanderous.

Concerning his label as the political monk, Hsing Yun only comments about his dilemma with the circumstances. "The media, not I," he says, "rant and rave over politics and hot topics like the future of the strait and the dissidents on the mainland. If I don't come up with a response, I'll be deemed unaware, unconcerned; if I do, overly political."

Friends in public office

Political monk or not, the rest of the world has come to know and appreciate Hsing Yun on a much deeper level. He does not worry over such a title. "Defamation in itself is incapable of spoiling a character," he says, "unless the character is an unwholesome and hollow one. The way to confront slander is not to try clarifying oneself, but to quietly reject the conflict." There are some political figures Hsing Yun does not try to shun, but rather treats without discrimination. Perhaps some come to him with dubious intentions at first. However, after interacting with them for a period of time, Hsing Yun has made a number of close friends.

Vice-chairperson Wang Chin-ping of the legislative council and legislatiors P'an Wei-kang and Shen Chih-hui are frequent visitors. P'an, the sole Buddhist in a family of Catholics, is so motivated by Fo Guang Shan's creed of "give others confidence, give others joy, give others convenience, give others hope," that she has adopted this creed as the foundation for her actions at work.

Also, secretary-general Wu Po-hsiung of the president's office, Judge Lin Fu-ts'un of the high court, Mayor Lin Shui-mu of Keelung, and chairperson Chung jung-chi of the Provincial Committee of the Kuomintang, often stay in touch with Hsing Yun. To commemorate the passing away of presidential political advisor Ch'iu Ch'uang-huan's parents, Hsing Yun conducted services for both. Former mayor of Kaohsiung Yu-Chen Yueh-ying regarded him as her personal consultant in municipal affairs.

His friendship with Chen Lian, head of the Supervisory Council, is almost legendary. Chen did not learn about Buddhism until age 50, but has since become a remarkably diligent and avowed protector of the Dharma. His family now shares the same devotion, and his eldest son Chen Yu-t'ing has entered the monkhood at Ling-ch'uan Temple. Moreover, with the unanimous endorsement of his siblings, Chen moved the remains of his parents, former vice-president Chen Ch'eng and his wife, from T'ai Shan to Fo Guang Shan three years ago. Hsing Yun assured the most dignified arrangements for the occasion. In last year's fundraising for Fo Guang University, the executive representative of the entire body of Fo Guang devotees literally packed two trucks of Chen's family antiques, paintings and calligraphic pieces off to Fo Guang Shan for auction.

Friends in business

Hsing Yun has more than a few business friends. Wu Hsiu-ch'i of President Corp. has been a great friend for over three decades and a strong supporter of Fo Guang Shan. Chang-Yao Hung-ying, whose semiconductor business Hsing Yun named Light of the Sun and Moon, played a key role in the founding of Hsi Lai Temple, Los Angeles. P'an Hsiao-jui, owner of the Grand Formosa Regent, Taipei, supported the master from the very beginning of Fo Guang Shan. "Dona- tions are the most delightful of all wealth," says P'an Hsiao- jui. The effect of years of charitable endeavors with his wife has resulted in a benevolent face which resembles that of Maitreya Buddha.

Ts'eng Liang-yuan and Huang Li-ming, a couple in the construction business, fondly address Hsing Yun as "old papa" instead of master. Having striven hard to initiate the fundraising of Taipei's new temple, they gave a hearty gift to the master who is more of a parent to them. They call themselves the gleeful, ultimate beneficiaries.

Friends in cultural circle

Some of Hsing Yun's best friends are from the cultural circle. "Few in the early years had the motivation to lend a hand in Buddhist cultural affairs," he says. "Those who did shall forever be my guests of honor." Academics Chen Ku-ying, Yang Kuo-shu, Wei Cheng-t'ung, Hu Fo, and others share warm memories of the days they used to teach at the Buddhist college and, in particular, the amount of respect lavished upon them – a rarity today.

A writer and artist himself, Hsing Yun knows well how to appreciate like minds when he runs into them. He conducted the painter Li Ch'i-mao's wedding. Script-writer Sun Ch'un-hua's daughter, now Venerable Miao Jung, is a disciple. Through various fundraising art auctions for Fo Guang Shan in the past two years, he has been able to build unprecedented affinities within cultural circles.

Writer of popular thrillers, Szu-ma Chung-yuan, a friend of twenty years, describes Hsing Yun as "insightful and visionary, positive and pragmatic, modern and unconventional." Szu-ma also calls him historically innovative in the spread of the Dharma and the expansion of Buddhism. Other literary figures include Chao Ning, who took refuge under Hsing Yun and was given the Dharma name P'u Kuang, and veteran author Liu Fang who, though Hsing Yun's senior in age, calls him master with unquestionable readiness.

Essayist Ying Wei-ch'ih once dined with Hsing Yun at P'u-men Temple. "Monastics receive their sustenance from all ten directions, as the saying goes," joked an apparently satiated Ying afterwards, "this pen-wagging bunch received ours from eleven today!" Members of the media Li Yu-hsi of the *Ming Sheng Daily,* Lu Chen-t'ing of *Central Daily News,* and Su Cheng-kuo of *Chinese Times* came thinking they were just visiting out of curiosity but could not leave without bowing their heads in awe.

The entertainment industry also has its fair share of Hsing Yun's followers, namely Kuo Hsiao-chuang, Chen Li-li, Cheng Pei-pei, Tien Wen-chung, Wang Hai-po, Kou Feng, producer of the mini-series *"National Master Yu Lin"* for television, Yang Ching-huang and Kuang Ming-chieh who played the leading roles, and many, many more.

Friends in need of a friend

Those around Hsing Yun marvel at what a good friend he is. Li Zijian, a painter from the mainland who found himself in the United States with virtually nothing, was given assistance and provided with a residence. Li was assured that his creative endeavors would not be interrupted and that his wife and child would join him. A year later, Li reciprocated his patron's kindness with close to a hundred works collectively titled *This World Needs Love*. Further aided by Hsing Yun, Li's work went in to exhibit at Hsi Lai Temple, Fo Guang Shan, and Taipei's city art gallery, and Li is currently taking his works across Japan, North America, and Europe.

Hsing Yun came to the rescue of Gao Ertai and Pu Xiaoyu, both on the faculty of Nanjing University at the time of the June 4th massacre in Tiananmen Square, [1989 C.E.], as both were forced into exile in the United States. The couple's fortunate encounter with him led to their eventual finding of both physical and spiritual peace. Like a new starting point to which the master had directed them, it was "the sighting of an image of light, by which images from ten thousand miles could be illuminated."

Qian Jiaju, an economist of international renown from mainland China who had expended a lifetime delving into materialism and Marxism, left for the same reason as Gao and Pu, and was also Hsing Yun's guest in the United States. After attending the master's lecture three times on the *Sixth Patriarch's Platform Sutra*, he became a Buddhist at the old age of eighty. As much mentor and pupil as good friends, the two are often heard addressing each others as "Elder Qian" and "Great Master."

Friends are forever

Wealth is not forever, friends are. All along, Hsing Yun has been surrounded by generous and undemanding friends. Chen Chien-ch'eng, a civil servant from Kaohsiung's department of financial affairs, was in the audience on every occasion when the master spoke, nodding in agreement as he listened. That nodding agreement has extended over twenty years now, from the early days in Shou-shan Temple to the contemporary times of P'u hsien Temple. The children and grandchildren of that first generation are becoming equally devoted. Lin Chi-sung, a devotee from an affluent background, is often spotted wearing an apron and a broad grin, working in Hsi Lai Temple's kitchen and serving in the dining hall during Dharma functions. Back in Fo Guang Shan, whenever there is the odd paint job needed, it is completed under the auspices of Chang T'ien-yung and Chang-Yun Wang-ch'ueh, a couple who run a paint business. The pair hardly ever get to greet the master in person, but year after year they have made their offerings, never faltering, never saying much. One of the most puzzling incidents of quiet devotion, however, was when an elderly devotee slipped a red packet into Hsing Yun's hands at the end of a Dharma service. Later the monastics discovered that the packet was stuffed with bundles of jewelry. But the whole incident happened so quickly Hsing Yun never even got a good look at her face.

Just what transpired in Hsing Yun's life to transform the lone monk from those early lean years into the magnetic individual attracting so much kindly affection? To put it simply, devotees feel close to Fo Guang Shan. They need only ask to be aided and supported in their weddings and funerals. They are updated about Fo Guang Shan's monthly events by an ample supply of journals and newsletters. Devotees are supported, both physically and spiritually, by attending lectures, Dharma functions, chanting sessions and workshops. They even receive occasional visits from the monastics when they are sick and more often when they are well and are up for a friendly exchange. They are given opportunity to pray for added well-being and to be rid of misfortune. Some of the older devotees are given birthday cards promptly a week prior to their special day. What better connects people to one another then such affection and commitment toward harmony?

Lin Ch'ing-chin, a follower for four decades, recalls how caring the master was to him: "I was in the army back in 1962 when the master visited the Chinmen front. He brought along a pack of Buddhist texts which were intended for me. But his schedule was far too tight and I was stationed out in the islands. We didn't even get to see each other. So he had to take the books all the way home and mail them back to me again. I honestly had no words for how I felt when at long last the package reached me.

After the draft, I was readying myself for further schooling. The master wholeheartedly supported me. I used to take advantage of the lecture hall when it was free from chanting sessions and work into the wee hours. Master would keep me company either doing his own reading or writing. At times he would pass snacks on to me given to him by devotees. 'I don't snack at night,' he would say, trying to ease my mind. I didn't fare that well but eventually I was accepted to a university. The master was thrilled with my progress and gave me a copy of the *Far East English-Chinese Dictionary*."

Upon graduating from National Taiwan Normal University, Lin returned to Hsing Yun's side and spent the next decade helping him found Chih-kuang, a school of commerce. He even helped transplant the shade-giving trees on campus. For a while Lin suffered with a painful stomach ulcer, but he was never remiss in fulfilling his commitment. "I didn't bring shame on the master," Lin voices his gratitude from deep down. He and his wife, both teachers, have been faithfully sending their monthly support for the last ten years – a commitment very rarely upheld even between children and their own parents today.

Receiving with wisdom

Director Kou Feng remembers how the master once received him with the most profound wisdom which, alongside vast compassion, was instrumental in drawing countless followers. "There seems to be this fully packed bookcase inside me," was the way that he described to the master his inner sense of unrest. "In trying to reclassify my books I knocked the bookcase over!"

"I'm troubled, too!" the master replied with a dash of humor. "Except that you're troubled a lot and I'm disturbed only somewhat; you can't let go but I can!"

Hsing Yun added, "I've a bookcase inside, too. Like yours it is not in good order. If it were I would be sitting inside there instead of here!" Hsing Yun then gestured in the direction of the shrine where the Bodhisattva was seated. What he intended to tell Kou was that one who is free from worldly cares is no longer an ordinary human but a Bodhisattva.

Such is Hsing Yun's way:

> *Whether you awaken instantaneously or*
> *cultivate over lifetimes of practice;*
> *Never abandon concern*
> *for any sentient being.*
> *Flow with the world and*
> *care for all living beings;*
> *Always help them to connect*
> *with the Buddha.*

"I won't desert anyone," Hsing Yun pledges. To him, nobility and commonalty are the same; everyone is one of the many. Best-selling author Lin Ch'ing-hsuan still recounts the details of the hospitality which Hsing Yun extended him long before his success. The master literally went out of his way to greet Lin on the latter's first visit to Fo Guang Shan. Last year, Lin went on a lecture tour in the United States on behalf of Buddha's Light International Association. The master, who had just returned to Los Angeles from Russia, made it a point to thank him in person. Lin ended up a quarter of an hour late for the appointment due to traffic congestion. But the moment his car drove through Hsi Lai

Temple's main gate, he could see a tall figure in the distance, cane in hand, waiting in the hot sun of July. The sight was quite unforgettable.

His sensitive considerateness makes working with him sheer pleasure. In fact, he always takes the initiative to have people comfortably settled before anything else. "To direct volunteers," he says, "one must first and foremost be the volunteer to the volunteers. Have stationary and seats in place before asking volunteers to write, have buckets and hoses at hand before asking volunteers to water the plants and tell them where the tap is, too."

Those gifted in the arts were exceptionally hard to come by during the early years in Ilan. When Yang Hsi-ming volunteered to paint the murals for the kindergarten, Hsing Yun was so thankful that he attended him day in and day out, preparing brushes, paint, palette, rulers, as well as tea and snacks like an apprentice. When Chu Ch'iao became editor of *Buddhism Today*, he often had to work into the night. Hsing Yun, too, would be there for him, cooking noodles or bringing him a glass of milk to keep him going.

To this day, during those tedious drives on the freeway, Hsing Yun is the one who keeps the driver entertained – and awake – while others nap.

All affinities are attributed to Buddhism

Though many have become devotees and supporters of Fo Guang Shan out of admiration and respect for Hsing Yun, all affinities he attributes to the institution. "These are Buddhist devotees, not my personal followers. Don't ask them for favors or donations unless absolutely necessary," the master tells his disciples. "Don't ever conduct monetary dealings with them. Don't lose your temper with them so that they lose their faith in you."

Hsing Yun continues to reiterate to disciples and staff what good affinities mean to him: "Coldness towards devotees is coldness toward me; leaving guests unattended is leaving me feeling hurt."

On one occasion, Hsing Yun heard that a young monastic in charge of a branch temple complained that devotees were becoming less compliant and that many were unwilling to do manual chores. The monk's distress troubled Hsing Yun visibly. "If my disciples should think such absurd thoughts," he said in shame, "I would have them mop the floor and scrub windows for ten years! Sure it's wonderful for devotees to serve, but it's just as well that they don't help at all. For they've come to pay homage to the Buddha, not to work!"

Preaching amidst the secular world

Many times the master has taught his disciples that, according to the Ch'an school, a monastery is compared to the plants in a grove. Just as a single plant cannot make a grove, nothing works unless in unanimity. Practice cannot be isolated, but must be carried out in such a manner that it deepens and opens one's heart to the world. Hsing Yun's recognition of the potency of the people is really the backbone of his acute sense of popularization, possibility, and public relations in spreading Buddhism in modern society.

The traditional Buddhist temple was generally either deep in the forested mountains or at the end of a blind alley, and always a picture of somberness. Devotees either could not find it or would not dare make the difficult journey. The monastics hardly ever stepped outside and appeared stern and uncaring. Fo Guang Shan and its branch temples have changed standards and created a distinctive, pleasant and upbeat temple image. As well as being places of worship, they function fully as premises for socializing and study. Some visitors even come away with a sense that anywhere can be ground for preaching. A few of the lecture halls are even upstairs from so-called beauty parlors and the like.

The newly opened branch temple in Taipei is right by Sungshan train station. Parking space is plentiful. The five stories below the 14th floor house the shrine, conference room, meditation hall, dining hall, reception room, audio-visual room, gift shop and art gallery. Directions outside the elevators are precise and clear, and the volunteer guides are very helpful. Plenty is always going on, and visitors are more than welcome to participate. In little over a year the temple has gained the notable favor of devotees in northern Taiwan.

> *Wherever red dusts[1] roll,*
> *the Bodhi is taught.*
> *Wherever the heart is pure,*
> *meditation is complete.*

Hsing Yun looks to the day when there will be no shortages of temples to visit so that Buddhism may truly take root in the lives and minds of all.

---

[1] Refering to the secular world.

Affinity before Buddhahood

Hsing Yun's affinity with millions of devotees and friends from all walks of life was not cultivated in a single day. In the minds of these people, the master's deep yellow robe and towering figure are "awe-inspiring to view and heart-warming to be near." And every move he makes, to them, reflects a childlike purity.

"Affinity with fellow humans comes before the attainment of Buddhahood." Fo Guang Shan today is best summed up in the verses which Hsing Yun composed for its main shrine.

> *Coming from the ten directions,*
> *going to the ten directions,*
> *In the ten directions,*
> *all endeavors shall be completed.*
> *Thousands of moments of cultivation,*
> *thousands of moments of letting go.*
> *For all the hundreds of thousands,*
> *affinities shall be completed.*

Part Four

Spreading the Dharma to Deliver All Beings

Handing down the abbotship of Fo Guang Shan to Venerable Hsin Ping (right), 1985

Visiting the ancient pyramid while propagating Dharma in Egypt

Enjoying the sights of Holland with devotees

A grand welcome by the locals while visiting Ladakh, India

Never one to emphasize self-importance, he ensures that all living beings are content

Reaching out to refugees in northern Thailand, 1988

Chapter 13
The baton, its passing and receiving

As the months and years have passed from the pioneering through to the cultivation periods, Fo Guang Shan has grown from infancy to assume the vigor of young adulthood. Hsing Yun, parent-like, thought the time was ripe for it to move forward on its own. He was determined to pass the abbotship on to Venerable Hsin Ping, his first disciple among the bhiksus, on the 18th year of Fo Guang Shan's founding.

A historical moment

September 22, 1985 was a moment of historical succession at Fo Guang Shan. As day was breaking in southern Taiwan, there were already a sea of devotees gathering in front of the main shrine. Plainly clothed seniors, casually dressed youths, formally attired men and women waited quietly, all kneeling with palms joined. In reverence they heeded the sounding of the bell and drum and the chanting of a dozen young monastics before the Buddha. They eagerly awaited what would be the grandest succession ceremony in the history of Buddhism in Taiwan.

At ten o'clock sharp, with the sun shining brightly, accompanied by senior Venerables Yueh Chi and Wu I as witnesses, and with thousands of devotees watching, Hsing Yun unrolled the Dharma scroll and started to read aloud the names of all the ancestral partriarchs of the Lin-Chi school. He then handed down the abbot's cassock and alms-bowl, the constitution and rules, the jade scepter, the Dharma staff and the whisk – all emblems of the abbotship. On receiving these, Venerable Hsin Ping pledged the following before the crowd:

> "The master's heart shall be my heart;
> the master's resolve shall be my resolve.
> [I shall] abide by the monasterial rules and ancestral directions;
> to spread the Dharma to benefit all sentient beings.
> Receive the people from all ten directions;
> and preach the Fo Guang ways to the ends of the world."

At that, music rose and thousands of doves flew skyward. Those on the ground felt both an enthusiastic welcome for the succession and yet, a reluctance to part with the master.

Hsing Yun, accompanied by the new abbot, executive director Venerable Tzu Hui, and over one hundred abbots and abbesses of the branch temples, bade farewell to the Buddha in the main shrine and then took the path down the hill. As he walked on he looked at the familiar objects and scenes one more time.

Meanwhile, along the one kilometer (0.6 miles) path between the main shrine and the gate of non-duality, emotional devotees lined up. Many were quite touched and pleaded:

"Master, please take care!"
"Master, come back soon!"
"Master, remember us!"

Waving good-by, Hsing Yun kept his smile to the end. Hard as it was to let go, hard as it was to walk on, one must walk on. Thus, he vanished beyond the mountain gate.

Handing over duties

Hsing Yun gave the public only a month's notice prior to the actual succession. But for those at Fo Guang Shan it was an expected move, not a surprise. The new abbotship meant a transfer of duties, not a change of an established system.

Hsing Yun was not only the dreamer of Fo Guang Shan's system, but also its facilitator. Clause twenty-two in chapter four of Fo Guang Shan's constitution states clearly: "The abbot of Fo Guang Shan is the director of the Religious Affairs Committee, serving a term of six years, with one re-appointment by popular vote and, under exceptional circumstances, a second reappointment by two thirds of the popular vote." Hence, toward the end of his second term, Hsing Yun was already searching for a successor both from within and from outside the community. By the time he completed his third term, his resolve to step down was unshakable. Venerable Hsin Ping was the unanimous choice to be the next abbot. Further, monasterial supervisory laws require the presence of an executive director, a position which Hsing Yun had also assumed while holding the abbotship. Venerable Tzu Hui was appointed in his place.

Venerable Hsin Ping, at fifty-eight years old, had been a

follower of the master through three decades since the master's time in Ilan. He was tonsured in 1961, received the precepts under Master Tao Yuan of Hai-hui (Assembly of Buddhas) Temple, Keelung, in 1963, and went on to attend Shou-Shan Buddhist College and the Chinese Buddhist Research Institute. For lengths of time during the earliest days of Fo Guang Shan, Hsin Ping was stationed in the construction quarters. In 1973, he was named the head of Fo Guang Shan's male monastics. Admired for his melodious voice in chanting and his kind, easygoing character, Hsin Ping was the best loved of the leading monastics.

Venerable Tzu Hui, age sixty, also from Ilan, hails from a prominent family. Acclaimed in the Buddhist circle for her excellent capabilities, she played her role as executive director like no other could. She began following Hsing Yun when he first set foot in Ilan forty years ago and has since been his personal interpreter in the Taiwanese dialect. She has indeed bridged the gap between Buddhism and the people of Taiwan. Venerable Tzu Hui graduated from Ilan's Lanyang Secondary School for girls with high grades and from Japan's Ohtani University with a Master of Arts degree in Buddhist Studies. She has also studied at Kyoto University in Japan. For many years she has been on the faculty of the Chinese Culture University.

Rule of law, not of people

To clarify his intentions, Hsing Yun wrote this verse just before he handed over Fo Guang Shan at the age of fifty-eight:

*Those of Fo Guang Shan are heading west,
while Mahakasyapa[1] heads east.
Coming and going in like manner,
[I,] in this world, [shall] always
be the calm, engaged yet free one.*

Effortlessly, Hsing Yun understands the affection of his disciples and devotees. He firmly believes that only a well developed system can ensure the continuous existence of a religious organization. At the succession ceremony he stated frankly the four reasons for his stepping down:
- Rule should be of law, not people
- No one is deemed indispensable
- Stepping down is not to be considered retiring
- Replacing previous leadership with new leadership reinvigorates Buddhism.

"I'm merely shedding the load of official commitments," he added. "A monk will always be a monk. I've no way of resigning as the master!"

Probably the only thing that troubled him, along with the passing on of the baton and renewal of the system, was the astronomical debts that were now laid upon his disciple's shoulders. Hsin Ping, though, never spoke of these to others. Nor did he say much about the burden. If many mouths had to be fed, he would do whatever he could to ensure that each was sated. That was the resolve for which he was most celebrated.

For Fo Guang Shan, the succession enhanced its metabolism from within and helped make a modern Buddhist

---
[1] Referring to Hsing Yun himself.

institution. For the rest of the Buddhist circle in Taiwan, however, it was like a gigantic rock hurled into an otherwise calm lake. The rippling effect left a long, lasting impact.

First-ever term set for abbotship

Transference of the abbotship is a matter of course in the Chinese Buddhist tradition. The succession can go by lineage; it is deemed the handing down of the law. When succession is done by inviting an eminent master from outside to take over the abbotship, it is called the "monastery of the ten directions" or "passing onto the sages." For the time being, Fo Guang Shan has followed the lineage tradition. But then, who can tell what may occur in the future? And, why did its first succession cause such a stir?

In a rhetorical article published in *United Monthly*, Buddhist scholar Yang Hui-nan lauds the master's decision and hints that others should follow suit. He further points out that the term system might not exist in the traditional Chinese Buddhist monastery, but the abdication of the abbot was not unusual, especially in an established monastery where succession was an integral part of the operation.

Buddhist monasteries during the pre-nationalist era were at best dubious in identity. Properties were never defined, the rich and powerful would assume propriety and run the sangha or the abbot would simply refuse to let go. As writer Li Ao once put it, the elders in China would not only refuse to hand over the baton but also have the younger generation batoned! The current government monasterial supervisory laws, though tough, have ironically been the factor behind many conflicts between the laity and sangha. More often than not, an old abbot's death within his term sparks triple-party contention over monasterial properties among his disciples, secular family and the director of the temple. Litigation, fist fights and other less honorable incidents make glaring headlines. In the end, monasterial serenity is no more.

Yang believes that Hsing Yun's abdication set the first-ever term for monasterial abbotship and pointed to a brand new direction in monasterial management. "Those abbots who harbor the intent of being there for thousands of years," Yang writes, "will have a lot to fidget about from now on. Should they follow what is right willingly? Or should they hold on to their titles until death? Hsing Yun! O Hsing Yun, what a portentous example you have set!"

As it turned out, Hsing Yun succeeded in setting the tone for the ensuing abdication of a number of elderly monastics, like Sung-shan (Pine Mountain) Temple's Master Ling Ken, Hua-yen Lien-she's (Avatamsaka Lotus Society) Master Nan T'ing, and Hui-jih Chiang-t'ang's (Wisdom Sun Lecture Hall) Master Yin Shun.

Living the spirit of baton-passing

As Fo Guang Shan continues to flourish, Hsing Yun's disciples – like him – uphold the conviction of "success not having to be about the individual" and take pleasure in their supporting roles. The senior monastics, in particular, are seen to manifest their master's baton-passing spirit and are willing to take a back seat to their up-and-coming juniors.

Venerable Tzu Chuang, known for her industriousness in the founding of branch temples, turned P'u-men Temple over to the younger generation of monastics ten days after its opening and proceeded to another construction project. Venerable Yi Kung's study at Tokyo University was arranged by Venerable Tzu Chuang, who also accompanied her there. When asked why Yi Kung was sent to such a prestigious institution while she herself had attended the lesser Bukkyo (Buddhist) University, Venerable Tzu Chuang simply replied, "That's the spirit of Fo Guang Shan."

One year, by coincidence, all the abbots and abbesses left their posts at the branch temples in Southeast Asia and Japan to join Hsing Yun on a lecture tour in Hong Kong. "Wouldn't the notion of your abbotship being overthrown on your return faze you?" Hsing Yun asked Hsin Ping, smiling. "It's one of the worst military maneuvers, you know, for the entire leadership to be away like that."

"In that case," Hsin Ping replied, also smiling, "let's build a second Fo Guang Shan!" Everyone who heard the exchange smiled. It evidenced the absolute desire of the master to let go and the readiness of his successor to lead and delegate. No matter who is at the helm, everything shall proceed according to the system.

Truly letting go

The first half-year after stepping down, Hsing Yun spent in the United States in order to enable a smooth transition in his absence. Over the past ten years, Hsing Yun has really and truly *let go*. Now he leaves the entertaining of guests at Fo Guang Shan to the abbot and all the construction and functions at the branch temples to their respective abbots or abbesses. Whenever he is asked for his opinion, he always asks, "Have you consulted the abbot first? What does he think?" He is neither compelled to intervene nor is he keen on giving advice any more – a definite show of confidence in the system and its operation, and the support for the new leadership. "I can't stand people putting down the bowl but not the chopsticks," he notes. "Stepping down, one must absolutely let go."

Official titles mean little to Hsing Yun. Now cleared of all of them, he works just as hard. "Editing journals, helping in the kitchen, and everything in-between," he says, "I promise to give all my efforts." One lunar New Year, devotees were again expected to swarm the place. A plot at the foot of the hill was allocated for parking so that devotees would no longer have to pay for parking nearby. It was New Year's Eve, and everybody was busy with assigned tasks. Hsing Yun was also assigned a job by the abbot – painting the lines in the new parking lot. By six in the evening dinner was ready but he was not. He quickly lay down his work and went over to the hordes of newly arrived guests. Afterwards, he sneaked back to the parking lot and picked up where he had left off. Not until four o'clock the next morning did he, together with a couple by the name of Tsai, finish eighty new spots for trucks and 800 for cars. As devotees started to take up those spots one by one, it was at last time for Hsing Yun to go to sleep.

Another time, the exhibition hall was vacated following the first auction of pieces of calligraphy and paintings to raise funds for Fo Guang University. In the middle of the night, Hsing Yun and a handful of disciples rushed to the scene and set up another display so that visitors would have something fresh the next day.

"Give a small chore to the competent," he explains, "and it will be maximized; give a big task to the incompetent, and it will be diminished." Undeniably, he is a monk of utmost competence.

Retreating as a form of advancing

Freeing himself of duties, the master had plans to meditate and teach, to read and write. But the discerning had no problem in predicting that, barely sixty and with his stamina, he could not possibly retire like that. Chang P'ei-keng, secretary-general of the Chinese-Tibetan Cultural Association of the Republic of China and a follower who is two years his senior, shared that opinion. "He knew too well," Chang observes, "that no matter what he did at Fo Guang Shan he would still be an abbot. He needed urgently to peck through the shell. Leaving the abbotship was in fact embarking on a new journey in his life." Hsing Yun's performance during the past decade has confirmed that view. He has emerged from his cocoon to create an all-round, global career in Buddhism as well as a radiant second spring in his own life. When asked to whom Fo Guang Shan now belongs, his answer is: "Fo Guang Shan is not owned by any one person. But it is yours to keep if you have it in your heart… I don't honestly feel as though Fo Guang Shan is mine. Rather, I feel the world, the universe are mine to keep. For I can lay it all down," Hsing Yun says. "In so doing, I can pick it up again."

This Buddhist verse contains the gist of Hsing Yun's sentiments ten years after his abdication:

*Transplanting green rice seedlings
all over the paddies with [my] hands;
Lowering [my] head to see
the sky in the water.
Purification of body and mind
to be in accord with the Dharma;
Retreating turns out to be
a form of advancing.*

Chapter 14
Like clouds and water[1]

The most well-known masters in *Biographies of Eminent Monks* are categorized in accordance with their cultivaion, learning, preaching, asceticism and so on. Hsing Yun will have to be ranked among the preaching masters.[2]

Buddha in his heart, the Way beneath his feet

With the Buddha in his heart and the Way beneath his feet, Hsing Yun has endured the unendurable in spreading the Dharma for the deliverance of all sentient beings. Taking over the editing of Venerable Master Tung Ch'u's *Life* magazine in the early years, he often traveled on foot to Sanchung rather than spend one dollar for public transportation. Some times he would oversee the formatter and printer at work for hours on end without eating anything the whole day. The unthinkable happened when he, then twenty-eight, began to travel, accompanied by followers, offering lectures on the Tripitaka across Taiwan. To protect the valuable but heavy sound equipment from being bumped or broken, he carried it in his own lap all the way eastward. Consequently, he suffered a case of arthritis that almost cost him his legs. Ano-

---

[1] In the original text, a bustling but not suffering *yun-shui seng*. *Yun-shui*, clouds and waters, qualifying the homelessness of the monastics; *seng*, a monastic.
[2] In the original text, *tu-hua seng*, a monastic who preaches to deliver all sentient beings.

ther time, enroute to Kaohsiung to spread the Dharma, he found himself penniless and without a ticket and had to hand over his fountain pen in lieu of the fare. Obtaining basic material needs was difficult enough at the time, but even more daunting was the task of breaking through the insulation and inflexibility that shrouded society at that time. Hsing Yun's resolve to spread the Dharma and deliver all sentient beings was to be challenged again and again.

Public gatherings under martial law were always mistrusted. In the shade or in front of the stage, men from the national intelligence bureau would lurk, chewing over each word for suspected treason or breaking up the session on the pretext of a failure to preregister. The speaker, though, soon learned that opening with praise about the leader of the people and his government would ensure the absence of prospective disruptions. Officials were equally suspicious of all campus activities, possibly an after-shock from the student movement that preceded the communist era on the mainland. Needless to say, Hsing Yun's Buddhist summer camps for college-level students in the 1960s were harassed, and attempts to speak on campus often barred. An already publicized engagement at National Taiwan Normal University was rescinded at the last minute without any explanation whatsoever. Many times he demanded to know why Catholics and Protestants preachers were permitted on school grounds but not the Buddhists. This demand was given nothing more than the cold shoulder.

Prisons, too, were out of bounds. As much as the Buddhists longed to reach out and bring peace to those in confinement, political dissidents included, the conditions were not right. Similarly, the hope to preach to the armed forces and the police remained a dream. The government largely controlled the media which did not appear any more accommodating. A day before *Gate of Faith*, the first national Buddhist telecast that was set to go on the air in 1980, Hsing Yun learned that the visual of his five-minute prologue would be deleted, leaving just the audio – the reason being that monks were not allowed to appear on screen. Trying to appeal his case with a cross-reference to monks portrayed in the popular soap operas, he was denied on the grounds that he was not an actor playing the role of a monk.

Political, economic and social progress within Taiwan has enabled the master preacher to spread the blossoms of Buddhism with perseverance and patience. Today, Fo Guang Shan and its branch temples are landmarks of Buddhist worship. Hsing Yun now takes the podium in the halls of government and other equally majestic venues. Twenty odd years since its inception, the Buddhist summer camps for college-level students have received into the arms of the Buddha tens of thousands of youthful intellectuals and, in the process, produced the most promising talent for Buddhism. Invitations and pleas from academia are endless. Hsing Yun has also taught a course on religion and life at Tung Hai University, established and chaired a research center in Indian culture at the Chinese Culture University and is responsible for the popularization of Buddhist studies among the new generations of intellectuals in Taiwan.

Popularizing Buddhism in prisons and among the armed forces

Speaking behind prison walls and among the armed

forces is now routine for the monastics of Fo Guang Shan. The department of legal affairs has conferred on Hsing Yun the official title of "educator of morality." He has spoken in almost every prison in Taiwan. "Prison is really the best place for practice," he often tells those serving sentences. "Take advantage of your time here to repent with deepest sincerity. What freedom of mind it is to be able to regard your sentence as a practice in solitude!"

Once a timid young man came to see Hsing Yun. "Master, do you remember me?" he asked stuttering somewhat. "I was serving time five years ago when you came to speak. What you said turned my life around." Another time, the master received a red donation packet on which was written: "An offering for the Master. In prostration, your disciple who has relinquished the wrong way for the right."

Spreading the Dharma among the armed forces, though relatively late in blooming, has been just as fruitful. The green light was not given until Hao Po-ts'un took office as Chief of the General Staff. Hsing Yun took the forces by storm when he toured the frontlines of Chinmen and Matsu in 1989 and was thereafter asked to speak by the Ministry of National Defense as well as the diehard Department of Central Intelligence at a range of events.

With much growth in social diversification, freedom of expression and the Buddhist populace, the media too, has rushed to amend their policy in favor of Buddhist content and the appearance of monastics. All three television stations in Taiwan are more than glad to include Buddhist programs. Contrary to past times when this monk bought air time for huge sums and the stations were thankless, they are now in hot pursuit of Hsing Yun and more than willing to reimburse him handsomely for every three-minute appearance.

Never leaving for the day

The master's preaching has actually attained new heights during the ten years since leaving the abbotship.

"The freeway is my bed and the car my cafeteria," is how Hsing Yun likes to describe his travel style. He used to set off from Kaohsiung just before dawn and return from his travels when the stars dotted the sky. In the sweltering heat of July last year he decided to go around Taiwan in three days. From Ilan, Hualien, Taitung, Pingtung, Kaohsiung, Tainan, Changhua, Miaoli, Hsinchu, Taoyuan, to Taipei. He gave a total of eighteen lectures and greeted 20,000 devotees. When the much younger members of the media touring with him were about to call it quits, the master was apologetic. "I'm so sorry to have caused you much stress," he said to them. "I've been long accustomed to this. The body is busy but not the mind!"

Another time Hsing Yun returned to Fo Guang Shan from Taipei at one o'clock in the morning. He was there to conduct a memorial service commemorating the 29th anniversary of the passing of the late vice-president Chen Ch'eng at six a.m.. He returned to Taipei at noon, and then presided over a committee meeting for a fundraising concert and informal talks on Ch'an over a vegetarian meal. At midnight he was at long last able to leave for the day. "It feels good to be off!" the master said, heaving a deep sigh. "Without any overtime compensation," his disciples chorused.

No time for idleness – that practically summarizes the

master's daily life. Almost under no circumstance will he take time off, for others would be let down. His right thigh bone was fractured from a fall in the bathroom in 1991. He was hospitalized and underwent surgery in which the bone was mounted with four steel pins. A lecture scheduled a week later for a literary society was canceled – only to be reconfirmed in three days. Newly discharged from the hospital, he took the podium in a wheelchair on that day and spoke for a full hour. Many were moved to tears at the sight of his paleness and frail health. "Even if he hadn't uttered a word," one was heard saying, "this is the very best lecture ever. What cultivation!"

Around the globe two and a half times yearly

Chasing the wind; racing the sun – that metaphorically describes Hsing Yun's life as a roving monk who takes the Dharma to the ends of the world.

According to his diary, Hsing Yun is estimated to have traveled 160 kilometers (100 miles) each day and around the world two and a half times each year. In the summer of 1993 alone he went to Russia, New Zealand, Australia, Hong Kong, England, Germany, Brazil, France, the United States and Canada; across four continents in a single month. He is probably the most frequent flyer among Buddhist monastics. President Shih Yung-kuei of China Television, a long-time friend, once joked, "Looks like you don't need a passport any more!" A couple of devotees once gave the master two dozen pairs of reading glasses, pledging that each would be kept at a different place for his convenience.

Although the sun has its daily recess, this wandering

monk does not. Adaptability must be instantaneous wherever he goes. Each year he averages 1,000 lectures, conducts refuge ceremonies for some 80,000, receives about 120 visiting groups and 1,000 guests, writes about a million words and records 300 telecasts. "I seem to have some kind of micro-adjuster inside," he says of his own flexibility. "My mood and attention are automatically capable of tuning to changing time and space."

Let us tag along on one his trips! The instant he sets foot in the airport, he is swamped by requests to say something or to have a photograph taken. Should a group show up for the latter, he holds his pose until everyone, even the occasional overzealous young female devotee, comes away with a satisfactory personal shot with the master. On board the aircraft, the crew, as well as fellow passengers, take turns sending hearty regards. Once on the ground, he is swamped again – virtually buried alive in leis and bouquets, blinded by the flashing of the cameras and deafened by greetings. Security is understandably tight throughout. Then he is sped on to the next public speech, the next reception of guests, the next lecture, the next conference. Every moment is occupied, and he does not seem to have a second in which to catch his breath. Finally when all is finished, he takes leave of each place – only to have the crowds of devotees swarm him again, though this time in the form of farewell.

Keeping busy is cultivation

Venerable Tzu Chuang remembers the record Hsing Yun set of visiting thirteen temples in Malaysia in one day.

Guests were at the door first thing in the morning. Lectures were delivered nonstop. Later, devotees would not let the master return to his hotel alone. The venerable herself did not get to speak with him until two or three in the morning. There were crowds to welcome him, to see him off, to dine with him, to bid him good night. He could barely find time to excuse himself to use the restroom. To ensure that others receive joy, he ate one generous meal after another.

"Too often I just sleep with my robe on," he says. "And, waking up, I am lost as to where I am." Some blame it on what they perceive to be an oversized ambition. Those who know him well know that it is spirited resolve:

> *Let me borrow the past month,*
> *the past day*
> *To pay back this month, this day;*
> *Let me borrow the next month,*
> *the next day*
> *To make up for this month, this day.*

Despite the strength of his eloquence, Hsing Yun is nearing seventy and weakening physically. More frequently he gets tired and needs a break. But there is so much to do and so little time. "It's easy for me to go away and practice in solitude," he says. "But so much preaching is waiting to be done. How can I take a recess? Disciples look up to me as their role model. Should I recede, they would all follow suit!"

Let us look at a breakdown of his daily schedule: speaking (lectures, classes, preaching, entertaining), eight hours; writing, four hours; traveling, four hours; sleeping, six hours; eating, washing, and miscellaneous, two hours. Driven as he is, some might ask, how does Hsing Yun find time to practice? Serving all sentient beings," he says, "satisfying the needs of all sentient beings, solving the problems of all sentient beings – keeping busy is cultivation. Anyone looking for leisure may find it in the grave."

Time management

With keeping busy as the norm, time management is essential. In fact, Hsing Yun is proud of his punctuality, which was inspired by a passage learned in childhood from a textbook at a nearby English school: "Off to school in shirts and shorts, [let us] always [be] on the dot." The master always wakes up on time for the earliest morning engagement, and he always leaves ample time for any appointment. Most unfathomable of all are the recording sessions for telecast, during which he keeps perfect timing of the four-minute shooting, has never had a retake and never needs to be edited. To the awestruck crew it is like "he carries a timer in his sleeve."

He is especially clever with planning and takes great advantage of intervals. The exceedingly harsh training in the monasteries – in which he would figure out how to ready his clothes, belongings, and bedding each night to enable himself to complete his toilet in three minutes the next morning – is the reason why, quite unruffled, he writes on planes, replies to faxed documents in vehicles and chants the name of Amitabha Buddha as he drives by each power pole. With disciples rallying around he is able to read documents, listen to reports and give verbal instructions simultaneously in order to make everyone happy.

The innumerable methods of practice always lead back to the path of the Bodhisattva. A decade of traveling has scattered lotus seeds far and wide and sown vast good causes and conditions.

In 1988 Hsing Yun, together with a volunteer medical group, traveled into the remote mountains and barren regions of northern Thailand in order to reach out to the illiterate and neglected. He went from traveling in a large vehicle to a small one, then to a donkey, and even a borrowed military helicopter at times. To those refugees and their offsprings of Chinese descent, he gave sustenance and medical care to their bodies, and the Dharma to their anguished minds to eliminate suffering and cultivate joy. Li Chien-yuan, daughter of General Li Wen-huan of northern Thailand's Third Army was in the audience during one of his presentations. She later visited Fo Guang Shan for three days and, on departing, became tearful. "Master," she said to Hsing Yun, "what you did for us in northern Thailand was like giving us another chance at life!"

Pearl of the Orient awash in Buddha's favor

The fruit of Hsing Yun's efforts is by far most visible in Hong Kong. The last British colony is understandably peppered with Christian churches, missionary schools and hospitals. Indigenous faiths were once piteously undefined and best manifested in the immense following commanded by temples attributed to Huang Ta-hsien[3] and the likes. The

---
[3] A sage by the name of Huang.

spread of Buddhism has been shouldered by a number of eminent masters. The endeavors of Masters Chueh Kuang, Yung Hsing, Ch'ang Huai and others in hospitals, schools and senior homes are exemplary. But somehow the average person remains woefully alienated from Buddhism.

Hsing Yun first preached Buddhism in Hong Kong seven years ago. Things have improved year by year ever since. These days auditoriums are bursting at the seams. Officials at Hunghom Coliseum reserve three days annually for his Dharma lectures. The coliseum now proudly stands as "a pure lotus in the Fragrant Harbor." And, as always, his schedules are packed with requests for interviews from the media and the public.

The master from Taiwan has added his touch to eradicate the erroneous public concept that monastics merely take without giving to society. Each year he actively participates in local charities by way of alms-round fund-raising for the government, Tung Wah Group Hospitals, Po Leung Kuk[4] and other institutions for the developmentally challenged.

As time goes on, more Dharma lectures by local masters are dotting public events, more notables openly acknowledge becoming Buddhists and the society has come to respect the sangha and the essence of Buddhism. The Pearl of the Orient is now awash in the favor of the Buddha.

Chiang Su-hui, Taiwan's information officer in Hong Kong and a resident for fifteen years, is sympathetic about the uncertainty of Hong Kong's future beyond 1997, and its people's quickened pursuit of spirituality. The timely entry of

---

[4] An orphanage with a long history.

Hsing Yun into their lives and the stability and assurance he has given them are the reasons behind his soaring popularity among them.

As one of the major gateways for import and export trade between China and the rest of the world, Hong Kong has the best of both worlds, East and West. Hsing Yun has become dedicated to the city. With the fluctuating worldwide emigration of the people of Hong Kong over the last few years, Hsing Yun's impact, too, mushrooms in every corner; England, the United States, Canada, Australia, and even South Africa. He is extremely grateful to the people in Hong Kong. He believes they have actually opened the way for spreading the Dharma across all five continents.

A mere monastic

As events of the decade continue their flow, the monastic who merely wanted to unload duties at the temple to focus on quiet cultivation, teaching, studying and writing, has carved out a braver, newer world with remarkable causes and conditions.

The Dalai Lama once shared his sentiments toward his Nobel peace prize, saying "I'm still a mere monastic. No more, no less." Hsing Yun gave the same reply when asked about his switch from being abbot to a roving monk.

Endurance is reciprocation of the Buddha's favor; labor is for the benefit of all sentient beings. Each step of his feet leave behind trails of lotuses, the rustle of his robe sweeps clean [the path to] the Pureland. Like Master Hsuan Tsang who, on his white steed, traversed to India through 800 miles of deep sand, vowing, "better to perish taking one step west than to survive taking one step east,"⁵ Hsing Yun in his modern transport creates the latest chapter in the history of Buddhism.

---

⁵ The west means destination and advance; the east, home and retreat.

Chapter 15
Heart for the isle, soul for the mainland

*F*rom Taiwan, Hsing Yun's teaching tours in the past ten years have covered the world except for the land he left behind four decades ago. On the mainland, still under communist ideology, religion is perceived as an anti-government activity infused with superstition and backward practices. The government preservation of a handful of monasteries and eminent masters is therefore only aimed at appeasement. On the other hand, the nationalists, licking their wounds, had sworn to block all channels of communication with the Mainland. Consequently, not even the rapidly maturing Buddhist practice in Taiwan was able to find its way home. Not until the late 1970s did President Chiang Ching-kuo give approval for family visits to the mainland. In time, this activated an economic and cultural exchange. These factors indirectly contributed to Hsing Yun's homecoming. They also constituted the position he would assume as the island and the mainland started to "nudge" each other.

A cough drop, a condition

Conditions can lead to such incredible happiness. The condition that led to Hsing Yun's homecoming was one tiny cough drop. In 1986, Hsing Yun and Ms. T'ien-Liu Shih-lun, during the 60th birthday gala of Thailand's King Bhumibol

Adulyadej, overheard the severe hacking cough of a lady seated in front of them. That was the wife of Zhao Puchu, chairman of the Buddhist Association of China. T'ien quietly pulled a cough drop from her purse and handed it to her. It pacified Zhao's cough in an instant and she was more than thankful.

Sharing the same roots, the encounter away from home touched off a spontaneous friendship between Zhao and Hsing Yun. That evening, Zhao Puchu delivered to Hsing Yun an autographed copy of his works.

Zhao, at eighty years old and ranked high in public office on the mainland, is an expert in Yuan opera and classical verses. He is one of the three foremost Chinese calligraphists of our time. Being a lifelong Buddhist, he has done his best to guard the Dharma during the worst of times. The last few years, he has been dedicated especially to the revival and repair of the severely damaged monasteries. One of Zhao's recent accomplishments is the towering bronze statue of the Buddha overlooking Lantau Island in Hong Kong. It is illustrated on the front of the city's electronic subway pass and is viewed as Hong Kong's most updated cultural symbol.

Despite an age gap of twenty years, Zhao and Hsing Yun became close friends and agreed to meet again.

Two years later in California, Hsing Yun was working on two major projects at Hsi Lai Temple: 1) the 16th general conference of the World Fellowship of Buddhists and 2) the 7th general conference of the World Fellowship of Buddhist Youth. With his heart in Taiwan and his soul in Mainland China, he struggled to bring both Buddhist organizations from Taiwan and Mainland China under one roof. He was hopeful that the ongoing conflict over the Chinese representation[1] would end.

To avoid political overtones, Hsing Yun clearly stated in the invitation that each delegation be representative of its organization, not its country. The only flags to be flown would be the United States representing the host nation, and that of the World Fellowship of Buddhist. No others flags would be allowed. He also suggested that the titles of the Buddhist Association of Beijing, China, and the Buddhist Association of Taipei, China, be used.

The ensuing negotiations, verging on collapse more than once, took a winding course before settling down to mutual acceptance of Hsing Yun's proposal. Setting aside their long-standing political deadlock, the two Buddhist organizations were able to compromise their differences and sit opposite one another at the conference table.

The breakthrough was announced at the opening ceremony. There was a standing ovation from more than 500 delegates representing 80 Buddhist organizations in 30 counties. Representatives from Hong Kong and Southeast Asia also supported Hsing Yun's mode. Zhao subsequently invited Hsing Yun to visit the mainland.

A whirlwind tour

This would be the first official visit by a Buddhist monastic to a country bound and shackled by materialist ideo-

---

[1] The delegation from the mainland withdrew in protest against the election of Taiwan representative T'ien-Liu Shih-lun as vice-chair during the 14th meeting in Shi Lanka. The Taiwan delegation was ousted altogether from the 15th gathering in Nepal as a result of pressure from Beijing.

logy for over half a century. How it was going to be justified to government authorities was the question. Lu K'eng, a respected journalist on the mainland, Taiwan, and Hong Kong, returned to the mainland to lay the groundwork. Finally in 1989, Hsing Yun led a Dharma Preaching and Family Visiting Group of the International Buddhist Progress Society to the mainland. It started a whirlwind that swept across the land. It opened the door to the bonding between Taiwan and Mainland China.

Academic consultant Charles W.H. Fu and T'ang Te-kang, along with over 70 authors, journalists, and monastics, together with groups of devotees from the United States, Canada, and Singapore, formed a delegation of more than 200. Starting from Shanghai in the east, this group traveled to Tunhuang in the west, Beijing in the north, and Ch'engtu in the south between March 27 and April 25.

The U.S.-based author, Wang I-ling, records the *highly formalized*[2] official reception for the international Buddhist leader and his much-publicized tour: "He shook hands and dined with every governor and mayor in every province and city he toured. No matter what time of day, droves of monastics and lay people greeted him at train stations and airports. The red carpet was rolled out everywhere he went. The bell and drum sounded as he visited each temple to offer incense and pay his respects to the Buddha. His motorcade was so popular that officials on bikes and on foot were needed to lead the way through the overwhelming crowds during the festivities at Lung-hua Temple in Shanghai."

---

[2] In the diplomatic terminology of the Chinese government. *Kao Kuei-ke* in the original text.

Enraptured audiences listened to the master's every word as he described the mind of Ch'an and the nature of human beings. Also, at the joint invitation of the universities of Beijing, Qinghua, and Renmin, he spoke at Beijing's National Library, causing a sensational and heartfelt response among those in attendance.

Visiting Sichuan, the great monk from Taiwan was the name on the lips of bustling shoppers.

"For years the nationalist government has been harping about pushing back," observed an amused reporter touring with him. "Today, against all odds, the master has made it!"

Indeed, Hsing Yun was an unprecedented speaker from Taiwan who took the podium in the People's Hall. His coming restored faith and hopes for Buddhists on the mainland and impressed the Buddhist masters residing there.

A borrowed freshness

Hsing Yun freely talked to the leaders of the communist regime, Li Xiannian and Yang Shangkun, about concerns over the pillage of religion during the Cultural Revolution. He requested that a religious policy be put in place and that monasterial management be returned to monastics. His plea was sincere: "Naturally, because you are communists, religious belief is not of utmost importance to you, but it is to your benefit to at least understand religion."

To an appreciative Zhao Puchu, the visit was like "ten thousand miles of fragrant blossoms bearing succulent fruits." Abbot Hsueh Fan of Ch'i-hsia Temple, Nanjing, was also deeply moved and stated "his rousing of the Buddhist morale from its long hibernation is exactly the breath of fresh air that

Buddhism in China needs."

Hsing Yun impressed everyone. He was precise, thorough, erudite and witty. Whenever he spoke to officials, Buddhist College students or the public, his words of praise or teaching advice were impeccable.

Also, he gave many generous gifts. To every monastic he encountered he gave a red envelope containing a monetary gift and to many monasteries he donated his own literary works and sets of the *Fo Guang Encyclopedia*. He also gave a jade Buddha and two new cars to Ch'i-hsia temple and made a generous donation to the Gallery of Modern Literature. The Buddhist Association of China received a generous sum of money and a tour bus. To his and his master's hometown, Chiangtu and Haian, he donated monetary gifts, and gave vehicles and ambulances to schools for deaf and mute children.

Professor Wang Yao of the Tunhuang Research Institute and Central Institute of National Minorities in Beijing called Hsing Yun "the embodiment of altruism". "It's been one hearty embrace between the master and the people of the land," Wang noted. He saw Hsing Yun's visit as a living symbol to a tormented, mortified nation that its innate spirit is alive and well on the international stage.

Dear, dear home

Finally, Hsing Yun returned to his hometown, Chiangtu.

Lu K'eng, the publisher of Hong Kong's monthly magazine, *People*, stated that: "It was the first time this journalist of fifty-one years saw a city empty itself onto the streets to salute someone. The rows lining both sides of the main street were three-people deep. Spectators were straining to see from buildings and people were perching in trees, all clapping and cheering. With this as a backdrop, he handed his mother a bouquet and grasped her hand.

'I'm home!' He told her, and could say no more.

'It's good to have you back!' She echoed. 'It's good to have you back.'

Their tears seemed endless, reflecting what it had meant to be without each other. Mother and son then greeted the crowds from the balcony. A band of monastics delivered a trilling *Ode to Mother*. T'ang Te-kang and I recited congratulatory verses for the reunion."

"This is Li Kuo-shen!" In plain Yangchou dialect the popular religious leader reintroduced himself to his townsfolk using his hometown name.

"At long last Yanchou has come up with a truly fine human being!" murmured a teary elder.

Hsing Yun, turning to depart, was stopped by a well-groomed mother, who raised her baby to him. He bent to touch the youngster's cheek with his own. Two dozen came- ras must have captured the shot…"

Despite her pride over brother Kuo-shen's achievements, sister Su-hua, who now resides in Kuanghsi province with her family, could not help feeling distraught by how long they had been apart. "I've turned gray," she said, as she strolled along the shaded path in Yuhua T'ai (Terrace of Rain-soaked Blossom) Park in Nanjing, "and he's grown old, too. He's but a child in my memory!" She could not fight back tears each time she relived their reunion.

On his return to Ch'i-hsia Temple, the principal and teachers of the Vinaya college, who had disciplined the fledgling Hsing Yun, received him with a ceremonial tribute. From the seat of the guest of honor, Hsing Yun rose to thank Ch'i-hsia for its nourishment of the Dharma and benefit of grace. Weeping as he spoke, he shared a poignant moment with a muted gathering of disciples and devotees. "May the radiance of Ch'i-hsia light up the future of Buddhism in China." Later he gave a lecture to the young monastics gathered there.

Back in Chiao-shan Temple, he joined those masters who had previously taught him to pray and chant. He amused everyone with candid confessions of childhood follies and an occasional escape or two.

Far-reaching consequences

With Hsing Yun on board the yacht Emei along the Yangtze, professor of religious studies Charles W.H. Fu of Temple University wrote about the revitalization of Chinese Buddhism and noted a revelation about the trip:

"First, it indirectly indicates the stirring of Chinese Buddhism in response to external aid and timely conditions. Buddhist moral in the country has reached new heights as a result. The lift that Hsing Yun gave the Buddhist circle was exactly what it needed. Buddhism was too economically suppressed to have bounced back on its own strength.

Second, it helps resume Buddhist cultural communication between the country and the rest of the world. While Buddhists from outside are astonished by the magnificent stone-sculptures of Tatsu[3], Sichuan, ancient monasteries, and other relics, the Chinese Buddhist circle is being updated, through the gifts of publications, as part of the new progress of modern Buddhism.

Third, it helps resume Buddhist scholarly exchange between the country and the rest of the world. Hsing Yun's seminar with research fellows of the Chinese Institute of Social Sciences was the first one of its kind. Together they probed the extent of religious modernization, and urged scholars to overcome their prejudice and ignorance that "religion is merely superstition."

Fourth, it transcends the political reality between Taiwan and the mainland. While the two continue to experience conflict over timeless political differences, a religious unification seemed the most probable with Buddhist organizations serving as the ideal mediators.

Political enthusiasts in the media both in Taiwan and Hong Kong seized this opportunity to expound from different perspectives. They questioned the legality of his visit to the mainland because of his status as a central advisory committee member. They speculated that Hsing Yun was playing messenger for the government of Taiwan and predicted that he would be bought by the communist rulers. Being aware of the generous donations he had contributed, they accused him of trying to buy his way through the mainland.

The Xu Jiatun Incident

All these speculations were mild compared to the dis-

---

[3] Images of the Buddha sculpted from cliffs that are masterworks dated from the T'ang dynasty.

ruption that was to occur one year later – the Xu Jiatun Incident.

Returning to Los Angeles, Hsing Yun and company stopped in Hong Kong to dine with Xu, then heading the branch office of the New China News Agency in Hong Kong.[4] Xu, now residing in the United States, is frank as he recalls their meeting. "I regard the master as an eminent Buddhist figure, a high official in the nationalist government, and a relatively significant target of diplomatic assimilation."

Chiangsu is hometown to both Xu and Hsing Yun. The former relates with fondness their first meeting. "Like old friends, we started to chat with the same regional accent." Hsing Yun then courteously booked their next appointment at Hsi Lai Temple, which Xu cheerily confirmed. Just prior to the June 4th disaster, a thank-you note reiterating the promised meeting reached Xu, who was somewhat tickled: "Hsing Yun's conspiracy letter is here."

Following the Tiananmen Square incident, the reformists were subdued while the government continued to rid themselves of dissidents, Xu, who had publicly sympathized with the student movement and never discouraged supportive demonstrations staged by his staff, was blacklisted for future retaliation. Dismayed over the lack of refuge offered within the system, he decided to take time off the following May and flew to the United States. He would accept Hsing Yun's offer to stay at Hsi Lai Temple.

Xu's disappearance shocked many on the mainland, in Hong Kong, and in the United States.

---

[4] A position some regarded as authoritative as the governor of Hong Kong.

For the past seven years, Hong Kong had come to cherish and respect the man who had been at the helm of the city's branch office of the New China News Agency for seven years. Also, the 50-year communist party member was the highest ranking official to flee since the flights of Wang Ming to the then Soviet Union in the 1950s and Lin Biao to Mongolia in the 1970s. The enigma of his whereabouts must have caused more than a few anxious, sleepless nights.

No one knew that Xu was at the temple, until two weeks later when Hsing Yun accompanied him on an excursion to San Diego and Las Vegas. Tourists from Hong Kong saw the two at a popular tourist attraction. Before they knew it, their pictures were in the papers. The temple was bombarded with phone calls day and night asking about Xu.

As the situation became more urgent, Hsing Yun informed his guest: "Monastics don't lie. Since you're here with us, I can't tell people otherwise. Neither will evading the calls solve anything. We have to say something."

Xu subsequently gave consent for a press conference in which Hsing Yun and Lu K'eng announced on his behalf, his four personal principles. They were 1) no seeking of political asylum, 2) no violation of national security, 3) no interviews with the media, and 4) no contact with exiled members of the June 4th movement.

Buddha gate opens for those who suffer

When the issues were resolved regarding Xu, there were still many unanswered questions about Hsing Yun. How could a monk, supposedly above and beyond the three realms, become involved in such a political turmoil? What was he after? Hsing Yun's attitude is one of "Let bygones be bygones." He has no regrets, as the Buddha gate is one of compassion. It will be always open for those who suffer. "I've never treated Mr. Xu as a political personage," he says. "Just someone in need."

Hsing Yun, refusing to become embroiled in the strife of politics, declined permission for a gathering at Hsi Lai Temple of exiled members of the June 4th movement and the conducting of Buddhist services on behalf of the victims of the Tiananmen killings. However, the communist government could not forget so easily. When Xu was officially expelled from the party the following year, he was also accused of involvement with subversive elements.[5] That was the extent of Hsing Yun's alleged guilt. Hsing Yun was banned from the mainland. The goodwill from his family visit and teaching tour vanished overnight. The Buddhist circle in the mainland remained quiet although some hastened to disassociate themselves from Hsing Yun rather quickly.

The visitation ban lasted two years until Jiang Zemin annulled it. Hsing Yun was allowed home again to see his mother, though not without the strictest *protection*[6] - a sign of sustained distrust on the part of the authorities.

Surprisingly, supportive affirmation of Hsing Yun during these troubled times came from Hong Kong, itself playing a questionable role in the China issue. The Master placed just after Jiang Zemin and before Li Teng-hui in a

---

[5] According to the communist government, Buddhist monastic Hsing Yun of Taiwan and subversive journalist Lu K'eng.
[6] Called *full-time accompaniment* in the protocol of the communist government.

public poll for the most newsworthy people.

Xu now lives reclusively in the United States. He often considers how much Hsing Yun has done for him: "For the entire time I've been here, the Master has consistently respected my privacy while attending to all my needs as far as personal health and daily life."

Looking back, Hsing Yun's virtue and gallantry were undeniable to many. However, some cannot condone how he was pulled into political muddy water. The subsequent rift with the communist government would considerably slow down the momentum from his first lecture tour and almost terminate all efforts to reinvigorate Chinese Buddhism.

Tangible exchange

Hsing Yun has enjoyed attention in China like no other individual. His *Taiwan Experience* will always be helpful should Chinese Buddhism be allowed to re-invigorate itself. Therefore, the communist government remains lukewarm towards him. It is clear to Hsing Yun that despite ostensibly opening the door to the outside world, in actuality the Mainland has little tolerance for religious development. Buddhist temples had been reduced to aesthetic gardens and ancient relics, unaccompanied by any religious practice or belief. For more than a thousand years, Buddhism has been an undercurrent in Chinese culture but to blossom again, it will have to wait longer for causes and conditions to mature. Before that happens, Hsing Yun must spread as many Bodhi seeds as he possibly can.

In the current context of tangible exchange, free issues of *Universal Gate* and *Awakening the World* are distributed regularly to the Mainland even though these might never reach the intended readers. The dozen or so letters each month requesting financial assistance for the sangha and monasteries are all answered. A joint effort between Hsing Yun and P'an Hsiao-jui provides annual scholarships for twenty students from the mainland to study in the United States. Scholarship are also given to two hundred local Buddhist college students. His publications continue to be widely reprinted; *Universal Gate* is considered a gem in many monasteries.

Hsing Yun's latest project is the publishing of *Anthology of Buddhist Scholarly Essays,* edited by Fo Guang Shan's consultant Chi Kuang-yu. The anthology's content centers around the problems and future of Chinese Buddhism. Contributing authors have been invited from the academia in China. The publication, to be produced in Taiwan and distributed in the mainland, is anticipated to be the instrument of scholarly exchange between both Buddhist circles.

Tending to a future cause

As long as the mainland continues with its economic advancement and political moderation, Hsing Yun foresees opportunities for communication. "All conscientious Chinese people want a unified China," he asserts. "It is not as if one side is swallowing up the other but rather a peaceful, equal form of unification."

"Prior to unification, attainment of the following must be complete: first, mutual strengthening of the economy; second, cultural dialogue; third, respect for religion; and fourth, political democracy. China isn't the exclusive property of a few. The country is the convergence of the majority."

On being labeled as unionist, he says: "No partisan politics for me, only this heart for Taiwan and this soul for China."

As a monastic, Hsing Yun does not intend to budge from the principle that "politics are politics and religion is religion." He hopes that both governments, with graciousness, will tend to the future of the Chinese people.

Part Five

Buddha's Light Held High

Showing the former California Secretary of State, now U.S. Ambassador, March Fong Eu the site of Hsi Lai Temple, Hacienda Heights, California

With graduates and faculty members of Hsi Lai University

With the President of the Commonwealth of Dominica,
Clarence Seignoret at the inauguration of Hsi Lai Temple, 1988

Surrounded by friends while on a visit to Ajanta, India

At the office of the President of the Philippines, Diosdado Macapagal, 1963

Delegates at the Buddha's Light International Association's Seventh General Conference in Toronto, Canada

Escorting the Buddha's Tooth Relic with the vice-abbot of Thailand's Dhammakaya Foundation

First-ever meeting with the leader of a Muslim country, Malaysian Prime Minister, Dr. Mahathir Mohammad

Chapter 16
The Dharma Coming West

*F*our decades ago, Buddhists were expelled from Mainland China. Hsing Yun rode the crest of Taiwan's economic boom and in doing so took the Buddha's light throughout the world. He traveled to Southeast Asia in the 1960s, Japan and Korea in the 1970s, Europe and the Americas in the 1980s and to Africa in the 1990s. The globalization of Chinese Buddhism has become an historical reality and its maturation phenomenal.

The construction of Hsi Lai Temple is perhaps the most momentous example of this maturation.

The Largest in the Western hemisphere

Hsi Lai Temple is approximately twenty miles east of Los Angeles and twenty minutes by car from Monterey Park, also known as *Little Taipei*. Spring breezes are always kind and gentle and daybreak is spectacular as the temple overlooks the largest and most dynamic city on the west coast. Less than an hour's drive from the Los Angeles International Airport, the road gently winds through the hills in Hacienda Heights. One is then pleasantly surprised. The temple's golden walls and glittering roofs light up the entire area. The colossal mountain gate welcomes all who pass through it. The inscription, designed by its' founder, reads *Fo Guang*

Shan Hsi Lai Ssu (Temple).
   Officially registered in the name of International Buddhist Progress Society [I.B.P.S.], Hsi Lai Temple is a milestone that marks the Dharma coming to the Western world. In addition, it is a major platform on which traditional Buddhism plays out its social role in modern society. The temple sits atop fifteen acres. The sprawling 102,432 square-meter structure was designed by U.S.-based architect Yang Tsu-ming. Groundbreaking was in 1986 and completion in November 1988. To symbolize the continuity of the dharma teaching and lineage over the centuries, Hsing Yun requested from India the traditional five-grain bricks, from the River Ganges its sacred sand and from Fo Guang Shan its soil. These traditional symbols of the roots of the Dharma were incorporated into the foundation of the Main Shrine.
   The palatial temple was featured in *Life* magazine, singled out as "the largest temple in the Western hemisphere" and dubbed "the Forbidden City in America", referring to its classic architecture. The temple was also the subject of a feature in *Reader's Digest* the following April.
   Hsi Lai Temple carries the torch of Fo Guang Shan as a spiritual and cultural center in America. It is a learning ground of Buddhism for Westerners, and the convergence of cultures, both East and West. Daily, devotees and visitors of all nationalities stroll the grounds. Lamas from India and bhiksus from Spain are frequent guests in the guest lodge and exchanges in various languages and dialects reverberate beneath the Buddha's feet.

Marvelous showcase of Eastern culture

Because of its direct descendancy from Fo Guang Shan, Hsi Lai Temple becomes an inevitable West Coast stopover for political and social celebrities from Taiwan. Former chairperson Hao Po-ts'un of the Executive Council, legislator K'ang Ning-hsiang, General Chiang Wei-kuo, presidential political advisor Li Huan, and former Kaohsiung mayor Yu-Chen Yueh-ying are among a few. Once Hsing Yun told Chang Ch'ing-yen, former head of the Los Angeles office of the Coordination Council for North American Affairs: "Please feel free to utilize the facility for hospitality and entertainment purposes!" More importantly, the temple transcends the tension between the isle and the mainland. It provides a buffer zone. The temple has hosted many celebrities including Zhu Qizhen, China's Ambassador to the United States; Xu Jiatun, former head of the Hong Kong office of the New China News Agency; Wuer Kaixi, leader of the June 4th Tiananmen student movement; and P'eng Ming-min, one of Taiwan's most vocal political dissidents. Also, local notables frequent the temple. California's Secretary of State, Dr. March Fong Eu, in particular, marvels at such a fine presence in her home state.

Today Hsi Lai Temple showcases Eastern culture and is recognized as one of the main headquarters for the spread of Buddhism in the West. However, it was an incredibly difficult and daunting struggle, which is typical of any pioneering effort.

The seed was sown when Hsing Yun first came to America as a guest of its bicentennial celebrations approximately twenty years ago. The country's cultural diversity and openness made a lasting impression. Hsing Yun was aware of the need for a spiritual anchor for the numerous Chinese immigrants in the United States. However, Hsing Yun also had to consider if the west could peacefully accept Buddhism. He was still influenced by the sometimes violent and intrusive manner in which Christianity was introduced to China in the last century. Could Buddhism be peacefully taught in the West?

Inspired by the urging of eager devotees, Hsing Yun sent Venerable Tzu Chuang, accompanied by the English-speaking Venerable Yi-Hang, to the United States with fifty thousand dollars. The two were to explore into the possibility of building a temple in America. Venerable Tzu Chuang, as it turned out, was utterly taken aback as she learned, firsthand, the price of real estate in California. A single house could easily sell for US$70,000 to US$80,000. Considering the entire endeavor too costly, she was ready to return to Taiwan when instead Hsing Yun joined them in their quest in California. They eventually located a church building for sale. While disciples ruminated over the notion of having to convert a church into a Buddhist temple, the master immediately finalized the purchase with twenty thousand dollars down payment. To him, a building designed for religious purposes would only make things easier, not harder. With the down payment, the loan application was approved, and the beginning of a new venture for Chinese Buddhism in America was established.

The monastics repaired the walls and painted images of the Buddha. The first chanting session drew devotees from a great distance and the ensuing gathering filled the temple each time. Due to its success, the Pai-T'a Temple (White Pagoda) was established in Maywood, California. This laid the way for a grander facility.

The resistance of Hacienda Heights

Hsing Yun's longtime follower, Chang-Yao Hung-ying, was a major driving force behind the vision. Her US $300,000 donation, together with others, helped purchase a hilly property in Hacienda Heights. However, the application for the state of California's approval to begin construction met with tremendous resistance from the affluent, conservative, and predominantly white suburb of retirees. The resistance of the Hacienda Heights community was bitter. Residents were concerned about everything from the annihilation of the natural landscape, disturbances from the chanting and festivities, negative impact of the monastic attire on the young, to the safety of their own household pets due to the mistaken belief that Chinese Buddhists dine on dog meat.

Subsequent legal proceedings took the form of six public hearings and over 100 explanatory sessions. Discussion centered around concerns that the temple would be too big, too tall and the colors would clash with the surrounding neighborhood. Actually the legal issues masked the true motivation behind many of the proceedings, which was fear and distrust of a different culture. This was occasionally expressed by rock throwing, name-calling and a general lack of understanding or respect for the intentions of the temple community. However, Hsing Yun, long skilled in insight, tolerance and preserverance, waited patiently for things to improve. Community representatives were invited for informal chats and to tour the site. The master, too, demonstrated his sense of community by leading disciples and devotees in many community service programs, and demonstrating that the temple is committed to sharing funds with local charities. Slowly the local residents became more confident of the true intentions of the temple community. During one of the public hearings, a Protestant minister literally pleaded on behalf of Hsi Lai Temple: "My wife is Vietnamese. She hasn't passed a day without crying about missing home since coming to America. The presence of Hsi Lai Temple is of great solace to her."

Home for the Buddhist body and mind

Hsi Lai Temple was established after a decade of struggle. Well-wishers both within the Buddhist circle and without were genuinely congratulatory. A message from U.S. congressman Matthew G. Martinez read: "The majestic Hsi Lai Temple will not only benefit its devotees and the local community with endless activities but also bridge the gap between cultures and thoughts of the East and West." The executive president, Venerable H. Ratanasara of American Buddhist Congress added; "Hsi Lai Temple is destined to be the lighthouse for the spread of Buddhism. A supreme glory for the Dharma in the Western hemisphere."

The temple set the stage for worldwide Buddhism when it hosted the 16th General Conference of the World Fellowship of Buddhists. This was the first time the conference was held outside of Asia.

During the past ten years, Hsi Lai Temple has evolved into an international and multifaceted center of cultural exchange. The Buddhist population in America finds sanctuary for its spirit and stability for its body and mind. Temple activities include the monthly dharma functions of the Great Compassion Repentance, the Eight Precepts Retreat, the Amitabha Buddha Seven-day Retreat and many Buddhist lectures. Counseling provided by the monastics assist the immigrants in finding solutions to their daily problems as well as helping them with the emotional and psychological frustrations which arise with the adjustment to a new culture. Sociologically speaking, the temple is where social interaction and social identification occur for many within the Chinese-American population.

Each lunar New Year, devotees of Chinese, (with roots in the mainland, Taiwan, and Hong Kong), Vietnamese, and Cambodian heritage join others of various backgrounds to pay homage to the Buddha. Many individuals drive two or three hours for the occasion. When the temple's two hundred parking spaces are filled, many must park quite a distance from the temple and walk uphill to the main gate. One incredulous bystander jokingly described the spectacle: "One closely behind another, they're like a line of focused, homecoming ants!"

Visitors are welcome to stay and are treated with genuine hospitality. One immigrant was allowed to stay at the guest house until he found a job and settled into his own residence.

To enrich the life of the entire community, the Hsi Lai Cultural Training Center offers classes in floral arrangement, vegetarian cooking, T'aichi, Chinese zither, calligraphy, and Dharma classes. To assist working couples who attend services, a day care center for children is being considered. An ideal weekend pastime for neighboring families is learning a craft or two, making new friends, and enjoying the vegetarian cuisine served at Hsi Lai Temple.

Those traveling from far and near

To serve Westerners who have traveled from far and near seeking the joys of the Dharma, Hsi Lai Temple sponsors Buddhist camps, dharma classes in English and hosts dinner for community residents. The temple also provides English interpretation for all regular Dharma functions. Western devotees accounted for approximately twenty percent of the three hundred people who annually participate in the traditional Refuge Ceremony that marks the official recognition of oneself as a Buddhist. Temple participation continues to increase with the most recent record showing twenty thousand temple members. The distrust and hostility expressed over a decade ago have been replaced with congeniality and enthusiasm. On average, eighteen thousand visitors from educational, religious and professional groups visit the temple each year. Seventy-five percent of the visitors are from the United States and the remaining are from Europe and other continents. Comprehensive guided tours in English are provided for groups, or the individual visitor may use a handy headset complete with an instructive tape to guide themselves around the beautiful temple grounds.

Last year, five large and thirty-three small conferences, were held at the temple. Composed of Buddhist, civic and educational groups, all were happy to take advantage of the temple's spacious location and up-to-date facilities. However, not only have others come to the temple to conduct their business, but the temple's role has been extended beyond its walls as well. A California State Council meeting was inaugurated by a Buddhist purification ceremony with Hsing Yun presiding.

Mondays and Thursdays on Channel 53, telecasts of weekly features and updates revolve around the topic, *"Buddha's Light Coming West."* The benefits of increased efforts by individual devotees to translate Buddhist literature into English are having a positive effect within the non-Chinese speaking community as well. A good example of this is Vice-chancellor Wayne Huang of City College, Los Angeles, who has just published an English translation of the *Diamond Sutra* and the *Heart Sutra*.

The five-year-old Hsi Lai University, temporarily accommodated in the temple, is a small and specialized institution of higher learning with distinguished faculty. Attending classes conducted entirely in English, students pursue bachelor's degrees in Buddhism and master's degrees in religious studies. In the words of Vice-president Venerable Tzu Hui: "Many of the most respected schools are one hundred to two hundred years old. It takes at least fifty years for any institution of higher learning to even begin to establish itself. The growth of a respected university takes a long time, so Hsi Lai University has a long, long way to go. But I have every confidence it will succeed."

French cyclist Bénédict Storme, originally intending to spend ten years traveling around the world, stopped at the mountain gate mid-way in her travels two years ago and continues to remain. Although raised as a Catholic Christian, she has taken both the Five Precepts and Bodhisattva Precepts at Hsi Lai Temple and studies at its university. "I used to be so frightened of the unknown future," she says, recounting the impact of Buddhism on her. "Twice I saw my own life imperiled. But I'm a Buddhist now and no longer fearful. I know that the Buddha resides in my heart, not [just] in the temple."

Karl Uth, a Buddhist of German descent, is preparing to publish German translations of the master's writings in his home country. He has spent countless hours of work to complete them. Not satisfied to stop there, he has also begun planning an early retirement so that he can devote all his energy to the development of his new faith. Also, Uth is presently in the process of donating a scenic family property in Germany as the site of a new temple. With construction slated to be completed in three years, it will serve as a base for the spread of Buddhism in Germany.

A global network

Like the master, Hsi Lai Temple has never failed to keep its word to the surrounding community. Aware that loud chanting may offend other neighbors, it is always done in a quiet and serene manner. Temple grounds are kept immaculate and pleasing to the eye to the many who pass by the temple as visitors and friends. Donations of funds and books are made to local schools on an ongoing basis. An example of Hsi Lai Temple's sincere concern for the well being of the community was demonstrated by the swift organization and allocation of funds to those in need after the most recent disastrous earthquake in Los Angeles. Conference facilities and services are free to educational and cultural organizations. Real estate prices in Hacienda Heights remain stable despite the general economic slump. The Chinese community knows that "it's safe to be around Fo Guang Shan."

The small step that Hsi Lai Temple has taken is one gigantic advancement in the evolving history of Buddhism. Following Hsi Lai's example, other Fo Guang branches have spread throughout the world, including twelve in Asia and thirteen in the United States and Canada. Others have sprung up as well in London, Berlin, Paris, and Switzerland. The International Buddhist Progress Society (I.B.P.S.) has also been established in Queensland, Australia and North Island and South Island in New Zealand. Brazil and Paraguay are the newest branch organizations in South America. Venerable Hui Li, the first Buddhist monastic in the history of Buddhism to spread the Dharma in South Africa, is currently planning construction of I.B.P.S. in South Africa. Last September Hsing Yun conducted the historic ordination of ten African Buddhist monastics in South Africa, many of whom hold doctorates and other academic credentials. For Chinese Buddhism, this was the epochal spreading of the light to the vast African continent.

Hsing Yun, with much humility, attributes the rapid spread of Buddhism to several facilitating causes. First, government policies in Taiwan since the mid-1970s have relaxed, resulting in the emigration of very well educated and affluent individuals. Second, from Hong Kong, where concern over uncertainties after 1997 intensified, there has been increased immigration to the British Commonwealth countries. Third, the influx of refugees from Indo-China countries has continued. Being of Chinese ancestry and of the Buddhist faith, they have helped to support the cause. Buddhism has been able to survive and grow.

Dreamer and doer

Both a dreamer and doer, Hsing Yun acknowledges the long and winding road ahead of him. Historically in America, Buddhism did not reach beyond the devotees of Asian descent until 1893 when the Parliament of the World's Religions met in Chicago. In Europe, the first Buddhist organization, Buddhist Preaching Society of Germany, was not formed until 1903 in Leipzig, Germany. Buddhism, which was first introduced in China from India, required more than 400 years of adaptation and harmonization within Chinese thought and culture before evolving into the "Chinese" version of Buddhism. Likewise, it might take hundreds of years before Buddhism will become established and influential in other countries. Therefore, the training of those who are to be instrumental in helping to introduce the Buddhist faith throughout the world will be essential.

In light of this, there are already many monastics pursuing higher education abroad. Venerable Yi Fa is expected to be the first bhiksuni with a doctorate from Yale University and Venerable Hui Kai is a Ph.D. candidate in religion from Temple University. Six years of teaching the Dharma in America has convinced Venerable Hui Kai that to open others' minds to the Buddhist teachings, one must first take into account their background, culture, customs, habits, and circumstances. Therefore, he has actively explored all aspects of Western culture, including religion, philosophy, sociology, and their interrelations. He has also studied other religions such as Christianity and Hinduism.

Knowing his master's goals, Venerable Hui Kai resides in a predominantly non-Chinese suburban neighborhood, befriends Christian ministers, and speaks often at neighboring institutions. He closely follows the daily news in order to gain a picture of the American mentality pertinent to the economy, education, family values, gun control, drugs, and other issues. In the process, he reflects on what the Dharma can do to help alleviate problems in America.

Sharon Silver, an ardent admirer of the Chinese culture and an elementary school teacher, visited Fo Guang Shan more than ten years ago. Each year she invites her good friend, Venerable Hui Kai, to speak to her class about the meaning of Buddhism. At the conclusion of the class, students are invited to participate in a simple meditation exercise. Mrs. Silver is always astounded to see her students, who usually cannot settle down for longer than a minute, sitting quite still during the entire exercise. In order to enrich the learning experience, the students have learned the proper way to greet their teacher and even to thank him using the Chinese language. Last year, their welcoming song for Venerable Hui Kai touched him deeply as it was *Fo Guang Buddhists in the Four Seas* – sung in Chinese, of course!

Integration of Buddhism and western culture

Ch'an meditation is therapy for both the body and the mind. Meditation is becoming more and more popular in the West. However, when compared to Tibetan and Thai Buddhism and Japanese Zen, Chinese Buddhism in the West has been a late development. One can only wonder what Buddhism will be like 500 years from now and which school will be the major source of influence at that time.

The Dalai Lama also addressed the same question following the completion of Hsi Lai Temple, "Interest in Buddhism in recent years has led to the construction of Buddhist places of worship in the West. We must be aware that, like the integration of Tibetan Buddhism and Tibetan culture or that of Chinese Buddhism and Chinese culture, Western Buddhism must integrate with Western culture. Integration of Buddhism with the existing culture facilitates societal acceptance and practice. As long as the fundamental doctrine remains intact, integration is only beneficial to and supportive of the normal development of Buddhism. While we practice, we should learn to respect other religions. This is especially vital for those of us who are new in our faith. Let us remember that personal inner cultivation and progress are far more important than any of the outer, more superficial trappings of religion."

Three decades of international efforts

Hsing Yun began dissolving international boundaries much earlier than would have been expected. He was only thirty at the time. In an article for *Awakening the World*, he wrote of his plans to lecture internationally and proposed training for English-speaking teachers of the Dharma. During the next two decades he traveled to India, Thailand, Malaysia, Singapore, the Philippines, Hong Kong, and Japan, laying the groundwork for the worldwide spread of Buddhism. On one occasion, in a refuge ceremony in Malaysia, offerings by devotees took three hours to complete. Another time, 3,000 people jammed the 2,000-seat Dewan Tunku Abdul Rahman to hear him speak. Those unable to find a seat were disappointed and frustrated at missing the event. "What happened this evening," stated Penang's chief minister Tan Sri Dr. Koh Tsu Koon at the opening speech, "reaffirms my resolution to put up an indoor stadium with a 10,000 − seat capacity. When Master Hsing Yun teaches in this city again, no one will be kept out."

Buddhist devotees in Islamic Indonesia, vowing to remain vegetarian for three months, ultimately influenced the government to lift the ban on the public teaching of Buddhism. Consequently, Hsing Yun was able to speak to a historic gathering of over 1,000 Buddhist devotees.

Last year in San Francisco, the master's lecture on the *Heart Sutra*, with simultaneous translation by Venerable Hui Qun, amazed his American audience. Journalist Lu K'eng observed: "In developing humanistic Buddhism, founding *Buddha's' Light International Association*, and organizing international events, you're the master of social movement. What we have failed to notice is that you are also a wonderful Buddhist scholar."

The spread of Buddhism has united Buddhists worldwide. It is also a form of religious diplomacy with disciples and devotees of various branch temples acting as informal diplomats. Fo Guang Shan's branch temples even surpass the number of Taiwan's foreign consulates worldwide. The language experts of Fo Guang Shan include over 100 of those conversant in English, over 60 in Japanese, over 40 in Cantonese, and others in German, French, Spanish, Portuguese, Tibetan, Thai, and Malaysian. "I'm afraid that Fo Guang Shan's pool of foreign language experts," Chiang Hsiao-wu, former consul to Japan, once lamented, "is more diversified than ours."

Fo Guang Shan also influences the overseas Chinese communities. In Paris, most residents of Chinese descent are concentrated in the 13th district. Incredibly busy running their restaurants, it is difficult to organize Dharma functions where all members can be present. Yet when Master Hsing Yun conducted a refuge ceremony there, over 2,000 members of the Chinese community were present.

Bodhi seeds from the East

Two thousand years ago, the Buddha spent four decades in propagating Buddhism across the five regions of India. Today, Hsing Yun, with the same spirit as the Buddha, has continued to spread Bodhi seeds from the East to the rest of the world. He truly is able to "let the Buddha's light shine through the great chiliocosm[1] of three kinds of thousands of chiliocosms, and to let the Dharma water flow across all five continents."

---

[1] A great number of universe.

Chapter 17
Buddha's Light International Association

*W*hat separates a human from a Buddha?
Buddha is a sanskrit word for the enlightened one.

It was well over 2,500 years ago that Sakyamuni Buddha attained enlightenment while meditating seated on the diamond throne beneath a Bodhi tree and gazing into the star-lit skies. He awoke to the innate goodness of all living beings, which is simply hidden or obscured by the five desires[1] and three poisons[2]. During the next forty-five years, the Buddha taught the Dharma in an effort to bring the deluded back to their true nature. Buddhism was then introduced to China, Japan, and Korea in the north, and Sri Lanka, Thailand, and others in the south.

Presently, Hsing Yun, expending a lifetime to uphold the Buddha's teachings and to transform humanistic Buddhism into a reality, has come to realize that the sangha alone cannot revitalize Buddhism. Buddhism's growth can be enhanced through the efforts of both the sangha and lay community. This empowering of the lay community became his goal after stepping down from the abbotship of Fo Guang Shan.

---

[1] Wealth, sex, fame, food and drink, and sleep.
[2] Greed, anger, and igrorance.

Correct knowledge and correct view

A Fo Guang Buddhist can be a member of the sangha, a student, a teacher, a staff member, a devotee, or anyone sharing a good affinity with Fo Guang Shan. Hsing Yun had the vision in the early 1970s that Fo Guang Shan would not simply be the birth of another school. It stands for a consensus, a set of principles, correct knowledge, correct view and the qualitative conditions of being a Buddhist.

The next decade saw Taiwan experience unprecedented economic growth, diversification in society, and universality in education. At the same time, Buddhism, after decades of cultivation and effort, was finally coming into its own. For the first time, the Buddhist lay community was composed of business, political and academic leaders.

However, there is a lack of unification in the now enthusiastic Buddhist community, as observed by Buddhist scholar, Cheng Chen-huang. There are a limited number of monasteries and monastics and there is not one leader or institution to organize the lay devotees. Hsing Yun agrees and believes that efforts to spread the benefits of the Dharma must be sustained by the vast number of devotees.

As the community of Fo Guang Buddhists expanded over three decades, the branch temples continued to be the center of Buddhist practice and refinement. The temples functioned in their role of social education in conjunction with public institutions, emphasizing that religion and life are interwoven at all times. Eventually, democratic policy was introduced in Taiwan by President Chiang Ching-kuo. The causes and conditions were perfect for the continuation of the spirit and principle of Fo Guang Shan. There was an end to martial law and permission was given for public organizations.

Alliance of the sangha and devotees

Buddha's Light International Association (B.L.I.A.), R.O.C. was formed on February 3rd, 1991 in Taipei. It was another pioneering feat in the history of Buddhism.

How would the organization be assimilated into Buddhism and society at large? In essence, B.L.I.A. is a manifestation of Hsing Yun's long-standing concern for the continuation of social involvement and his worry for a society lacking in order, values and faith. He is optimistic that with the sangha and the lay community joining forces, people will be assisted in their study of the Buddhist Canon and upholding the Five Precepts. As a result, society will be able to achieve a state of purity and serenity.

Hsing Yun was specific about his goals for B.L.I.A., R.O.C.:

"People used to think that Buddhism was mainly for monastics, not for lay people. The coming of B.L.I.A., R.O.C. marked the transition of Buddhism for the sangha only to Buddhism for everyone. Buddhism will no longer be isolated from the world. B.L.I.A., R.O.C. shall re-energize Buddhism for its altruistic function.

In the past, people believed that there were Buddhists only in Taiwan. However, due to the establishment of B.L.I.A., R.O.C. it is now possible to spread Buddhist teachings to every corner of the world. In the past, although a lay person may have developed a very deep understanding and practice of Buddhism, they were still viewed as spiritually inferior to any monastic. Only by becoming a monastic could they assume the status of a teacher. The coming of B.L.I.A., R.O.C. enables qualified devotees to join the sangha and teach the Dharma to assist others in their spiritual growth and contribute to the happiness and prosperity of society and the nation."

That is, B.L.I.A., R.O.C. has encouraged the direction of the development of Buddhism to proceed from:
- the sangha to the lay community
- the monastery to society
- self-cultivation to altruism
- a stationary state to an active state
- the status of disciple to that of teacher
- Taiwan to the rest of the world

Those who understand Buddhism know how much vision and courage are required to promote such ideals. In the traditional Buddhist circle, monastics are thought of as superior and lay people inferior. B.L.I.A., R.O.C. emphasized the inclusion of lay people in "shouldering the family task of the Tathagata." This could have easily been misinterpreted as the decline of monastic sovereignty. However, Hsing Yun is not inclined to submit to the pressure of convention or promote class distinction. Hsing Yun believes that those who have renounced their homes and those who practice from home, the monastic and lay people, should share equal importance and join hands in bringing Buddhism into a new flowering.

The mushrooming effect

Built on the solidity of Fo Guang Shan, B.L.I.A., R.O.C.

began with a membership of over three thousand from branches under the four district associations in the North, Central, South, and East of Taiwan. In addition, there are lateral branches such as Tainan's Buddha's Light subchapter for teachers, Tathagata subchapter established within the immigration department, and Pao-kuang (Precious Light) subchapter organized by finance and business professionals.

The whole mushrooming effect has been phenomenal. Hsing Yun once sanctioned the establishment of fifteen subchapters in one single day. Membership is categorized into individual, group, and preliminary. There are also fami- ly and associate memberships. The list of benefits is extensive; Buddhist studies, career and general counseling, social activities, consultation for weddings, funerals, etc. Wherever B.L.I.A. is, the familiarity of the golden vest embroidered with the nine-petal lotus trademark invariably induces kindred warmth.

The inauguration of Buddha's Light International Association World Headquarters a year later, May 16th, 1992, at Hsi Lai Temple, Los Angeles, was a prompt response to devotees overseas regarding the growth of Fo Guang Shan. It also illustrated the strength of B.L.I.A. as an international organization.

The impact

Four thousand members representing fifty-one districts from thirty countries on five continents were present for the opening ceremony of Buddha's Light International Association. Many international dignitaries also attended. This was a milestone for the further development of Buddhism into the next century. During the inauguration ceremony of B.L.I.A.; Sir Clarence Seignoret, President of the Commonwealth of Dominica, Dr. March Fong Eu, Secretary of the State of California, Mr. Jung-chi Chung, Chairperson of the Social Workers' Association, and Venerable Sharma Rinpoche of Tibet came to celebrate this auspicious event. To commemorate the occasion, Monterey Park mayor Samuel Kiang expressly proclaimed May 16th, 1992, the city's Buddha's Light Day.

The festive gala was a historic union for the Buddhist sangha and devotees. Participants came from countries and regions such as China, Japan, Korea, India, and Tibet. The various schools within Buddhism were also represented, such as the northern and southern schools and the Sutric and Tantric. Nishihara Yuichi, president of B.L.I.A., Tokyo, was elated to have become friends with 4,000 fellow Buddhist in a single day.

Prior to the opening, Los Angeles erupted with riots in the inner-city due to severe racial unrest. The turmoil shocked the world and intimidated visitors. It was against such a backdrop that Hsing Yun scheduled the auspicious event. He rallied Buddhists from all countries and races in "joy and harmony," in true openness and mutual acceptance. Hsing Yun's attitude exemplifies the peace and tolerance of the Buddhist doctrine.

At the end of 1994, the international organization of B.L.I.A., founded by the Chinese Buddhists consisted of one head association[3], seventy-nine chapters[4], and seventeen pre-

---

[3] A country with more than 4 chapters is eligible for the establishment of a head association.

liminary chapters.

The omnipresent Fo Guang Buddhists

B.L.I.A.'s golden vest worn with various skin colors is living proof of the prevalence of Fo Guang Buddhists everywhere. The B.L.I.A.'s five-color, striped flag, symbolizes the ultimate transcendence "across ten directions and throughout three times."[5] It now flies in 51 countries and regions on all five continents. These include Canada and the United States; Central and South America; the Commonwealth of Dominica, Brazil, Paraguay, Argentina, and Costa Rica; France (Paris), England (London), Switzerland (Zurich), Germany (Berlin), Russia (St. Petersburg), and Holland; South Africa; Australia and New Zealand; Taiwan, Japan, Hong Kong, Macao, Malaysia, the Philippines, Indonesia, Thailand, Singapore, Sri Lanka, Sikkim, and India.

Why has B.L.I.A. spread so rapidly? Legislator P'an Wei-kang, a member of the board of directors of B.L.I.A., R.O.C. and a veteran of board meetings, marvels at the open sharing and delightful harmony that typify the association's meetings. Vice-president Chang Nai-pin of the Los Angeles chapter, founder of a social service hotline in Taiwan, speaks for the Chinese community in America. He says, "The presence of B.L.I.A. calms the anxiety of living overseas, uncovers the infinite treasure of our mind, and links together the hearts of every Chinese person around the globe."

Hsing Yun, known for his organizational capabilities,

---

[4] A chapter has 10 subchapters, and a subchapter has 100 members or more.
[5] The ten directions are north, south, east, west, NE, SE, NW, SW. Above and Below. The three times referring to the past, present, and future.

has devised for B.L.I.A. an ingenious developmental strategy that serves a dual function. First, influential public figures are invited to chair the local chapters and help recruit local members. Second, both regular and special functions are designed to encourage individual participation. For example, to assist the members of the Chinese community in Germany, most of whom are in the restaurant business and do not have the time to socialize, Venerable Man Che of I.B.P.S., Berlin, has established a form of a non-alcoholic happy hour. It is held from midnight to two in the morning each Tuesday. Participants are able to forget the discomforts of kitchen grease and the noise of the workplace for a friendly chat, a Dharma class, or a philosophical exchange. President Ting Cheng-kuo, of the Berlin chapter, was among the many thankful attendees of these gatherings. After completing the refuge ceremony with Master Hsing Yun in Paris, the over 2,000 participants immediately became B.L.I.A. members as well.

Awash in the Dharma rain together

Membership is approaching one million, and more and more Buddhists of other races and origins are joining B.L.I.A.

For example, Fred Webb, one of three vice-president of the Los Angeles chapter, has been diligent in his service and devout in his faith for the past two years.

Approximately thirty English-speaking members who make up the Hsi Lai subchapter hold group discussions on Fridays at the home of B.L.I.A. President, Al Duffy. They also attend the English Dharma program each Sunday. Duffy, who is of Scottish descent, has received the Five Precepts and is proud to be Buddhist. He volunteers at Hsi Lai Temple, and greets all he meets by lowering his head, joining his palms, and with his American accent, saying: "Ni hao, O-mi-t'o Fo[6]!" His visit to Fo Guang Shan made such a strong impression that he is planning to become a Hsi Lai Temple resident in two years. The 30-year veteran in marketing is preparing himself for more active participation in spreading the Dharma among the English-speaking community.

Not just another religious body, Buddha's Light International Association is also a cultural bridge leading from Taiwan to the rest of the world. For example, when the second annual convention was held in Taipei's Lin-kou Stadium, 30,000 representatives from around the world assembled. President of the Republic of China, Li Teng-hui addressed the audience. The international visitors were invited on an excursion to see the present Taiwan. This was another outstanding public-relations event.

Hsing Yun hopes that eventually there will be 100 more national head associations and the entire world shall bask in the Buddha's Light and all humankind will be freshened by the Dharma rain.

Integration and coexistence

The theme of the second annual convention emphasized the richness of B.L.I.A.'s universal message of integration and coexistence. Its theme originated from the ancient Buddhist goal of cultivating universal kindness and common sympathy.

---

[6] "Hello! May Amitabha Buddha bless you!"

Hsing Yun's elaboration was this: "When I came to Taiwan four decades ago, I was called a monk from the Mainland; after four decades, I'm still called a monk from the Mainland. Then, when I returned to the mainland after an absence of four decades, I was only to be called the master from Taiwan! After years of traveling in America, Europe, and Australia, however, I don't see the bridge of my nose rising or my eyes turning blue; nor has anybody called me American or Australian. I can't help asking where I belong.

It is all self-interest and intolerance, I've come to realize, that brew conflicts among nations and bias between races. So long as the planet Earth doesn't desert me, I'll just be an earthling. After all, we are all members of the same human family. So let's treat male and female, old and young as one; let's treat rich and poor, noble and ignoble as one; let's treat all cultures and races as one. Buddhists should not limit their helping activities to other Buddhists alone; Chinese should no limit their aid and assistance to other Chinese alone. Let's all share the same existence on earth."

The concept of integration and coexistence gives hope and security for those who live in this turbulent age. At the opening of the Paris Chapter, President Chiang Chi-ming of the third subchapter tried to articulate the inner struggle he experienced as a multi-cultural Chinese person. "I'm Chinese-Cambodian, but I fled to France when the communists took over my country. However, China wouldn't acknowledge me as Chinese. Back home, Cambodia would not acknowledge me as Cambodian. Now that I live in France, the French will no acknowledge me as French either. For the longest time I was pained and disheartened. That is, until what the master said struck me. I finally got it! I need to grieve no more. From this day on, I'm simply going to be an open-minded, compassionate, joyful, and generous earthling."

Affinities of beauty

Its tolerance and selflessness enable B.L.I.A. to extent its influence as far as Moscow in the upper north to the mountain city of Ladakh, India, 15,000 feet above sea-level. Venerable Sanghasena, president of Ladakh's Buddhist Association, recounts what it feels like to be part of B.L.I.A.: "In the long eight years I have served in Ladakh, my reputation, my influence, and my efforts had no way of reaching beyond Ladakh. Now, as Vice-president of B.L.I.A. Ladakh chapter, I am able to make contact with Buddhists the world over, letting Buddhists everywhere know of our country and our needs."

In addition to providing devotees with everything ranging from a spiritual haven to study and discussion groups, lectures and cultural trips, meditation classes and visits, the association opens windows in their lives. Feng Te-jung, who works in the department of economy and has just taken over the presidency of the Pao-kuang subchapter from his wife, Kuo Li-fen, is equally animated. He states that "from the home base of Taiwan, I can bond and walk with the rest of the world. How global networking maximizes the space and scope of life for me!"

Behind B.L.I.A.'s charitable undertaking is an all embracing theme: All living beings belong together. The various branches in the United States responded immediately in providing emergency relief for the recent disasters, such as the flood in the mid-west and the fire in Los Angeles. The winter before last, the Los Angeles chapter donated 300 relief packages of everyday necessities to the homeless. They were given shelter by the First African Methodist Episcopal Church in south central Los Angeles. The sight of the humble, tired men as they received warmth and help from the Chinese Buddhists so moved the thankful Reverend Murray of the church that he called it "a flight across the gigantic racial and religious gap, and the transformation of love into a beautiful affinity."

Such potency of resolve

As Hsing Yun handed over the abbotship of Fo Guang Shan to ride the crest of yet another set of causes and conditions, he was swept to an even more commanding state. Indeed, those that give to others receive the rewards[7].

Watching him travel from place to place and establishing one B.L.I.A. branch after another, one has to wonder how he has survived. Hsing Yun has had to adapt, maximizing his use of time and bearing the unbearable. A flight from New York to Sao Paulo, Brazil took 26 hours instead of the scheduled 11 due to engine problems. Another time, almost everyone in his party became ill with acute mountain sickness due to Ladakh's high altitude. In Ladakh, the temperature ranges from thirty-seven degrees Celsius (ninety-seven degrees Fahrenheit) in summer to subzero degrees in

---

[7] *She-te* in the original text. The two characters are usually put together to mean willing to give. They are also separated here to illustrate the process of giving which often results in getting.

winter. The annual rainfall averages ninety-two millimeters (3.6 inches). While others rested, Hsing Yun continued to conduct ceremonies and visit with guests despite a splitting headache, swollen cheeks, and shortness of breath.

Hsing Yun's fortitude propelled the three-year-old B.L.I.A., R.O.C. into being recognized as one of the most outstanding organizations in Taiwan for two consecutive years. In 1994, B.L.I.A. placed first out of almost 2,000 candidates. Additionally, it is the world's fourth largest private organization. Notably B.L.I.A. is in the process of applying for non-political group membership in the United Nations, even though the government in Taiwan has not yet been accepted. B.L.I.A. may break the diplomatic deadlock.

Of wheels, of wings

The big brother of the Buddhist circle, the Chinese Buddhist Association, is slowly being replaced by B.L.I.A. It has been speculated that B.L.I.A. is Hsing Yun's declaration of independence after years under the Chinese Buddhist Asso- ciation and possibly even a challenge. He has never for- mally responded to this idea except to say that "the founding of B.L.I.A. is to the Chinese Buddhist Association like the implementation of a courier service to the freeway system, both of which are good."

In reality, the two *are* different. The Chinese Buddhist Association primarily consists of monastics, while B.L.I.A. primarily consists of lay devotees. Many are members of social and intellectual circles with a much higher and more progressive attitude toward their faith than traditional Buddhists. Hsing Yun ensures that devotees play the lead role with monastics lending support and guidance to the devotees.

Hsing Yun views Humanistic Buddhism as the map for worldwide living Buddhism where monastic-run temples collaborate with the devotee-run B.L.I.A. For a strong foundation, the sangha is the cement and the devotees are the sand and stones. For progress to be made, the two must work together like wheels on a cart and the wings of a bird.

A century ago, British colonists sailed the four seas and, through military conquest, built an empire where "the sun would never set – its flag rising wherever the sun rises." A century later, a Chinese monk emulating the compassion, wisdom, vows, and practice of the four great Bodhisattvas[8] sowed seeds of the Dharma throughout the world. With peace and tolerance, he founded Buddha's Light International Association and, thereby, let the Buddha's Light shine and Dharma water flow wherever the sun rises.

---

[8] Avalokitesvara, Manjusri, Ksitigarbha, and Samantabhadra. Other lists exist.

Chapter 18
Holding space in an embrace

Religion is one aspect of human civilization that is constantly evolving along with the always changing cultural and social structures. For example, Christianity evolved into both Catholic and Protestant schools. The Western church has many branches, sometimes formed after bloody conflict. History records innumerable battles between warring religious factions, leaving deep scars which affect people groups, even to this very day. Seemingly, religion has not yet developed a cure for the prejudice and selfishness of humankind. Living beings have yet to learn compassion and tolerance on a grand scale.

Many doors to cultivation
How exactly did Buddhism, as a religion, evolve?
Over 2,500 years ago, Sakyamuni Buddha taught various methods of cultivation in accordance with the diverse natural capacities of all living beings. Following his death, disciples interpreted his teachings based upon their own understanding, and later disciples compiled a written record of his teachings. Generations of eminent masters have studies these works and formulated their own interpretations, resulting in various Buddhist schools.
The wandering masters took the Dharma south to Cam-

bodia, Burma, Thailand, and Sri Lanka, and north to China, Japan, Korea, and Vietnam, developing Theravada Buddhism and Mahayana Buddhism respectively. In the process, the Buddhist faith interacted with the cultural and social conditions present at the time. Additional subdivisions were established, as evidenced in Japan, which has over fifty schools.

Buddhism in China was introduced during the reign of Emperor Ming of the Eastern Han dynasty [58 – 75 C.E.]. It intermingled and harmonized with the existing religions, Confucianism and Taoism, and ultimately blossomed into eight primary schools, each with its own school habits, practice and emphasis – as presented in the following verse:

> *Tantric for the rich,*
> *Ch'an for the poor,*
> *Pureland for the convenience of all,*
> *Yogacara for the patient,*
> *San-lun[1] for emptiness,*
> *Hua-yen for orthodoxy,*
> *Vinaya for cultivation,*
> *and Tien-t'ai for structure of doctrine.*

The T'ien-tai school emphasizes teaching and its organization. The Hua-yen, Yogacara, and San-lun schools emphasize textual study. The Vinaya, Ch'an, Tantric, and Pureland schools emphasize practice. The Tantric school is also known as Tibetan Buddhism due to its prevalence there. The Tantric cultivation requires the guidance of masters.

---

[1] *Chia-hsiang* in the original text, who founded the San-lun school during the reign of emperor An of the Eastern Chin dynasty (397-419 C.E.).

Devotees make a practice of generous offerings to the masters, which only the more affluent can sustain. The Ch'an practitioners, with their straw sandals and chipped alms-bowls, aspire to enlightenment by way of simplicity, frugality, and freedom from desires. Regardless of intellect, gender, or location, those who chant the Buddha's name with utmost dedication shall attain rebirth in the Pureland, hence the method of convenience.

Unlike other religions, each of the Buddhist schools was established through independent, spontaneous growth rather than through struggle and conflict. In China, all eight Buddhist schools took center stage to further enhance the cultural pageantry of the Sui and T'ang dynasties. More than once,[2] fickle imperial favoritism ignited persecution of the sangha, yet the harmony and respect between Buddhism and other religions, or among the Buddhist schools themselves, has never been tarnished.

One master, one way

Throughout history, some of the eight schools of Mahayana Buddhism faded while others emerged more vibrantly than ever. The evolution of Buddhism as an integral force in world history was delayed when the southern, northern, and Tibetan divisions drifted apart due to geographical and cultural factors, and barriers were established. Visionaries

---

[2] Textual mention of the four most catastrophic cases in Chinese history in which enraged monarchs ordered the annihilation of texts, images, and the sangha, or monastics were forced to renounce their vows. The incidents took place, namely, in the 7th year (446) of the reign of emperor T'ai-wu of Northern Wei; the 2nd year (573) of the reign of emperor Wu of Northern Chou; the 5th year (845) of the reign of emperor Wu-tzung of T'ang; and the 2nd year (955) of the reign of emperor Shih-Tzung of Later Chou.

across the years requested the unification of teaching of all eight schools to establish harmony between the Sutric and Tantric[3], and the dual practice of Ch'an and Pureland. Hsing Yun made these dreams a reality.

Hsing Yun's believes that there is only one master, Sakyamuni Buddha, and only one direction for us to go. All beings should be mutually caring and supportive, nondiscriminating and collaborative. Modern Buddhism must be able to rely on the stability of this kind of outlook in order to foster its own growth and development.

Efforts during the past ten years have led to healing within the Buddhist circle. A feat worthy of celebration was the friendship between Hsing Yun and the Dalai Lama.

Tibet has been cautious regarding relations with Taiwan due to political and cultural differences; thus explaining why the exiled Dalai Lama has never visited the island of Taiwan. However, the construction of Hsi Lai Temple changed everything. This temple in the West played a key role in the developing relationship between the Tibetan sangha and devotees and the emerging Buddhism populace in Taiwan. In July, 1989, the Dalai Lama and his entourage visited Hsing Yun at Hsi Lai Temple, chatting for over three hours. Their chat was followed by a speech by the Dalai Lama.

The following day, on the Dalai Lama's 55th birthday, Hsing Yun and approximately 1,000 guests attended festivities. The Dalai Lama requested that Hsing Yun be seated with him during dinner so they could continue their dis-

---

[3] The two fold categorization of Buddhism according to practice. The Sutric division or *Hsien-tzung*, comprises seven of the eight schools except the Tantric school or *Mi-tzung*, which stands in its own division.

cussion. Many attending noted the historic nature of the encounter and were encouraged by the atmosphere of the entire event.

In five days the two eminent masters convened four times and established a specific agenda: 1) scholarships at Hsi Lai University for the Tibetan sangha, and 2) student exchange between Buddhist colleges in India, Tibet and Taiwan. As an immediate result, Venerable Yi Hua is currently studying at International University, India[4].

The Tantric and Sutric joining forces

The meeting was no coincidence. It was the product of years of painstaking cultivation and the sowing of good seeds for the alliance of both Sutric and Tantric.

Early in 1985, Hsing Yun initiated the Chinese-Tibetan Cultural Association of the Republic of China. Subsequently, a joint Dharma function of the two traditions for the preservation of the nation was held in Taipei. This was the cornerstone of the collaboration. Approximately ten thousand Chinese and Tibetan devotees were present.

The next year, Fo Guang Shan hosted the World Sutric and Tantric Buddhist Conference to discuss harmony in relationship to the evolution of global cultures. Three hundred participants from 19 countries and regions attended, including lamas and scholars from Nepal and India.

"Modern Buddhism is no longer regional or divisional," Hsing Yun stated. He offered a slate of concerns which included the following: "Buddhist development should be a

---

[4] Venerable Yi Hua obtained her master degree from India's university, and is now the Dean of the Buddhist College at Fo Guang Shan.

harmonization between Mahayana and Theravada, between the lineage of both North and South, between the sangha and the lay community, of all four orders[5], and between orthodoxy and modernity. However, most crucial is the harmony between the Sutric and Tantric traditions."

The sad state of affairs in Tibetan Buddhism was clearly communicated when the head of the Tibetan Saskya school spoke: "Buddhism, which has been vital to the life of Tibet, has been devastated by the communists. So I am especially elated to see it back on its feet in Taiwan."

The historic meeting between Hsing Yun and the Dalai Lama set the stage for further advancement. During the following years tantric monastics were ordained at Hsi Lai Temple and many furthered their studies at Fo Guang Shan. Lamas and rinpoches also began to spread the Dharma in Taiwan. Hsing Yun's vision of harmony between the Sutric and Tantric was finally beginning to take form.

Mahayana and Theravada under one roof

Sutric or Tantric, Mahayana or Theravada, Hsing Yun wants to see all schools united. The various schools of teachings resemble flowers with different hues and shades, which, when gathered together, form a delightful bouquet. "After all," he asserts, "there is but one Sakyamuni Buddha!" Hsing Yun's book of travels, *Traces of Wandering in the Seas and Skies*, indicates that he also visited the Thai monarch and head monastic in 1961. His visit has been reciprocated many times by visiting Buddhist dignitaries from that country.

---

[5] Bhiksus (monks), bhiksunis (nuns), upasakas (male devotees), and upasikas (female devotees).

Hsing Yun has become aware that not only is the status of female monastics depreciated in Theravada Buddhism, there is also no full ordination for bhiksunis. Consequently, he daringly proposed that the sangha of bhiksunis be restored.

In 1988, a remarkable number of Theravada participants attended the month-long Triple Platform Ordination at Hsi Lai Temple. In the process, the wall of regionalism that has separated the South and North for more than 1,000 years began to crumble. Those invited to pass on the precepts included eminent masters from the Southern and Northern schools. Among the approximately two hundred preceptors were monastics of the Theravada tradition as well as disciples of the Tibetan Tantric schools. Many of them were monastics of high seniority seeking to repeat their vows. Others possessed advanced academic degrees and were devoting themselves to Buddhism.

Mandarin, the Taiwanese dialect, and English were spoken for the precept ceremony, and the preceptors were passed on irrespective of gender or school. So overwhelming was the number of participants, nations, and schools that the success of the event was unprecedented in the history of Buddhism.

At the end of the perceptual period, preceptors learned a great deal from a stimulating exchange among themselves in regard to traditions, concepts, ceremonies, discipline, and doctrine. Many designated this event as the most inclusive and global experience thus far in the history of Buddhism.

Last spring, Hsing Yun visited Thailand's Dhammakaya Foundation, a sister temple, for the casting ceremony of its golden Buddha. He was driven through streets strewn with flowers and lined with 100,000 persons there to greet him. This was an unprecedented honor for a Mahayana monastic in a Theravada country. White Pagoda Temple in Los Angeles, which was the forerunner of Hsi Lai Temple, has been turned over to the Dhammakaya International Society of California to serve as the base of Thai Buddhism in America.

Others closely associated with Fo Guang Shan include Todai Temple in Nara, Japan, the Japanese Buddhist pilgrimage group, the Nichiren school, and the Ts'ao-tung school. Venerable Jung Woo of Tong-do Sa (Temple), Korea, heads the Asian liaison committee of B.L.I.A.

Dual practice of Ch'an and Pureland

For the harmony of both the Sutric and Tantric schools, the inclusion of the Mahayana and Theravada, and the collaboration of all eight schools, Hsing Yun's resolution has never faltered. He even chooses to view in a positive light the criticism of sectarianism from Taiwan's Buddhist circle. He states that it is an indication of prosperity and a sign of versatility. "Like the four legendary mountains in China coexisting over time," he says, "It is from the school of Sakyamuni Buddha that all Buddhists invariably descend."

Despite the similar dominance of Ch'an and Pureland in Taiwan, Hsing Yun, being the 48th patriarch of the Lin-chi school of Ch'an, will not be confined to a certain school. In creating the first chanting sessions in Ilan, he also boosted the Pureland method of aspiring for rebirth in the Land of Ultimate Bliss by calling on Amitabha Buddha's name. Hsing Yun is also given credit for the resurgence of popularity in the practice of meditation. Meditation instruction is now a regular feature in all branch temples of Fo Guang Shan. The Fo Guang Shan's new meditation hall is the largest and best equipped in Taiwan and is already most renowned for its vigorous discipline. The Taipei temple's meditation hall close to the Sung Shan train station serves the busy city folks as a convenient location for practice.

Revering the masters, motivating the newcomers

Hsing Yun is cordial and courteous to all the venerables and masters in Taiwan. Master Ching Kung was invited to the Buddhist College to speak on the study of Yogacara and Master Liao Chung spoke on the *Sandhi-nirmocana Sutra*. Master Tung Ch'u discussed the monastic system. Master Yin Shun, together with Nan-Huai, was invited to teach Dharma and conduct seven-day meditation retreats respectively.

Universal Gate magazine, headquartered at Fo Guang Shan, reports monthly on temples all over Taiwan and serves as a clearing house for communication throughout the Buddhist community.

Hsing Yun is very supportive of the generation of monastics which has succeeded him, and has encouraged the formation of the Chinese Buddhist Youth Association and the founding of Venerable Cheng Yen's Ching-ssu Vihara. Each time he lectures in Hualien where Ching-ssu Vihara is located, he opens by saying: "What a wonderful place Hualien is! The landscape is so lovely, and the air so fresh. Above all, Hualien is where the Buddhist Compassion Relief Tzu Chi Foundation[6] is!"

---

[6] One of the most acclaimed Buddhist charitable organizations in Taiwan. Its founder is Reverend Cheng Yen.

His advice for young monastics is to break the stubborn habit of previous generations in not fostering communication among themselves. He urges dialogue and teamwork regardless of differing opinions. The common goal is to bring Buddhism to new heights. Over time, many of the younger generation come to rally around these sentiments, showing their support by joining Hsing Yun on his lecture tours.

The beauty of religious harmony

What does it mean to hold space in one embrace and measure worlds as numerous as the sands of the Ganges?

Hsing Yun upholds harmony both within and without Buddhism. He once described the human quest for the true, the good, and the beautiful as a journey to a common destination. The yearning being the same, it is only the ways that differ. Whether we choose to bike, drive, ride, fly, or sail to get there, different religions actually are heading towards the same end.

Once in the early years, approximately eighty Dominican priests and nuns traveled to Fo Guang Shan with the purpose of learning the Dharma. More recently a Bishop from the Vatican also visited. Hsing Yun and Archbishop Lo Kuang once held a stimulating exchange on religion, philosophy, life, and faith. The two masters, both compassionate and wise, agreed that religions must be tolerant of one another. There will always be differences amidst similarities and similarities to be found amidst differences. In their mutual concern for the welfare of all and the elevation of human minds, the respect and affirmation they had for each other was beautiful to behold.

Later, at the request of the archbishop, Hsing Yun spoke on the wondrous use of Ch'an at Fu Jen Catholic University.

Sharing concern for their chaotic society, a gathering was hosted by *Global View Monthly*. Hsing Yun joined Archbishop Lo Kuang, Protestant minister Reverend Chou Lien-hua, and vice secretary-general Chang Ch'eng-ch'i of the Taoist Association in an in-depth discussion on the reconstruction of social values as prevention against social disintegration.

Following the completion of the Taipei Temple in February, 1994, a forty-nine day lecture series was offered to the public. The series, entitled *The Running Water of Life*, featured such animated speakers from various religions as Father Ting-sung-yun of the Catholic Institute of Kuang-ch'i She and Shih Yung-kuei, a Muslim. The event itself, as well as the lectures offered, was a wonderful display of the beauty of religious harmony.

On another occasion, Chung Jung-chi invited many religious leaders including Muslims, Protestants, and Catholics. Hsing Yun hosted the event with a discussion on Ch'an over a vegetarian meal.

Last year, he donated the royalties from his writing to six needy organizations. They were the Taipei Relief Foundation for Women, Sunshine Foundation, Hsin-lu Cultural Foundation, Christian Ch'en-hsi Society, Yi-kuang Society for Volunteers, and Shan-mu Society for Catholic Nuns. Like the showering of mandara flowers on all living beings, his own all-inclusive showering is rooted in his understanding that: "To give is not just about asking society to give alms to Buddhism. We as Buddhists must give alms, too!"

Tolerance for folk religions

What about the numerous folk religions in the world?

Hsing Yun could not have phrased it better when he commented: "Correct belief surpasses superstitious belief, superstitious belief surpasses non-belief; and non-belief surpasses *evil belief*."

Beliefs, like learning, are widely varied in depth and sophistication. As long as they are committed to doing good, Hsing Yun believes that they should all be valued.

"I remember back home in Yangchou," he recounts, "there wasn't a police station within ten miles or a courthouse within one hundred. So what could be done when people got into a dispute?

What happened was that the parties concerned would pray at the temples of the earth gods and all would eventually be solved. The townsfolk were unwavering believers of the law of causality and harbored a perfect willingness to try their cases before the deities."

Hsing Yun, although viewed as an orthodox Buddhist, has never ventured to set himself apart from others. Quite the contrary, he remains affirmative about the positive effects which deities such as Ma-chu and the earth gods have given the common folk. He takes a stance of tolerance and respect toward folk religions. However, he does not tolerate the charlatans whose practice does nothing but jeopardize social well-being under the pretense of supernatural powers. They belong to what Hsing Yun describes as *evil belief*, because of the way they dupe well-meaning but naïve people into parting with hard earned money for the supposed benefits of association with supernatural powers.

Buddhism is not a superstition; nor is Hsing Yun superstitious. Many, speculating on the sophistication of his personal practice, bombard him with questions about divination, physiognomy,[7] and geomancy.[8] They are also curious about the supernatural powers he may or may not possess. These are his least favorite topics. Instructions in the *Sutra of the Buddha's Exhortation Left After His Passing* instruct the Buddhist practitioner not to engage in divination and not to practice astrology. These are not in accord with the Buddhist understanding of causes and conditions, correct livelihood, nor the rules and principles. One of Hsing Yun's favorite sayings is: "When joy is in the heart, every day is a good day and every place a good place."

Ahead of his time

History has been riddled with human strife and conflict, and all the world's wars have yet to awaken the innate goodness in us. As the end of another century looms, wails of carnage and destruction have not ceased. This, most certainly, is a time when Hsing Yun's example can serve as a light leading us out of the darkness. The visionary and gallant Hsing Yun has expended half a lifetime patching and repairing Buddhism, bonding with other religions, tapping social resources, and creating a diversified and all encompassing religious mode. Ahead of his time, Hsing Yun sheds a light on peaceful coexistence among human beings and does so in a superlative style.

---

[7] The art of determining character from the form or features of the body.
[8] Divination by geographic features or by figures or lines.

Part Six

Returning on Wings of His Vows

Celebrating his 60th birthday at Fo Guang Shan 1987

Always with a smile and tender loving heart for the young

reeted by BLIA members from all over the globe at a General Conference

With Australian dignitaries at the inauguration of Nan Tien Temple, Australia

Awarded the Top Honor Medal by the Ministry of Interior Affairs, R.O.C.

At the ground-breaking ceremony for Fo Guang University, 1993

Presenting the Fo Guang Buddhist Canon to Professor Lancaster of the University of California, Berkeley

The master with devotees of Fo Guang Shan

Chapter 19
Heart of a child

Once somebody asked the master, "What is the reality of life?"

"Life," he replied, "is half in the Buddha's world and half in the samsaric world; it is half advancing and half retreating."

At the end of close to seventy winters and summers, he is able to "be free in accordance with the heart, settled in accordance with the environment, acting in accordance with joy [for others], and living in accordance with conditions", because he has mastered this *half-and-half* principle.

Living in the spiritual and material worlds

Considered by many to be enlightened above and beyond the three realms,[1] Master Hsing Yun has chosen to remain engaged within the context of everyday activities. To those who don't know him personally, he is as enigmatic as he is approachable. Understandably, many are eager to catch a glimpse of his personal life and private feelings. Those who know him concur that he has always been the master of his own heart; in his own independent way, he has managed to balance spiritual and material concerns.

---

[1] The Three Realms are Formless, Form and Desire.

Inexperienced as he was in his early days as a monastic, he naturally missed his mother, siblings and home. However, having entered the monkhood, the austere discipline and his master's expectations kept him away from his family much more than he might have initially desired. Through this difficult experience, Hsing Yun learned to cope with his personal emotions with the help of religious practice. Later, on the eve of his flight from the mainland, he chose to bid farewell and reveal his plans of spreading the Dharma in Taiwan to his master rather than to his mother. His family had not the slightest inkling of where he had chosen to locate himself during the next four decades.

In Taiwan, the pursuit of establishing schools and housing for the sangha and sacrificing for the Dharma in myriad ways left little time for his individual needs. However, thoughts of his loved ones would often invade the stillness of the night. Now, ever since reconnecting with them a few years ago, he has taken upon himself the responsibility to care for them – 100 or more relatives in all – as though he were repaying some mountainous debt of forty years. He was willing to bend in any way possible to bring pleasure to his mother, who was stunned when she eventually met the thousand or so monastics inhabiting Fo Guang Shan.

"Do they all answer to you?" She asked him.

"Yes," he replied, "but I answer to you alone!"

He made every effort to be with her on her birthday the past two years. Back in Yu-hua (Rain-soaked Blossom) Vihara, Nanjing, the master was but the son of a local family once again. He would carefully cool her porridge before allowing his mother to eat it, or sit by her bedside and encourage her to reminisce with him. A master of international repute then became the humblest of listeners.

Caught up as people sometimes are in the stress and strife of everyday life, at times we find out too late that we have failed to appreciate the people and opportunities in our lives. A tree, about to fall down, finds the wind unceasing as ever; a child, prepared to repay his parents, discovers they are nowhere to be found. While he treasures every chance to fulfill his duty to his mother, Hsing Yun is filled with regret for his earlier lack of appreciation for his teacher, Master Chih K'ai. It took him years to fully comprehend the proound caring and concern beneath the stern façade of the master, who was killed in the Cultural Revolution. On his homecoming five years ago, a stricken Hsing Yun broke down completely at the graveside of Master Chih K'ai; on subsequent visits, he makes it a point to go and chant a sutra there.

Repay a drop of water with an overflowing spring

For Hsing Yun to be tenderly and gratefully mindful of his biological mother and ancestral master is thoroughly consistent with his character, just as he bears in mind anyone who has helped or supported him. To all who have aided him, he is sure to repay every single drop received with an overflowing spring.

It was a time of extreme turmoil when he graduated from Chiao-shan Buddhist College and became principal at White Pagoda Primary School in 1947. To evade the bandits, guerrillas, and soldiers, he was compelled to go into hiding with his teaching staff for days. A loyal worker at the school would bring them food daily despite the extreme perils.

Never has Hsing Yun forgotten him. On his first homecoming in 1989, he made a point of reestablishing contact with this worker. Eventually, Hsing Yun located the man's family and, braving a heavy downpour, visited them, bearing gifts and good will. "Even though the man [who had helped us] is no longer with us," he told his disciples later, "his son is, and I'm no less grateful. That's why I have every reason to go on taking care of his offspring."

Another person to whom he shall forever be thankful is Sun-Chang Ch'ing-yang. From the time he came alone to Taiwan, to the founding of Fo Guang Shan, Mrs. Sun treated Hsing Yun as one of her own and protected the Dharma with all her might. During her last days, Hsing Yun took time out to be with her whenever he could. When he could not, he would ensure that his disciples would take his place. Upon her death, he conducted her funeral and undertook efforts to execute her will with utter meticulousness. Chang Fo-ch'ien, a writer, described the memorial service presided over by Hsing Yun for Mrs. Sun as the most impressive and solemn he had ever seen.

This tender care is extended to his teachers as well. As an expression of his gratitude, he had Masters Yuan Chan, Hsueh Fan, Ho Ch'en, and Hui Chuang flown to America. When Master Sheng P'u fell ill last year, Hsing Yun made sure that his Chinese language teacher be amply provided for and properly treated.

Although tradition has it that monastics are to see everything as empty and act like withered wood, this is not quite Hsing Yun's way. When it is time to be warm and tender, his warmth and tenderness surpass most.

More than a few embarrassing moments

Many wonder about the private world of his inner feelings. Those who have known Hsing Yun since the early days, and those who have chanced upon photographs taken in his youth, usually comment on the young monk's handsome and distinguished looks: his tall stature and his piercing eyes, his stately bearing and his eloquence. Obviously esteemed as very attractive, the question arises as to whether or not he has ever been attracted to others in a way unbecoming to a monk. Some are also curious as to whether others have sought his presence as more than simply a Dharma lecturer.

A seasoned master today, Hsing Yun has no qualms about telling how, when he was a twenty-something monasterial director at Ta-chueh Temple, overly doting parents were seized by the wishful thought of adopting him with the happiness of their daughters in mind. Often they would try to dissuade him from pursuing the monastic life. More than a few young women devotees were seen to frequent the two temples, Lei-yin and Shou-shan, out of a special regard for the attractive young monk rather than for the Buddha.

Su Hsiu-ch'in, a longtime follower in Kaohsiung, recalls how she and others used to share the purest admiration for the attractiveness of the master's Dharma appearance. Unlike some others, they were able to appreciate the master for his spiritual contributions, drawing the line between feelings for the Dharma and feelings of love. Still, from time to time, the media would publish what they deemed to be clues to the secret life of a master monastic. These days, these reports no longer bother him nearly as mush as they used to, and he dismisses them all as sheer unfounded gossip.

One of the more drastic cases of unsolicited attention was that of a woman in her seventies who was obsessed with what she considered an ongoing relationship with the master through seven lifetimes. One day, she dropped by Fo Guang Shan, and as usual, demanded to see the master. This time, however, her two handsome young sons accompanied her. While on the grounds of the temple, the trio ran into the master, who was giving visitors a tour of the premises. The next instant, the woman ordered the young men to get down on their knees, claiming: "This is your father! Bow to him right now!" The young men, visibly embarrassed, had to comply. They returned later to apologize for their mother's obsession. While Hsing Yun remained totally unfazed by the episode, it is anyone's guess what the members of his tour group thought.

An equally obsessive high school teacher used to approach the podium with copies of books midway through Hsing Yun's lectures. When asked about her intent, her reply was a cryptic: "I want to pluck that cloud from the sky"[2]. Once she caught Hsing Yun totally by surprise as he was waiting for an elevator. Emerging from nowhere, she deftly reached over and adjusted the master's collar for him, leaving the others present totally flabbergasted. Unable to do anything about the bizarre incident, Hsing Yun simply proceeded into the elevator.

Still another time, one of Fo Guang Shan's most ardent supporters suddenly announced her dissociation for the most ludicrous of reasons: the master was supposedly taking a fifth concubine, or so she had heard. It turned out that the insti-

---

[2] A pun on the master's name, which translates into "stars and clouds" in English.

gator of the vicious rumor was a former teacher at the nursery school who had been dismissed for her misconduct. The master had not even the slightest inkling of who she was.

Faithful for half a century
Throughout half a century since his tonsure, Hsing Yun has abided by the monastic precepts, and his conscience is clear in the face of temptation and distortion of any form. To Buddhism he has been faithful, never allowing any personal affections to distract him from the task at hand. He has been true to his commitment of sharing his love with all sentient beings. Deep within is a boundless world of sentiment, and his love is not for one, but for all. "Both monastics and lay people have a sense of love. But the monastic is committed to a more boundless and sublime expression of love. This love is for the benefit of all beings, not simply a partner or family members," he explains.

Hsing Yun's faithfulness extends to all people. "All elders under heaven are my folks," he says. "All children are my own, and all people are my family." He wisely resists individual attachment while rendering his devotion to everyone, saying, "Unlimited love becomes compassion, while asking for no return is true wisdom."

Many seek to repay his kindness with demonstrations of love and respect. Not satisfied with just a birthday party, devotees from every corner of Taiwan came to Fo Guang Shan on the master's sixty-eighth birthday in 1993 and gave him a three-evening gala salute.

Love for all creatures

He loves all creatures large and small. Pigeons have been his favorite companions since he was young, and for years they would stop by and feed on his windowsill at Fo Guang Shan. Whenever he had to go away, he would hand over his tending chores to another so that the birds were cared for consistently.

Hsiao-chun, a stray puppy who took shelter at the Buddhist College, displayed the Buddha nature by attending every lecture with amazing concentration. Hsiao-chun, as a young puppy, would always rise on the approach of Hsing Yun but started to slow down visibly as he advanced in years. One day, Hsing Yun was speaking with students in the corridor when he spotted Hsiao-chun struggling to get up. Out of consideration for the aging dog, the master simply slipped into an office, allowing Hsiao-chun to save his energy without having to inconvenience him any further.

Lai-fa, another puppy, was barely a month old when he was taken to Fo Guang Shan. His home for the next six or seven years would be Hsing Yun's door. There he stood guard whether the master was entertaining or out lecturing. Then, one day, Lai-fa was missing. Hsing Yun missed him a bit. A few months later, someone brought along another puppy which strangely enough, resembled Lai-fa in color, disposition, and even movement. Everyone called it Lai-fa, Jr. Hsing Yun cared for Junior the same way he did Senior until the second Lai-fa died of old age. A chanting service was held in his memory.

Keeping it simple

Visitors at Fo Guang Shan marvel at how a temple can be so magnificent, so modern, and contemporary all at the same time. The aesthetic appeal of the temple is meant to be enjoyed by everyone. It is an extension of goodwill and, most of all, a reflection of the *advancing* aspect of Hsing Yun's life. Yet watching him conduct himself daily, one also becomes aware of the existence of a *retreating* aspect.

In contrast to the splendor of the temple grounds, the master has different views regarding clothing. He lives by the maxim: "Simplicity is basic for a monastic." The master alternates between a couple of robes all year round, adding thermal wear or a knit sweater underneath when the temperature plunges. A curious, small, centipede pattern on his left shoe turns out to be a tear which he neatly sewed himself. In fact, both shoes are quite battered in the sole, their linen padding showing through. When asked why they are not replaced, he quips, "They've been like this for a while. I guess they can't get any worse, can they?"

The manner in which he eats is sometimes astonishing. He will run into a room holding a bowl of steaming plain noodles, cool it before the air-conditioner, devour it, and dash off again to his next commitment. Hsing Yun has rushed through decades in this way, and it can be said that he has mastered the art of eating on the run. Dining with him is both a pleasure and a pressure. While acting as host, he keeps helping his guests to sumptuous amounts of food, yet he himself merely touches a couple of the dishes closest to him. He never replenishes his bowl by taking from more than one dish, and he completes his meal quickly.

A little-known fact is that Hsing Yun takes after his father, who was skilled in vegetarian cooking. In the long list of Hsing Yun's culinary creations, peanut tofu, tomato noodles, imperial bean noodles, and arhat soup are among Fo Guang Shan's most requested dishes; all the cooking staff are required to know how to prepare them. Whenever the temple was swamped with visitors in the early days, Hsing Yun could be seen in his apron helping out with the fried noodles. He has not done much of that lately, but last year in Hong Kong, I was thrilled to have feasted on a heavenly dish he made for everyone: twisted fritters and tender pea shoots. Our plates were emptied in no time.

His favorite food is a simple dish of plain noodles sprinkled with soy sauce and sesame oil, or rice soaked in water and served with fermented bean curd from Ilan. As he travels from one place to another, his tastes have become quite eclectic; he is perfectly at home with anything from Japanese or Korean pickled vegetables to American bread. The only things that he excludes from his diet are fruit, health tonics, and vitamins.

His home is everywhere

"Even heaven and earth feel small when the heart is bound, but a bed feels spacious when the heart is free," Hsing Yun says. As spacious as Fo Guang Shan is, for years his quarters consisted of only a cubicle in the corridor of Chuanteng Chamber, until he moved into the Founder's Quarters, which Venerable Hsin Ping built in his honor two years ago.

Without a permanent home, the roving monk is equally comfortable aboard a trans-Pacific jet as he is in a car on the freeway, and he is certainly at ease in both. However, what really bothers him is extravagance. Once on a lecture tour, the Korean master who was the host reserved for him the presidential suite in a five-star hotel. Hsing Yun did no more than sit in one of the chairs; pulling up a corner of the bedding, he curled up for the night. Totally unaccustomed to luxury, he could not bear to spoil the impeccable setting. Like many who have seen the worst of times, Hsing Yun learned to be frugal the hard way, and fame has not changed that. There is an anecdote that his disciples love to tell to illustrate his thriftiness. Each time the master is abroad preaching, he has at hand a sizeable amount of ready cash to help those he meets along the way who may be in need of financial help. At the same time, whenever the master uses paper napkins on a plane, in restaurants, or in washrooms, he folds each piece neatly and keeps in his pocket after one use, conscious of the fact that it can be used again. Once, upon his return, an attendant helping him unpack his bags found seventy or more paper napkins stashed in his pocket. "The master left home with U.S. dollars," the attendant declared, quite amused, "and returned with napkins!"

Vimalakirti[3] once said: "With the Dharma joy, I no longer relish worldly joys." Hsing Yun, too, rarely buys for himself, and the last time he did so, he had to borrow money from Venerable Tzu Hui. While in transit in Japan, he borrowed the money to purchase a wristwatch with large numerals because his eyesight is failing.

---

[3] A wealthy householder who represents the Mahayana lay believer, as described in the Vimalakirti Sutra. Vimalakirti advocated the non-dual nature of Ultimate Reality.

A disciple was moved beyond words one day when she saw the master pull out forty dollars in bills with utmost caution and hand it over to someone, saying: "Respect it, and there will be more!" Willing to relinquish all things, he views the five desires and six defilements as illusions; willing to receive all things, he views incalculable, beginningless time and all living beings within it as his wealth. His enlightened perception of the ebb and flow of the universe makes him magnanimous and open, able to give and receive.

Hard on himself, easy on others

Hsing Yun has always demanded much of himself but not of others. Conscientiously, he sees to it that offerings from devotees are channeled directly to the temple to facilitate a multitude of projects. "I don't know whether it's a positive or negative aspect of my character," he remarks, "but I am not able to keep any money. I tend to look for every chance to part with it." With his stipend, for instance, he loves bringing everyone a little something each time he comes home from a trip. These small souvenirs, coupled with his care and appreciation, are his way of expressing his gratitude and connection with all who work alongside him.

His heaviest *investment*, as such, is in the young. Fo Guang Shan finances all the disciples currently studying abroad. Moreover, Hsing Yun visits them whenever he can and leaves them extra funds from his own pocket.

The summer before last, he met Venerable Chi Ch'un and Hsiu Yung from Hsiamen Buddhist College in Hong Kong, and they had a cordial exchange. Hsing Yun gave them a handsome collection of texts, including the *Fo Guang*

Encyclopedia and *Hsing Yun's Lecture Series*, and urged them to return home to work hard for Buddhism on the mainland. Parting, they prostrated to thank him. Hsing Yun hastened to help them up and handed over a gift envelope of financial support, which he had just received from a devotee some ten minutes before. The pair left with tears in their eyes. Monetary matters may be mundane, but, when given from a sincere heart, money can become an important means of benefiting all beings in the universe.

Indeed, as a monastic, Hsing Yun lives a simple and frugal life. "I've never held the key to my room," he notes, "nor are any of my letters ever hidden, or my whereabouts unknown."

The world is as large as the heart that can hold it

Truly, the world is as large as the heart that can hold it. In the same way, how much we can achieve depends on how much we can tolerate. Hsing Yun's ability to create the most expansive Buddhist body worldwide hinges on the broadness of his mind, which has enabled him to break through monastic conformity.

Author Lin Ch'ing-hsuan and director Liu Wei-pin were filming a documentary on location at Fo Guang Shan years ago when Liu was suddenly smitten with the idea of shooting from the top of the offering table before the Buddha, normally off limits for such things. Pleased with Liu's innovative spirit, Hsing Yun's approval was just as prompt. Liu also recalls his wonder and glee in watching the sangha engaged in a game of basketball at Fo Guang Shan – led by the master himself!

Hsing Yun once said that what holds the most indelible place in his heart is not the majestic structures of Fo Guang Shan but the basketball court in Tung Shan. Sports enthusiast that he is, he almost faced expulsion when he resorted to building his own hoop because the Buddhist College curriculum then did not include physical education. Since that time he yearned for a basketball court, especially when he came to have his own temple. He used to have the time of his life playing in the evenings with the disciples, the only detraction being the occasional interruption which would force him to quit half way and hurry off to greet visitors – still sweating from the game.

An advocate for basketball among the sangha, he hopes that more exercise will foster better health for all of the monastics. Hsing Yun, in typically teacherly fashion, outlines the benefits of playing basketball as a means of personal development that fosters fairness, justice, openness, personal progress, valiance, and speed. It encourages group spirit, collaboration, and glory for all. The sport engenders honesty, humility, obedience, and kindness. Furthermore, it develops love for the opponents, without whom there could not be a game in the first place.

On the basketball court, between master and disciples, the Dharma – not just the ball – is passed on, and bonding – not just competition – occurs. Although his doctor has banned him from the sport after fracturing his leg, he still shoots his three-pointers, though from a wheelchair. For twenty-seven years, those at Fo Guang Shan have all turned out to play in the annual basketball tournament celebrating the master's birthday!

Heart of a child

Those close to him often describe him as a personable and fun-loving character. Author Yao Cho-ch'i spent a month with Hsing Yun on his homecoming in 1989. Yao remembers how the master bought a panda hand puppet at the entrance to the Ming tombs in Beijing and became very dexterous, handling it with three fingers. He would hide it in his sleeve and pull it out to greet whoever passed by, winning laughs and hearts.

A good number of those traveling with him at the time were lay devotees for whom the abrupt switch to a totally vegetarian diet was somewhat taxing, especially in view of the delicious meat dishes included in the cuisine. Finally in Xian, seven of them could no longer refrain and, at the direction of the local guide, were about to sneak out for a feast of mutton when they bumped right into the master.

"Why," he laughed, "going somewhere for a bite?"

Sheepishly, the troupe confided their plan to the master.

"Watch out," he cautioned. "It's probably safer to have the chef at the hotel prepare it for you."

The next day, a full-course non-vegetarian meal was laid out before them – including mutton. Everyone had a pretty good idea where it all came from. Another time, at the close of the B.L.I.A. executive meeting in Japan, he amused himself – and others – holding his cane at his chest as though it were a rifle and saluting everyone at the hotel entrance.

The sweet smell of joy

To be a monastic of exceptional caliber in an age of

professionalism must be trying. But exceptional is exactly what Hsing Yun is, and what he has achieved is professionalism. His meticulousness makes him an infallible host who makes sure that all lights are on and the roads are clear before a tour commences, seats are in order, air-conditioning functioning, and tea ample before a meeting begins, all so that guests will feel at home.

After three years alongside Hsing Yun on the television program *Hsing Yun's Dharma Words*, producer Ch'en T'ai has only this to say: "He is top-notch!" Ch'en recalls the mas- ter having no misgivings whatsoever about going to great lengths for a perfect shot. Once, after three or four hours un- der seven 5,000-volt spotlights, the master remained as com- posed and smiling as ever. His disciples, though, were ready to cry, "Enough! The master is going to be roasted!"

Although nearing age seventy, Hsing Yun is nonetheless young at heart and receptive, an impeccable role model to disciples and followers. In the way he walks, opens the door, or pulls a drawer, he causes no disturbance. He takes care of his own chores: shaving his own head, laundering his own clothes, and cleaning up after himself at each bath – even in hotels. As the saying goes: "Even the power that moves the water of one thousand rivers cannot disturb the heart of the practitioner."

Demonstrating mindfulness and humility, the master teaches by example. He is most attentive to thoughts of the young and the needs of disciples and followers, and rarely negates them. Never chastising, his words for anyone acting out of line are: "If I were in your place, I might try another approach – it may bring better results." Hsing Yun's manner of dealing with people embodies the maxim, "Criticism should not be too harsh, for it must be acceptable; instructions should not be too demanding – they must be feasible."

Unlike the stereotypical graying monk lost in meditation, Hsing Yun heartily supports having fun. "Joy," he often tells those who are downcast, "is the indoor sunshine." He refuses to be persuaded that anything is unsolvable. Coming up with the perfect analogy, the master adds, "Joy is like perfume. When we spray it on others generously, we're sure to catch a few drops ourselves."

A wise person said, "When one rule is understood, all else shall be clear." Striving to build good rapport with all beings, over time Hsing Yun has developed a certain fluidity and sophistication in his interactions with others. "Failing in work is acceptable," he often says, "but not in getting along with others." Only when time, space, and human relationships are pursued to perfection can all be happy.

A self-made bibliophile

Hsing Yun's credentials, though informal, stem from a lifetime of self-directed study. Text after text has gone from his side and desk to the various collections of Fo Guang Shan's many cultural departments and libraries. He relishes the few pages he reads before bedtime no matter how long the day has been. His reading selections include the biographies of the eminent Buddhist masters, the classics, martial arts fiction, science fiction, journals, and newspapers.

He frequently gives books as gifts to disciples and friends, and he speaks often of reading as a source of happiness. It must not result in defilement but joy, he says, and must accord with one's nature and inclinations. The force of learning, not paper qualifications, should underlie true professionalism, he believes. Most of all, the truly learned person should be a thorough reader of the texts of life and humanity.

Many are curious as to how a monk reared in such seclusion actually has such a good understanding of everyday problems and affairs. His listening skills are the reason for this. Visitors, friends, devotees, and disciples he heeds with patience and humility, and he learns a great deal from them. He once compared himself to a sponge soaking up information and retaining it, or a computer storing select views and ideas and turning them into his own.

Writing for the benefit of all beings

T'ang poet Tu Fu once said: "One who reads thousands of texts composes with utmost spontaneity and eloquence." Hsing Yun is one of the most prolific authors among the monastics in Taiwan. He took years to train himself. He will never forget the lean years in which, lacking pen and paper to jot down his thoughts, he could only keep them close to his heart. He used to compose mental drafts while at meals or in line for the shrine and still does the same while on the road. Perhaps that is one reason for the spontaneity and compactness of his writing.

Understandably, Hsing Yun's style is easy and popular. He does not hesitate to pick up colloquial phrases and incorporate them into his writing. Critiqued as "seasoned and essential, simple and lasting," his format is lively and his language unpretentious, but his intent is profound. His own favorite author is Kumarajiva, a brilliant translator of some of the most popular sutras. Hsing Yun's principle in writing is that it should be simply understandable, readily accepted, and easily incorporated into life:

A living treasure-trove

Followers have long realized that the master is a living treasure-trove. A recent discovery is his calligraphy. In his spare time – if any – he renders Dharma sayings in brush and ink. He gives these to devotees in appreciation of their dedication. He is humble about his own ancestral background, which was nowhere near an academic one, and about his lack of practice, which he says has consisted of no more than writing up posters and couplets for lecture halls. That he is able to make gifts of his calligraphy is, first and foremost, a surprise to him.

Hsing Yun has dedication of character, forgetting both the world and the self, and treating oneself and others as one. This quality permeates his calligraphy, which has become increasingly sought among collectors. Some of these now fetch hundreds and thousands of dollars, as in the recent fundraising art auctions for Fo Guang University. At the same time he does not think twice about rendering a piece expressly for a twelve-year-old who only pledged NT$100 (US$3.30).

Living is joy; dying is not necessarily grief

Despite basking in the Dharma for half a century, Hsing Yun, like all others, is merely sojourning in a physical body, which is subject to the changes of birth, aging, infirmity, and death. Long principled in creating joy for others, he rarely mentions his health concerns. However, the fact is that diabetes is affecting his vision and memory somewhat, and even his skin is showing the effects of the disease. Disciples and followers often ask him to slow down, and some have offered herbal medications and other remedies. Li Wu-yen, a follower of thirty years and a radiologist, has pleaded on his knees many times for the master to go for his medical checkup.

"There is only one human," he answers with characteristic lightness, "one life, and one heart."

Others have not been as casual about the master's increasing age and the condition of Hsing Yun's health. "The position can be replaced, but not the person or the prestige," they say. Understandably, many speculate about the future of Fo Guang Shan after the master passes away. To that, his answer is ready. "I have no fear of death," he says, "for death is a matter of course. This is not to say that we as Buddhists won't die. No, it's just that, in the face of death, we know that it is not the end but the beginning of another existence."

"I often use the analogy of death as moving to a new residence or changing into a new garment. Life and death, death and life, are really two in one, one in two. Living is certainly joy; dying is not necessarily grief."

"Do not worry about Fo Guang Shan when I'm gone. Hasn't it fared well since I left the abbotship? It's been established to be in accordance with the Dharma and it is systemized under healthy leadership. This is pure, harmonious, and joyful sangha. There's no need to draw any connection between the fate of Fo Guang Shan and mine," he assures his followers.

Free to follow conditions

Irrespective of others' admiration, concerns or doubts, Hsing Yun's self-evaluation is this: lifting the weighty as though it were light; following the conditions of freedom through one's life. Ch'an master Chih Hsien of Hsiangyen (Fragrant Rock) gave verse to the same sentiment: "Devoid of marks and traces anywhere, splendor rules beyond sights and sounds." Thus, Hsing Yun wrote in his diary:

> *I embrace the vow of compassion to deliver all beings,*
> *I float like an untied boat in the Dharma sea.*
> *Ask me what merits have I over a lifetime,*
> *they are the Buddha's Light across the land.*

Indeed that is how he views his whole existence. Simply put, everyone is the architect of her or his own fate. A Buddhist who has undertaken to revive his own faith and who lives out his life, marches on, never turning back. While leading a sincere and pious life, Master Hsing Yun is an ordinary monk who is quite an extraordinary leader.

Chapter 20
Devoted to the Buddhist path

*V*iewed in his totality, Hsing Yun is a vigorous monastic who weaves his way in and out between the Buddha gate and the secular world. He possesses a marvelous gift of discernment and easily ranges over the past, present, and future. The master is an erudite man of letters who writes and speaks with the utmost eloquence, a peaceful character of countless affinities who befriends all levels of beings. He is a dynamic manager of international repute who originates and handles enormous corporate planning and financial tasks. Such versatility makes one consider whether he might be one-of-a kind. Critics have even suggested that he has strayed far afield of the traditional monastic concerns.

A scrutiny of his past – his thoughts, sayings, and deeds – reveals a life that has been principled in Buddhahood and little else. Bearing the surname of Shih,[1] the same as the Buddha himself, Hsing Yun is committed to vitalizing Buddhism and, moreover, to aiding the world by means of the Dharma.

As the study of life, the teachings of the Buddha are about the truth of all matters and things within the universe. Methods of interpretation and dissemination may vary to

---

[1] As in Shih-Chia Mo-ni, the Chinese transliteration of Sakyamuni Buddha. Hence, the surname Shih is given to all Chinese monastics.

agree with changing times and circumstances, but the doctrine and spirit are essential and inextricable from their Buddhist ancestry. Hence, in advocating humanistic Buddhism, Hsing Yun aspires to transform traditional Buddhism into a new tool for the resolution of contemporary issues.

The Dharma, environmentally friendly for the mind

The world of the twentieth century seems to be spiraling, both visibly and audibly, into a maelstrom of natural disasters, human hostilities, deceit and corruption. All living beings find themselves struggling to catch their breaths or trying to survive amidst constant fear, uncertainty, and restlessness. Environmental preservation of the physical world is crucial on a planet stricken with problems of waste management, air pollution, sewage, and unrelenting land exploitation. Social concern must address a society afflicted with problems of politics, crime, and family dysfunction; many people seem to be plagued by loneliness, futility, and confusion.

In the particularly engaged style of the Humanistic bodhisattva, Hsing Yun offers a rational and workable approach to solving the problems of living. The master teaches people how to live with family and interact with relatives; how to love spouses and care for friends; how to relate to society; how to handle everyday life; and how to tackle matters of finance, religion, health, medicine, and politics.

Apart from its manifestations in education, culture, and charitable causes, Hsing Yun's humanistic Buddhism also assumes many other forms, including classes taught by qualified speakers from both the sangha and lay community, consultation for those seeking guidance and advice in careers and family, emergency relief and shelter for the aged and disabled.

"Believers are many, but practitioners are few," comments Lian Chen, head of the supervisory council in Taiwan. He is aware that there is a greater enthusiasm for material donations to gather personal merits than in spiritual cultivation for the elevation of the mind and betterment of society. Hsing Yun agrees, and he looks forward to a more deeply rooted understanding of the Dharma, not blind adherence. He hopes to see a much broader adaptation of its values.

Laying the groundwork

Many today proclaim the coming of a new epoch in Buddhism, one of unprecedented influence, esteem, and promise. Upon hearing this, Hsing Yun is both elated and wary. He is astutely aware that, beneath the apparent prosperity of the Buddhist faith, a range of structural issues remains unresolved.

For years Hsing Yun, whose life is pledged to the Triple Gems, has called for a progressively solidified groundwork: the establishment of a modern system; the betterment of the quality of the sangha; the expansion of Buddhist efforts, and the promotion of humanistic Buddhism.

In fact, the absence of a unified system in Buddhism worries him greatly. The state of affairs in Taiwan, in particular, resembles loose sand. On the one hand, the increasingly affluent society has little problem supporting a proportionately growing sangha. On the other, even monastics relatively superficial in spiritual cultivation and knowledge are now able to attract a cadre of devotees, establish their temples, conduct Dharma functions, receive their own disciples, confer precepts, and enjoy their share of financial contributions. Ungoverned by any administrative body, many are susceptible to fraudulent or lawless practices.

This tendency, however, is directly addressed by Fo Guang Shan's comprehensive systemization covering all possible areas: personnel, finance, monasterial administration, preaching, Dharma functions, tonsure, precepts, and many more. A far cry from the traditional feudal monastic hierarchy, the systematic rules and disciplines in Hsing Yun's mind are modern and convenient. They are instrumental in the unification and progress of Buddhism as a whole.

A lame-duck law

The existence of a lame-duck law has kept a unified system from prevailing in the Buddhist circle of Taiwan. The supervisory regulations for monasteries implemented by the Nationalist (Kuomintang) government as far back as 1929 are mandatory only for Buddhism and Taoism. No other religions, even the occult, are subjected to any kind of supervisory agency. Alive and well to this day, the consequences of this law are grave. With the abbot playing second fiddle to the monasterial supervisor, too often either the sangha is overpowered by lay people or the two groups are in constant battle with horns locked. The ambiguity of the existing laws creates confusion over such matters as the legitimate boundaries between purely monastic affairs and those of the laity. No legal stipulations exist concerning the selection of a qualified abbot or monastics. Consequently, the monastics often use the absence of a defined term for abbotship as an excuse to develop an individual monopoly.

Hsing Yun has, on many occasions, made public pleas for fairer, healthier circumstances under which all religions may be enabled to grow. He insists that both the congregation and monastery be integral parts of Buddhism at large, and therefore not dependent on individual followings or private ownership. He also advocates that administrative supervision by lay people be abolished, making way for professional management by the sangha and ending the strife between the two once and for all. He insists that abbots be required to train in orthodox Buddhist colleges and to hold legitimate and professional credentials; and that terms for abbotships be clearly defined to facilitate proper succession.

Pleas for Buddhist education

To elevate the quality of the sangha, Buddhist education is the key. In Taiwan, Fu Jen Catholic University has a full-scale religious studies department and curriculum, and the Protestant Tung Hai University has its own legitimate school chapel. The courses offered by the Buddhist Colleges are not officially recognized by law, therefore Buddhist college graduates do not enjoy the same status as the graduates of other religious universities simply because their opportunity to study certain subjects is curtailed by existing laws. Worse yet, within the very governing body that gives other religious institutions their full endorsement, there still arises the suggestion to abolish the Buddhist Colleges altogether. Even the communist regime of the mainland runs a centralized educational operation that includes religious studies, despite its intrinsic atheism. All Buddhist colleges are funded and directed by the government, and their faculties are salaried like their counterparts in the teachers' colleges. By contrast, in America, all types of theological institutions are allowed to thrive. Likewise, both national and private universities in Japan are known to facilitate well-developed religious studies programs.

Somehow, in Taiwan alone, the Buddhist College seems orphaned within the educational system. After promoting Buddhist education for three decades, Hsing Yun is still fighting for legitimate status for Buddhist education. He is calling for official registration of all Buddhist colleges, the general acceptance of official guidelines from the Taiwanese ministry of education, official recognition of student credentials, and official permission to recruit students publicly.

Hsing Yun's proposals for the promotion of Buddhist education are that:
- the elementary, middle, and university levels should be clearly defined
- eligible teachers are certified by examination and standard qualification procedures
- the curriculum and facilities are standardized
- educational administrators are trained and recognized
- the leadership is centralized
- outstanding graduates are encourage to pursue higher learning
- intercollegiate activities such as lectures and contests are conducted
- student credentials are recognized
- positions such as dharma teachers, abbots, and directors

are assumed by Buddhist college graduates only
- joint examinations are devised for Buddhist student bodies in college-level institutions to enable eligible examinees to serve in the Buddhist circle in the future and
- scholarships, grants, and loans are obtained within the Buddhist circle

History reveals that a nation's power is directly linked to its foresight in education. By the same token, as much as religion is accountable for educating society, how can it purify minds and affect moral trends if the qualifications of its proponents are questionable?

The question of self-sufficiency

Traditionally, as long as monastics carry on their efforts in chanting sutras and conducting Dharma functions, they can make a decent living and the temple will thrive. An old saying describes the monastic mindset as thus: "As clouds of incense gather above me, I can be assured a vegetarian feast awaits me." This adage proves true even today, and it is evident that these attitudes about monastic livelihood have not changed much. Monastics still compete for devotees and solicit donations for the purpose of maintenance of the monastery itself – a sign of material dependence and one of the reasons that Buddhism has yet to command the respect of society.

The agrarian–Ch'an livelihood which Ch'an master Huai Hai of the T'ang dynasty led and advocated was committed to self-sufficiency by way of day-to-day labor and productivity. Master T'ai Hsu, in 1911, went to the extent of urging that factories be set up and run by monastics not only for self-sufficiency but also to benefit society. In the same tradition, Hsing Yun, sharing the same orthodox training as the two Ch'an masters, believes firmly that the Buddhist circle should be as productive and service-oriented as the Catholic and Protestant circles so acclaimed for their medical and educational undertakings. The Buddhist circle in Japan, too, has ventured into the retail and hotel businesses, and society appears to have no objection. The master insists that Taiwan's Buddhist circle cease regarding business enterprises as taboo, and become economically resourceful to better serve society and benefit all living beings.

As for Hsing Yun himself, his business ventures span decades, starting some thirty years ago with his founding of Chih-kuang, a school of commerce, with fellow monastics Wu I and Nan T'ing. From P'u Men High School at Fo Guang Shan eighteen years ago to Hsi Lai University; the newly launched and feverishly pursued project established in 1990 by Fo Guang University, Hsing Yun has occupied himself with a whole range of ongoing enterprises. Add to these Fo Guang television and radio stations, a Buddhist daily, and a mass-communications center, and the master's ongoing vision of the development of Buddhist enterprises becomes quite clear.

Fo Guang University represents Hsing Yun's ultimate dream, which is about to come true. On a sprawling fifty-six square hectare property overlooking the sea in Linmei (Beautiful Woods), Chiaohsi (Rocky Brook), in the county of Ilan, the groundbreaking ceremony was held in October 1993. Initially scheduled to begin with seven departments – Chinese, philosophy, mass communications, business management, foreign languages and literature, fine art, and drama – it began accepting applications for its graduate school in 1995.

Hsing Yun's vision of Fo Guang University is one of breadth and depth and balances academics with applications to daily life. Its first chancellor is Dr. Kung P'eng-ch'eng, a young scholar of Chinese literature.

In the meantime, effective fund-raising through public donations and auctions has amassed a remarkable financial foundation for the institution and demonstrates a mutually supportive connection between Buddhism and society at large. None other puts it better than Hsing Yun himself does: "Who owns Fo Guang University? Certainly not myself or Fo Guang Shan. This is an institution that belongs to society. Indeed, Fo Guang University belongs to everyone!"

Riding the crest of universal wave

More often than not, the master's concerns for the state of affairs around him, when articulated, either annoy a privileged few or simply fall on deaf ears. But Hsing Yun knows too well that the home base, one's own grass roots, is where everything begins.

So this branded liberal in the Buddhist circle has vowed to create a monasterial institution of modern character named Fo Guang Shan, whose system is healthy and viable, and whose operation is organized and efficient. Its Buddhist colleges have to this day generated over 1,000 graduates, all vibrant new blood in the monastic lineage. What is more, in recent years other Buddhist bodies have been seen to pattern themselves upon Fo Guang Shan in the network establishment of educational, medical, charitable, and cultural enterprises.

Hsing Yun is never overly excited or afraid of anything; instead, he holds to the principle of Buddhahood, and Buddhahood only, and rides the universal crest of undertaking. Nevertheless, problems abound, and perfection is yet to be attained. Indeed, the fruit of Buddhahood takes much more than a mere lifetime to mature. Hsing Yun has great faith that the undertaking of Fo Guang Shan shall continue through succeeding generations, and someday soon, Chinese Buddhism will enjoy a shining new lineage.

Chapter 21
No regrets whatsoever

Out of the clear, cool nocturnal blue above southern Taiwan rain gold and silver and loose diamonds – fireworks! Among the shadows of trees and groves, ornate lanterns sway back and forth. Applause and cheering rise and fall... and rise again.

This is the Dharma function of the Lanterns of Peace, featured each lunar New Year at Fo Guang Shan from the first to the fifteenth day of the first moon. Then, on the first day of the second moon – also the anniversary of Hsing Yun's entrance into the monkhood, called renunciation – devotees converge again for the annual general meeting which happens year after year without fail. In that month alone, hundreds of thousands of devotees from all over head toward the Great Welcoming Buddha, the Main Shrine, or, simply, home sweet home.

From the rubble of postwar poverty, Taiwan rose like a phoenix out of the ashes of changing world events. The legend of Hsing Yun was wrought from a similar foundation. But then again, Hsing Yun's is much more than a fabulous tale, for he inherited no lineal prominence and earned no formal credentials; nor was he ever anywhere close to being a child prodigy. Still, as a child, he lost a parent; becoming a novice, he faced infinite chaos; he was a loner, yet he survived.

His odyssey is an inspiration to those of us who seek the extraordinary despite our own ordinariness. He is like a borrowed light for the revelation of our inner nature, as well as for projecting into our future.

Focus, then strive on

"Focus, then strive on to the end" is the motto that summarizes his career and characterizes his life. This determined focus brings him success. Choosing monkhood over home at the tender age of twelve, the child was driven to implore his mother to allow him to leave and enter the sangha. Thereafter, he braved a decade of tribulations in monastic training by the sole realization of what honor meant – to fulfill the initial inspiration of his vows.

Again picking a winding path to Taiwan in 1949, the young monk found himself a total stranger in a strange land, with limited means and no knowledge of the language. He was hungry; he was cold; he was sick; he was jailed; he was wronged; he was battered; he saw many around him succumb to similar circumstances. What kept him going was the pact with Master Chih Yun to fend for their faith in the mainland while carrying the Buddha's light across the strait, and the overall commitment to the renaissance of Chinese Buddhism. This involved four years of learning how to live under someone else's roof, twelve years learning how to lay the groundwork for the future, and many years of learning to build Fo Guang Shan. All the time, when things and people around him changed, the life choice of living his faith did not.

Like the economic progress of Taiwan and the maturation of its social conditions, Hsing Yun's diligence, too, has borne bountiful fruits. His first-generation disciples, torch in hand, have taken their positions in an astounding global network, and the second generation is ready and waiting. The body of Buddhist enterprises known collectively as Fo Guang Shan embraces close to one hundred branch temples worldwide. The branch temples are joined by 180 peripheral establishments such as Buddhist colleges, high schools, kindergartens, nurseries, publishing houses, hospitals, and seniors' homes.

Forever and ever handing down the light

Hsing Yun has been very successful in rearing the young for the Buddhist faith. Whether viewed from the standpoint of modern education or that of orthodox formality, the fact that Fo Guang Shan has produced a total of over 1,100 monastics is a phenomenal record in the history of Buddhism. Hsing Yun believes that the act of handing down the light continues forever and ever.

To make sure that development of all forms be strong and lasting, Hsing Yun harmonizes the orthodox monastery with the modern institution. He has come up with a versatile system that is capable of keeping up with the times in terms of administration, economy, finance, personnel, education, and welfare. According to Hsing Yun's design, all those who head the hundred or so branches abide by the system as the core of a network built upon monastic fellowship. A mighty mechanism, it is fair and open, yet finely tuned and efficiently run.

Thematically, Fo Guang Shan embodies the spirit of

Mahayana Buddhism, which Hsing Yun seeks to manifest in the forms of humanistic Buddhism and realistic Buddhism. Employing modern preaching methods, he seeks to spread such concepts as life preceding death – emphasizing the importance of living mindfully, here and now – and Buddhism as a religion of blessedness. In the meantime, Taiwan's economic boom, social diversity, and educational progress together have formed fertile ground for the growth of humanistic Buddhism. Presently, Fo Guang Shan's devotees number over one million, along with hundreds of thousands worldwide. Overall, Buddhism has become a popular faith among the rich, the famous, the intellectual, as well as the common folk.

While it is true that Fo Guang Shan began with Hsing Yun's creative vision, "the Dharma, not the preacher, is to be relied on," he says, and the system must be adhered to. A decade ago, to make sure that Fo Guang Shan's growth would never cease, the master decided to pass the baton of abbotship on to Venerable Hsin Ping.

Laying down in order to pick up once more

One has to "lay down in order to pick up once more." As if liberated from some cocoon, Hsing Yun went on to preach across the continents and eventually founded Buddha's Light International Association (B.L.I.A.). Destined to be a major player in the future of Buddhism, B.L.I.A.'s 100 or so chapters are already injecting new strength into the dissemination of the Dharma all over the world.

Hsing Yun is frank about his inward journey: "All my life I have deplored, most of all, broken promises. To me, honor is of the essence. Reality is such that, regardless of how many trials and tribulations you have endured, people seem to care only about the result [and not your efforts]. I just set my goal and thereafter refuse to be shaken or to change my mind no matter how bitterly trying it is along the way. The knottiest problems can be solved, just like that. Indeed, one who is determined always has hundreds of thousands of solutions, while one who is undetermined, hundreds of thousands of obstacles." Hsing Yun's philosophy is that, irrespective of our role upon the stage called life, we should always play it as though we were the protagonists.

A thoroughfare to modernity

The *Diamond Sutra* states: "All things going, they resemble dreams and illusions, bubbles and shadow, dew and lightning. That is how things should be viewed." This means that whatever is seen and heard is empty, lacking any substantial, independent reality. On the other hand, for the public to appreciate Master Hsing Yun from an everyday point of view, it makes sense to trace and analyze his career and contributions in the light of history and as a projection into the future.

A lifetime of engagement has aged him markedly. His greatest achievement is that, in bringing orthodox Chinese Buddhism to Taiwan, he has transformed a desert deprived of the Dharma rain into a Pureland blossoming with bodhi growth. Furthermore, he has opened up for Buddhism a thoroughfare to modernity. Under Hsing Yun, the doctrine remains orthodox while the format is contemporary; thinking remains transcendent while undertakings are very practical;

lifestyle remains conservative while preaching is progressive." As more and more people become drawn to Buddhism, some even attribute Buddhism's comeback to Hsing Yun – in Taiwan, if nowhere else.

Second, he has reared generation after generation of talent for the perpetuation of the Dharma lineage. Especially noteworthy is that he has been far ahead of his time – and certainly above his peers – in acknowledging the [equal] giftedness and competence of the bhiksunis, female monastics, and in promoting them to positions [historically beyond their reach]. For the Buddhist convention has it that the bhiksus (male monastics) always come before the bhiksunis. The latter are subjugated to the extent that in Thai, Sri Lankan, and Tibetan Buddhism, no bhiksuni precepts are conferred.

Not so in Taiwan, which has produced a constellation of brilliant bhiksunis, like Venerables Hsiao Yun, Cheng Yen, and many others, together with Hsing Yun's first-generation disciples, Venerables Tzu Chuang, Tzu Hui, Tzu Jung, Tzu Chia, and Tzu I. In fact, Fo Guang Shan's bhiksu and bhiksuni population is a record 3:7 proportion. Added to that is Venerable Tzu Hui's vice-presidency in the World Fellowship of Buddhists under the auspices of Hsing Yun. Traditionally the domain of representatives from the Theravada tradition and closed to women, the tight-knit executive circle has been broken with the addition of Tzu Hui. In the hearty words of Venerable Chao Hui, "He has genuinely attained the equality among all living beings as taught by the Buddha."

Third, Hsing Yun has established an order for the coexistence and mutual respect between the sangha and devotees. Contrary to the traditional view of monastic superiority regardless of personal dedication or practice (which has historically been a factor in the alienation of the two groups), Hsing Yun stresses a Fo Guang Shan free from distinctions of class or status.

"Just as a nation cannot be without people," he says, "a temple cannot be without devotees." In his eyes, nothing invigorates Buddhism more than the joining of forces between the sangha and the lay community. An outstanding group of lay preachers and teachers of the Dharma has been elected in Buddha's Light International Association, which is the consummate affirmation of the role of the lay community in Buddhism.

The master's vision of Buddha's light

Even beyond the realm of religion, Hsing Yun has never stopped giving, directly and indirectly. Taiwan's four million Buddhists are appropriately a major source of stability, and their practice of Buddhism helps to regulate individual behavior amidst the nation's political, economic, and social strife. His own sensitivity to his status as a monastic originally from the mainland helped him to demolish the barrier of regionalism by leading a majority of indigenous devotees in Taiwan. In truth, the breakdown of regionalism is giving Buddhism in Taiwan a fresh outlook.

Overseas, the intricate web of organizations under Fo Guang Shan and Buddha's Light International Association smoothly executes its function in diplomacy. From the chateau in France, to the grassland of Australia, to the desert of South Africa, Hsing Yun and his followers have replaced the centuries–old impression of an isolated nation with a glittering new image of a vibrant people – the Chinese of today.

"Look to the future, and do whatever is closest at hand. Willingly consider the doubtful as well as the probable, and use your energy where it is needed most" – these are the principles of Hsing Yun's undertakings. Some consider his religious leadership a product of Taiwan's social evolvement and see the master himself as a heroic figure made by circumstance. However, even if that proves to be so, Hsing Yun, in dispatching the message of Buddhism across the world, can still be considered a master who has carved out a unique and remarkable vision.

Hsing Yun, the name and its meaning

If slander is a twin to acclaim, now and again Master Hsing Yun finds himself in some whirlpool of controversy. These encounters are helpful in reflecting the kaleidoscope of views that are held concerning Hsing Yun. While some wait in awe on the temple grounds, hoping to catch a glimpse of his elegant figure, others snort at how completely uninspiring those cement Buddha images are. For those whose hearts have been touched in some way, there are tears while they sit listening to the Dharma teachings. Others consider his presence in the national political arena to be totally unsuitable for a monastic. While most devotees donate in earnest to gather merits for themselves and loved ones, others attempt to profit under the shingle of Fo Guang Shan. Even while many pay homage and offer incense, there are others who scrutinize each record book of donations and speculate on how much he must have pocketed.

The ultimate irony is how harsh people tend to be on

the subject of their hero-worship, which they happen to have created themselves. But, is that truly the intent of the hero himself?

"Who am I?" Hsing Yun asks. "Only a regular monk! Only a peasant!"

Criticism and praise to him are as swans across the sky and snow on the ground, for he has always formed his own definition of life.

Once, while he and a group of monastics traveled together, the weather forecast on the radio predicted: "Satellite pictures of the clouds indicate…" At that, Venerable Tzu Jung was struck with a question: "Master, first the grand master named you Chin Chueh. Then you named yourself Hsing Yun. How did your naming actually come about?"[1]

"I remember while learning to use the dictionary in the monastery, I stumbled upon the term *hsing-yun-t'uan* (masses of stars and clouds)," Hsing Yun replied. "I read on and its definition ran like this: 'Huge, ancient, and without bound.' There was a union of countless cloud-like stars before the universe took form. How I admired that state! While I vowed to bring light to those in the dark, I ventured to be always above and beyond care and bondage. So I took the Dharma name *Hsing Yun*."

On his portrait rendered by Li Zijian, Hsing Yun wrote a verse, which is in essence a summary of his life:

---

[1] Wei-hsing Yun-t'u in the original text. Venerable Tzu Jung was struck by the words *hsing* (star, as in *wei-hsing* or satellite) and *yun* (cloud, as in *yun-tu* or picture of clouds) in the weather report. Hence her question.

Who was he?
Living atop Buddha's Light Mountain,
founding it twenty-seven years before.
Speaking the Dharma
through forty fall seasons,
Teaching disciples,
one thousand and more.
Spreading the light
over five continents,
Donning the mantle
countless the roles,
Always befriending
and purifying the world.

Paving the way for the next 500 years

Against the backdrop of turbulent times, Hsing Yun has emerged from ordinariness to attain extraordinariness through broad-mindedness, insight, flair, and resolve. In an article titled *The Next 500 Years in Buddhism*, U.S.-based historian and author T'ang Te-kang summarizes Hsing Yun's role in religious history as follows:

In teaching the major religions of the world, I make sure that students bear in mind the old Chinese proverb: "Every 500 years a benevolent king shall rise." This is an easy way for them to keep track of historical events.

As regards the dates of various religious founders, that of Jesus is the easiest to remember. 500 years before him came Sakyamuni Buddha (563 – 483 B.C.E.), Lao-tzu, and Confucius. Still another 500 years earlier is the time of Moses, founder of Judaism.

Moving forward in time, it was Mohammed (570 – 630?), founder of Islam, who came 500 years after Jesus. Five hundred years after that came Martin Luther (1483 – 1546), founder of Protestantism. Now, as the clock ticks toward the end of another 500 years since the religious reform [in Christianity] of 1520, apparently the next epochal leadership in religion is again anticipated.

A circumspect look at the world's cultural, philosophical, political, and economic developments today reveals that Buddhism is the source of a new life force... For Buddhism today is not only sweeping across Southeast Asia but also penetrating the five continents. So potent is its impact and so excellent are its conditions that it has long surpassed the Christian reform [of the 16th century].

With the emerging four young dragons[2] of the Pacific Rim and China racing feverishly to catch up, the enormous middle class that results is asking for a religion of their own – a Buddhism which is adaptable to modern circumstances, and one which is home-oriented instead of monastery-oriented as in orthodoxy. Hence a Buddhist reform is in the works, and a reformer is here.

The new state of Buddhism is such that, at long last, the Mahayana and Theravada, along with the ten schools are at last joining forces, and together they shall take China and the rest of the world by storm. The question arises as to who is capable of leading Buddhism into what appears to be a new era of prosperity and growth. Apart from Venerable Master Hsing Yun, founder of Fo Guang Shan, I honestly cannot

---

[2] Taiwan, Hong Kong, Singapore and Korea, the first three being of Chinese descent, and the last being of relative descent.

think of anyone else.

Once a monk, always a monk

Like his mother giving her son away to the world, Hsing Yun, too, has long given himself to all living beings. Over his lifetime, has he ever regretted that decision or contemplated another way of spending his life?

"The greatest blessing in this life of mine has been attaining monkhood," he remarks. "I pledge to be a monk in my next life, and in the many, many lives to come." Emperor Shun-chih of the Ch'ing dynasty once penned poetry to honor monkhood. It ran thus:

> *"As rare as gold and white jade are;*
> *Rarer still is the wearing of the robe."*

For Hsing Yun, monkhood has been a task for a man of fortitude and courage, something beyond even what great generals and ministers must tackle. Should he return as a monastic in the next life, he would still have no regrets.

Appendix 1
Chronology of Venerable Master Hsing Yun

1927   Born on the 22nd day of the 7th month of the lunar calendar in Chiangtu, Chiangsu province, [China]. Named Li Kuo-shen. Father Li Ch'eng-pao, mother Liu Yu-ying. Third of four children, with older brother and sister and a younger brother.

1931   Became vegetarian alongside maternal grandmother, a Buddhist.

1934   Entered rural school.

1937   Father missing on a business trip to Nanjing.

1938   Midway to Nanjing with mother in quest of his father, took the tonsure under Venerable Master Chih K'ai at Ch'i-hsia Temple. Given the Dharma names Wu Ch'e and Chin Chueh. Became a disciple of the 48$^{th.}$ generation of the Lin-chi division in Ch'an Buddhism.

1941   Ordained at Ch'i-hsia Temple.

1944   Studied at T'ien-ning Temple, Ch'ang-chou.

1945   Transferred to Chiao-shan Buddhist College.

1947   Arrived in Ta-chueh Temple, Pai-t'a Mountain. Became principal of White Pagoda Elementary School. Founded monthly *Raging Billows* with schoolmate Master Chih Yung. Was arrested by the communists.

1948   Became director of Hua-tsang Temple, Nanjing.

	Edited *Splendid Light* supplement of newspaper *Hsu Pao*.
1949	Arrived in Keelung, Taiwan, with monastic relief group. Arrested with Master Tz'u Hang and others on allegations of subversive activities and incarcerated for twenty-three days.
1950	Took shelter at Yuan-kuang Temple, Chungli, under Master Miao Kuo. Also stood guard in the mountains around Fa-yun Temple Miaoli, where he authored *Singing in Silence*, his first work.
1951	Took charge of academic affairs in a Buddhist seminar conducted by Venerable Ta Hsing. Edited *Life Monthly* and learned Japanese.
1952	Elected an executive of the Chinese Buddhist Association. Raised funds for emergency relief of the flood in Hualien.
1953	Spoke on the Dharma at Lei-yin Temple, Ilan, on the invitation of Li Chueh-ho. Published *Discourse on Avalokitesvara's Universal Gate Chapter*.
1954	Stationed at Lei-yin Temple and started preaching in rural areas and prisons. Venerables Tzu Chuang, Tzu Hui, and Tzu Jung took refuge in the Triple Gems.
1955	Preached around Taiwan while promoting the reprint of the Buddhist Canon. Suffered severe arthritis in the legs. Published *Biography of Sakyamuni Buddha*, the first-ever hardback Buddhist text published in Taiwan.
1956	Completed the lecture hall for the Ilan Chanting group. Founded the first kindergarten, Tz'u-ai, and

tutored in arts and sciences, Kuang-hua. Preached in prisons.

1957 Published *National Master Yu Lin*. Founded and became chief editor of *Awakening the World*, a magazine which was published three times a month.

1958 Conducted the Dharma function for the preservation of the nation held by the Chinese Buddhist Association in Taipei. Venerable Hsin Ping was tonsured.

1959 Supported the Tibetan Buddhist movement against communist suppression. Organized the first float parade in celebration of the Buddha's birthday. Established a Buddhist cultural service in Sanchung, Taipei. Published *Biography of Sakyamuni Buddha's Ten Great Disciples*.

1960 Published the *Enlightenment Sutra*.

1961 Became publisher of *Buddhism Today*. Led the Ilan youth choir and cut the first six Buddhist records in Taiwan.

1962 Took over the publishing of *Awakening the World*.

1963 Organized a Buddhist visiting group alongside Venerable Pai Sheng and toured India, Thailand, Malaysia, Singapore, the Philippines, Japan,, and Hong Kong. Met with King Bhumibol Adulyadej of Thailand, President Diosdado Macapagal of the Philippines, etc. Petitioned for the release of 700 Chinese and rescued two fishing vessels in Kaohsiung.

1964 Completion of Shou-shan Temple, Kaohsiung, followed by the founding of Shou-shan Buddhist College. Established a school of commerce named

Chih-kuang together with Venerables Wu I and Nan T'ing. Published a book of travels and a range of bilingual Buddhist texts in Chinese and English.

1965 Published a series of lectures titled *Awakening the World*.

1967 Construction began for Fo Guang Shan. Shou-shan Buddhist College renamed Tung-fang Buddhist College. Took over a Christian mission service, which was turned into a home for the aged and poor.

1969 Held the first Buddhist summer camp for college-level students. Founded the first Buddhist Sunday school for children. Built Pilgrim's Lodge at Fo Guang Shan.

1970 Founded Ta-tz'u Nursery. Established pilgrims' group.

1971 Completion of the Great Compassion Shrine, followed by the blessing of the Buddha's image. Founded P'u-men Vihara, Taipei, which later became P'u-men Temple. Elected president of Sino-Japanese Buddhist Association.

1972 Introduced the constitution of Fo Guang Shan's Committee of Religious Affairs.

1973 Chiang Ching-Kuo, head of the executive council, visited Fo Guang Shan for the first time. Basketball court at Tung Shan officially opened. Founded Fo Guang Shan Ts'ung-lin College, which was renamed Chinese Buddhist Research Institute.

1974 Groundbreaking of Fu-shan temple, Changhua.

1975 Foundation laid for the Great Welcoming Buddha and the Main Shrine. Conducted a three-day lecture

at the National Arts Hall, which was the first-ever Buddhist lecture held in the halls of government.
1976 Attended the U.S. bicentennial festivities and preached the Dharma for the first time in the country. Ran Buddhist summer camp for seniors and started an English Buddhist center. Was founding publisher of *Fo Guang Scholarly Journal*. Launched a clinic at Shou-shan Temple, Kaohsiung, and P'u-men Hospital.
1977 Lectured at Chung-shan Hall, Taipei. Founded P'u-men High School. Established the editing and publishing center for the Fo Guang Buddhist Canon. Chinese Buddhist Research Institute and University of Oriental Studies, U.S.A. became sister schools. Ten Thousand Buddhas Triple Platform Ordination deemed a preceptoral model.
1978 After becoming president of R.O.C., Chiang Ching-Kuo visited Fo Guang Shan again. Held Dharma function for the preservation of the nation in Dr. Sun Yat-sen Memorial Hall. Raised funds for the establishment of a Chinese Buddhist Youth Association. Received honorary Ph.D. from University of Oriental Studies. Became first president of International Buddhist Progress Society. Raised funds for the establishment of Hsi Lai Temple.
1979 In view of strained diplomatic ties between Taiwan and the United States, held Buddhist concert at Dr. Sun Yat-sen Memorial Hall to raise funds for a national foundation of self-sufficiency. Launched *Universal Gate* magazine; first Buddhist program,

	Sweet Dew televised. Led pilgrimage to India. Held first Buddhist summer camp for children. *National Master Yu Lin* adapted for the stage at the National Arts Hall.
1980	Produced the first set of Buddhist bookmarks and calendar. Became director of Chinese Culture University's Indian Research Institute. Telecast of the program *Gate of Faith*.
1981	Held Buddhist summer camp for mothers. Taught Buddhist philosophy at Tung Hai University.
1982	Became brother temples with Tongdo Sa, Korea. Conducted the 5th International Buddhist Scholars' Conference.
1983	Honored by the ministries of legal affairs and education for outstanding educational achievements.
1984	Met the Dalai Lama. Established a mobile clinic to offer free medical care. Founded the first Buddhist city college at P'u-hsien Temple, Kaohsiung.
1985	Held World Buddhist Youth Scholars' Conference. Passed the abbotship of Fo Guang Shan onto Venerable Hsin Ping. Practiced in isolation at Hsi Lai Temple, Los Angeles. Served as executive officer of the Chinese-Tibetan Cultural Association of the Republic of China. The *Platform Sutra of the Sixth Patriarch* televised, as well as *Venerable Master Hsing Yun's Lecture Series*, which was honored by the Department of Information.
1986	World Sutric and Tantric Buddhist Conference held at Fo Guang Shan. Took office as advisor of nationalist party affairs. Launched new annual lecture

series at Kaohsiung Chung-cheng Cultural Center.
1987 Became founding president of the American Buddhist Youth Association. Visited Chinese Buddhist Temple, Sarnath, India. *Hsing Yun's Ch'an Talk* televised.
1988 Inauguration of Hsi Lai Temple, where the 16th World Fellowship of Buddhists Conference and the 7th World Fellowship of Buddhist Youth Conference were held. Conducted purifying service for the opening of the California State and Los Angeles municipal meetings. Preached in Hong Kong for the first time at the City Hall. Held the first alms-round fundraising event for the Fo Guang Shan Cultural and Educational Foundation. Traveled to northern Thailand with medical team and preached there. The *Fo Guang Encyclopedia* honored by the Department of Information.
1989 Held International Ch'an Conference at Fo Guang Shan. On his first homecoming in four decades, paid homage to ancestral stupas in Ch'i-hsia and visited his mother in Chiangtu. The Dalai Lama was a guest at Hsi Lai Temple. *Hsing Yun's Ch'an Talk* honored by the department of information. Spoke on the Dharma to the armed forces and their respective academies.
1990 Invited to attend the inauguration of U.S. President George Bush. Received his mother at Fo Guang Shan and Xu Jiatun, head of the New China News Agency in Hong Kong, at Hsi Lai Temple. Began an annual three-day lecture at Hunghom Coliseum,

Hong Kong. Went on preaching tour in England, Holland, Belgium, France, Switzerland, Austria, Yugoslavia, and Italy. Plans for the construction of International Buddhist Association of Australia under way on a thirty-six acre property donated by the city of Sydney, Australia.

1991 Hsi Lai University, temporarily housed in the temple, opened. Founded Buddha's Light International Association, R.O.C. and raised funds for floods on the mainland. Hospitalized for a broken right thigh. *Hsing Yun Dharma Words* televised. Established a branch temple in a chateau outside Paris and began the spread of the Dharma in Europe.

1992 Buddha's Light International Association established and its first meeting held at Hsi Lai Temple. Devotee Chang Sheng-Kai donated his own residence for the establishment of the first branch temple in South America, I.B.P.S. Do Brasil. Was requested to put up a temple in Johannesburg, South Africa by Dr. Hennie Senekal – the first step in the spread of the Dharma in Africa. For the second year honored by the ministry of education for outstanding educational undertakings. Fo Guang Shan Cultural and Educational Foundation also honored.

1993 *National Master Yu Lin* televised on CTS. Second B.L.I.A. World Conference held in Taipei. Registration of Fo Guang University officially approved by the Ministry of Education, followed by groundbreaking ceremony in Linmei, Chiao-hsi, in Ilan county. Buddha's Light International Association named the most outstanding social organization in Taiwan.

1994 Extensive fundraising for Fo Guang University through art auctions. Taipei Temple inaugurated. Received city key to and honorary citizenship of Austin, Texas. Third B.L.I.A. world conference held in Vancouver, Canada. Fo Guang Shan provided emergency relief for the massive floods in August at the request of President Li Teng-hui. *Hsing Yun Says* opened on TTV. *Diary of Hsing Yun* published in 20 volumes. Ten monastics of African descent tonsured. Held honorary presidency of World Fellowship of Buddhists and presidency of B.L.I.A.

Fo Guang Shan Global Distribution of Branch Temples, 1999

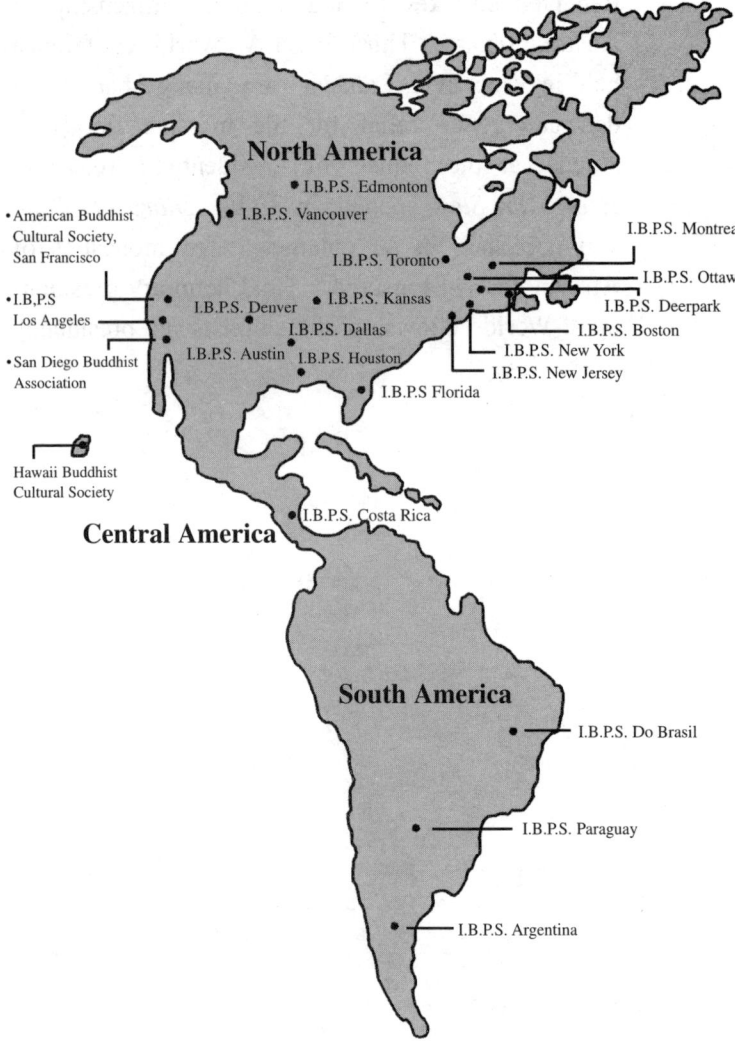

I.B.P.S.- International Buddhist Progress society

Buddha's Light International Association Global Distbution of Chapters, 1999

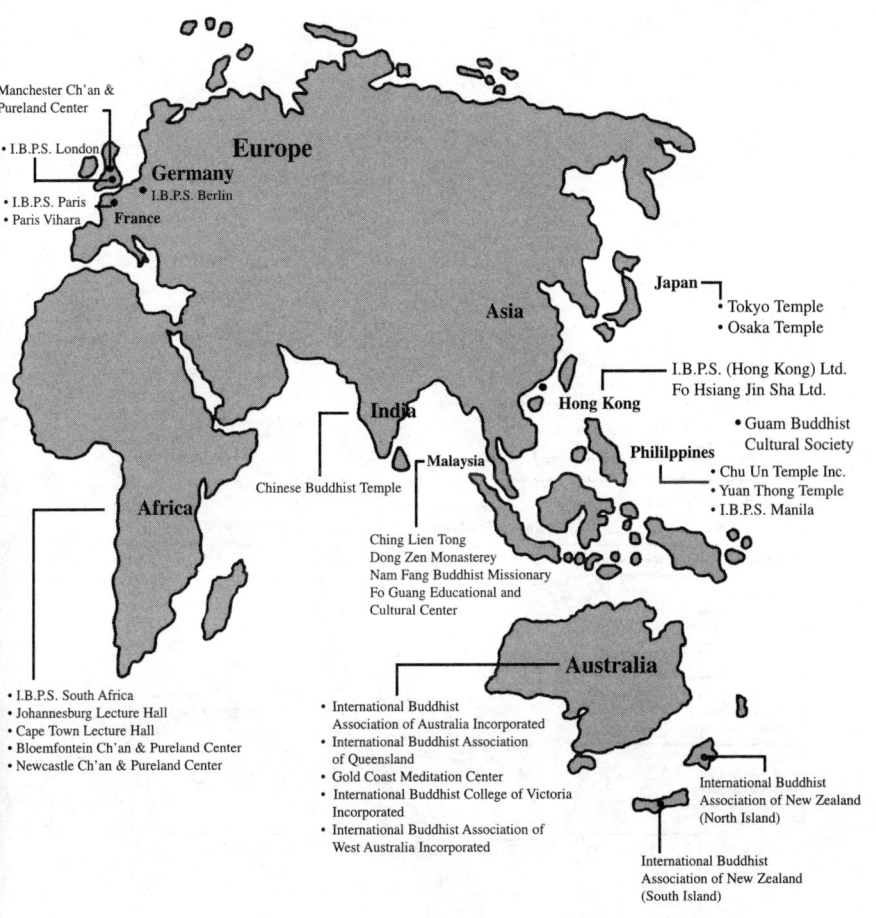

Fo Guang Shan Distribution of Branch Temples in Taiwan, 1999

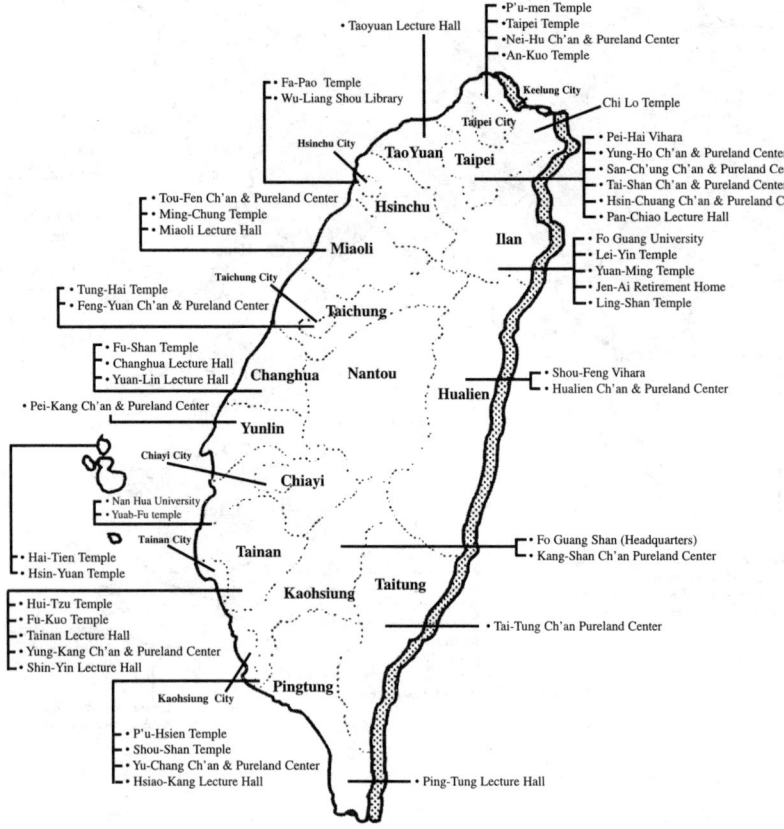

Directory of Fo Guang Shan Branch Temples in the Americas

USA
Hsi Lai Temple
3456 S. Glenmark Drive,
Hacienda Heights, California 91745.
TEL: 1 (626) 961-9697   FAX: 1 (626) 369-1944

San Diego Buddhist Association
4536 Park Blvd.,
San Diego, California 92116.
TEL: 1 (619) 298-2800 / 299-5360   FAX: 1 (619) 298-4205

American Buddhist Cultural Society
1750 Van Ness Ave.,
San Francisco, California 94109.
TEL: 1 (415) 776-6538   FAX: 1 (415) 776-6954

I.B.P.S. Las Vegas
4189 St. Jones Blvd.,
Las Vegas, Nevada 89103.
TEL: 1 (702) 252-7339   FAX: 1 (702) 252-8923

International Buddhist Association of Arizona
6703 North 15 Place,
Phoenix, Arizona 85014.
TEL: 1 (602) 604-0139   FAX: 1 (602) 604-0171

I.B.P.S. Denver
2530 West Alameda Ave.,
Denver, Colorado 80219.
TEL: 1 (303) 935-3889   FAX: 1 (303) 935-1196

I.B.P.S. Kansas
10129 Wenonga Lane,
Leawood, Kansas 66206.
TEL: 1 (913) 642-3068   FAX: 1 (913) 642-3850

I.B.P.S. Dallas
1111 International Parkway,
Richardson, Texas 75081.
TEL: 1 (972) 907-0588   FAX: 1 (972) 907-1307

I.B.P.S. Austin
6720 N Capital of Texas Highway
Austin, Texas 78731.
TEL: 1 (512) 346-6789   FAX: 1 (512) 346-3346

I.B.P.S. Houston
12606 Jebbia Lane,
Stafford, Texas 79477-3302.
TEL: 1 (281) 495-3100   FAX: 1 (281) 495-6622

I.B.P.S. Florida
127 Broadway Ave.,
Kissimmee, Florida 34741.
TEL: 1 (407) 846-8887   FAX: 1 (407) 870-5566

I.B.P.S. New York
154-37 Barclay Ave.,
Flushing, New York 11355-1109.
TEL: 1 (718) 939-8318   FAX: 1 (718) 939-4277

I.B.P.S. New Jersey
1355 River Road,
Piscataway, New Jersey 08854.
TEL: 1 (732) 418-9627   FAX: 1 (732) 418-9657

I.B.P.S. Boston
C-1, 950 Massachusetts Ave.,
Cambridge, Massachusetts 02139.
TEL: 1 (617) 547-6670 / 547-9984   FAX: 1 (617) 491-8862

Hawaii Buddhist Cultural Society
6679 Hawaii Kai Drive,
Honolulu, Hawaii 96825.
TEL: 1 (808) 395-4726   FAX: 1 (808) 396-9117

Guam Buddhism Society
408 A Boman Street,
Borrigada, Guam 92921.
TEL: 1 (671) 639-8678   FAX: 1 (671) 637-8679

Canada
I.B.P.S. Vancouver
#6680-8181 Cambie Road
Richmond, British Columbia V6X 1J8.
TEL: 1 (604) 273-0369   FAX: 1 (604) 273-0256

I.B.P.S. Edmonton
10232 103 Street,
Edmonton, Alberta T5J 0Y8.
TEL: 1 (780) 424-9744   FAX: 1 (780) 424-9745

I.B.P.S. Ottawa
176 Rochest Street,
Ottawa, Ontario K1R 7M6.
TEL: 1 (613) 232-6626   FAX: 1 (613) 236-7743

I.B.P.S. Toronto
6525 Millcreek Drive,
Mississauga, Ontario L5N 7K6.
TEL: 1 (905) 814-0465   FAX: 1 (905) 814-0469

I.B.P.S. Montreal
200 Rue de Castelnau Est.,
Montreal, P.Q. H2R 1P5.
TEL: 1 (514) 278-0808   FAX: 1 (514) 278-6361

South America
I.B.P.S. Costa Rica
773-1200 Pavas,
San Jose, Costa Rica.
TEL: (506) 231-4200 / 290-2635   FAX: (506) 290-1584

I.B.P.S. Do Brasil
Estrada Municipal Fernando Nobre,
1461 Cep.06700-000 Cotia
Sao Paulo, Brasil.
TEL: 55 (11) 7922-2895 / 492-2335   FAX: 55 (11) 492-5230

I.B.P.S. Rio de Janeiro
Rua Itabaiana 235,
Cep. 20561-050, Grajau,
Rio de Janeiro.R.J. Brasil.
TEL: 55 (21) 576-8976   FAX: 55 (21) 576-8976

I.B.P.S. Paraguay
Av. Adrian Jara 660. Piso 5
Centro Shopping International
Ciudad Del. Est., Paraguay.
TEL: 595 (61) 500-952 / 511-573   FAX: 595 (61) 510-269

I.B.P.S. Argentina
Av. Cramer 1733,
1426 Capital Federal
BS.AS. Argentina.
TEL: 55 (11) 4786-9969   FAX: 55 (11) 4788-6351

Other English Publications by Venerable Master Hsing Yun

1. *Hsing Yun Ch'an Talk*
2. *Perfectly Willing*
3. *Happily Ever After*
4. *How I Practice Humanistic Buddhism*
5. *Where is Your Buddha Nature?*
6. *Being Good: Buddhist Ethics for Everyday Life*
7. *Only A Great Rain: A Guide to Chinese Buddhist Meditation*
8. *The Carefree Life*
9. *Humble Table, Wise Fare: Hospitality for the Heart (I)*
10. *Humble Table, Wise Fare: Hospitality for the Heart (II)*
11. *Cloud and Water: An Interpretation of Ch'an Poems*
12. *Lotus in A Stream: Basic Buddhism for Beginners*

If you would like more information regarding these publications or interested in ordering the above titles, you may contact us at: Phone: (626) 961-9697
Fax: (626) 369-1944
Email: itc@blia.org

Fo Guang Shan
International Translation Center

In view of the ever increasing interest in learning Buddhism in the Western world, Venerable Master Hsing Yun established the Fo Guang Shan International Translation Center in 1996. Works on a wide spectrum of topics had since been translated into English, Spanish, German, French, Russian and a number of other languages. Free English monthly booklets on various Buddhist topics are published for distribution in the branch temples of English speaking countries.

Some of the booklets published include *Nirvana, Conditionality: The Law of Cause and Effect, Speaking of You and Me, Living the Dharma, When We See Clearly.* Other publications include *Humble Table, Wise Fare (Parts I & II), The Carefree Life, Being Good* and *Only A Great Rain.*

We appreciate any comments or suggestions that you may have toward our publications. You may forward your comments and suggestions to:

Fo Guang Shan International Translation Center
3456, South Glenmark Drive, Hacienda Heights,
CA 91745, U.S.A.
Phone: (626) 923-5151
Fax: (626) 369-1944
Email: itc@blia.org